The Internet Guide for Accountants

The Internet Guide for Accountants

Alexander Kogan
Rutgers University

Ephraim F. Sudit
Rutgers University

Miklos A. Vasarhelyi
Rutgers University

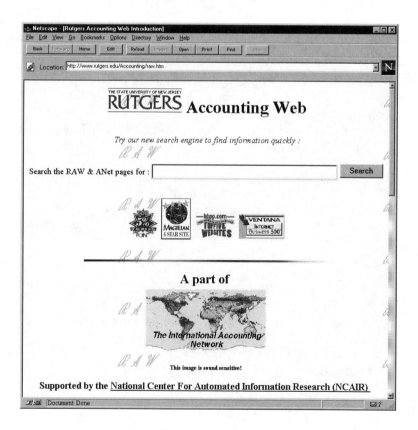

PRENTICE HALL, Upper Saddle River, New Jersey 07458

Editor-in-Chief:	P.J. Boardman
Editorial Assistant:	Jane Avery
Production Editor:	Susan Rifkin
Production Coordinator:	Cindy Spreder
Managing Editor:	Katherine Evancie
Manufacturing Buyer:	Alana Zdinak
Senior Manufacturing Supervisor:	Paul Smolenski
Manufacturing Manager:	Vincent Scelta
Marketing Manager:	Deborah Hoffman-Emry
Senior Designer:	Suzanne Behnke
Cover Design:	Bruce Kenselaar
Composition:	Impressions Book and Journal Services, Inc.
Cover Art:	Mark Murphy

Copyright© 1998 by Prentice-Hall, Inc.
A Simon & Schuster Company
Upper Saddle River, New Jersey 07458

Library of Congress Cataloging-in-Publication Data

Kogan, Alexander, 1961–
    The Internet guide for accountants / Alexander Kogan, Ephraim F. Sudit, Miklos A. Vasarhelyi.
        p.   cm.
    Includes bibliographical references and index.
    ISBN 0-13-270968-6 (alk. paper)
    1. Accounting—Computer network resources.   2. Internet (Computer network)   I. Sudit, Ephraim F., 1943– .   II. Vasarhelyi, Miklos A.   III. Title.
HF5625.7.K64   1997
025.06′657—dc21   97-16613
                                                                                                                CIP

    ISBN 0-13-270968-6

Prentice-Hall International (UK) Limited, London
Prentice-Hall of Australia Pty. Limited, Sydney
Prentice-Hall Canada, Inc., Toronto
Prentice-Hall Hispanoamericana, S.A., Mexico
Prentice-Hall of India Private Limited, New Delhi
Prentice-Hall of Japan, Inc., Tokyo
Simon & Schuster Asia Pte. Ltd., Singapore
Editora Prentice-Hall do Brasil, Ltda., Rio de Janeiro

Printed in the United States of America

10 9 8 7 6 5 4 3

Contents

Preface

This is a book about accounting on the Internet. Its main purpose is to present accounting students, educators, and practitioners with a comprehensive, up-to-date guide to accounting materials and related resources on the World Wide Web. At the same time, it also provides a detailed introduction into the Internet technology and electronic commerce. The book is self-contained in the sense that it is designed to provide readers who are not experienced Internet users with basic information about the Internet structure and the use of its basic services.

Accounting is an information and decision support system. So is the Internet. The growing interface between the accounting profession and the Internet is a very exciting and important development. The future impact of the Internet on accounting is likely to be profound. It is therefore essential for accountants who prepare for the twenty-first century to keep abreast of the explosive trends in the use of Internet technology in accounting.

The book is designed for the accounting students and professionals who wish to become simultaneously familiar with the Internet and its accounting content. This is a book that is extremely suitable to serve as a companion to any accounting course. It gives accounting professors an opportunity to achieve the dual objective of covering the traditional Internet materials and educating the readers about accounting on the Internet.

Since this book is self-contained and assumes no prior knowledge of the Internet or accounting, it can be easily and effectively used as an independent study guide for students in introductory accounting courses. In busy courses, instructors need to devote little, if any, time to cover the book in class. Indeed, instructors can assign and use this guide without being experienced Internet users. On the other hand, topics in the book lend themselves to easy and useful integration with a variety of accounting issues in courses where some time can be spared for additional coverage.

The book is nontechnical and is written for novices. All cyberspace terms used are defined and explained. Almost every important statement is followed by an example or an illustration that is easy to follow. To the extent possible, technically complex issues are avoided. Whenever such issues are raised, they are explained in a simple, straightforward manner.

Website Outline

A part of this guide will form a "living book" accessible to its users on the Internet http://www.rutgers.edu/Accounting/raw/book. This part will "live" and regenerate the book mainly through periodic updates of developments concerning accounting on the Internet related to topics discussed in the text. Thus, the readers will be able to update themselves of new developments by connecting to this "living" site of the book on the Web. This Web site will also contain an up-to-date Instructor's Manual with access restricted only to instructors who register as users of this guide. Tabs at the left of the page will provide references to be persued by the reader in the living book's Web site. For example, the tab in this paragraph will point the reader to the living book's outline on the Web.

At the end of most chapters in the book, you will find a set of problems designed to motivate students either to think about important outstanding issues or to apply their newly acquired knowledge by performing tasks on the Internet. The problems are designed so that students should be able to handle them mainly on their own with little or no help from busy instructors. However, instructors have the option to expand some of those problem and integrate them into the course work. Answers to some problems are provided on the Web site of this living book.

The basic structure and functions of the Internet are described in Chapter 1, leading to a discussion of the actual and potential importance of the Internet to accounting and accountants. Chapter 2 focuses on the role and use of the World Wide Web. It explains the main features of Web browsers and demonstrates how they can be used. This chapter prepares the reader for independently surfing the Web in the search for desired information.

The reader is taken on a maiden accountant's voyage through cyberspace in Chapter 3. This journey illustrates the wealth and diversity of accounting information to be found on the Internet. The participants in this surfing voyage are left with a general impression and a bird's eye view of the scope and depth of the accounting material available on the Internet. They are encouraged to revisit these sites on their own and utilize their links to look for new ones.

The discussion in Chapter 4 ranges beyond Web surfing and browsing. The reader is introduced to many other important Internet services including electronic mail, remote login, and file transfer. This chapter gives the reader the basic skills to communicate and move information over the Internet, as well as to gain a degree of access to and control over remote computers on the Internet.

Exciting personal publishing opportunities on the World Wide Web are the subject of Chapter 5. Readers are taught how to establish their own personal homepages and how to use the HTML markup language to put their own material on the Web, cross-reference it, and link it to other pertinent materials.

A systematic survey of the accounting resources currently available on the Internet is presented in Chapter 6. Standard Internet search engines are shown to be ill-structured and sporadic in their capabilities to locate accounting information, and the need for well-organized directories of accounting resources is demonstrated.

Chapter 7 focuses on Internet security. As accountants transfer and communicate sensitive and confidential financial information over the Internet, they have to secure it against potential interception of messages en route over the Internet and break-ins into databases in computers hosting Web sites. The relative merits of alternative safety systems securing on-line sites and on-line information flows are discussed in this chapter.

The historical development and current state of electronic commerce are discussed in Chapter 8. Direct-selling practices over the Internet are reviewed, and direct-selling Web sites for selected products are highlighted. The examples range from products and services for whom most phases of the selling transactions are carried out electronically over the Internet to those products for whom only part of the selling is performed on-line. Systems of electronic payments, including various forms of electronic cash, anonymous and identified, on-line and off-line, are explained. The roles in facilitating electronic commerce of support activities such as electronic-mail systems and electronic file transfers are also discussed in this chapter.

Key legal issues likely to affect Internet users including accountants in forthcoming years are reviewed in Chapter 9. Among the major topics discussed are legal laws and court decisions pertaining to censorship, libel, jurisdiction, intellectual property rights (e.g., copyrights, trademarks, patents) with special emphasis on their effects on electronic communications, electronic publishing, and electronic commerce.

Chapter 10 is futuristic in nature. It contains a discussion of the future of accounting, electronic commerce, and their likely interfaces. The prospect of a fully networked world, with most organizations and business enterprises connected to the net and having Web sites, is considered. In this world most professional accountants will access the Internet through their respective organizations, as well as privately using home access through on-line providers. The likely implications of these developments on disclosure requirements, on-line auditing, distance auditing, intelligent agents, accounting expert systems, interfaces of accounting systems with business intelligence information flows, and continuous on-line professional accounting education are among the issues discussed in this chapter.

The book contains four appendices. Appendix A describes how to transfer financial data from the Web to a spreadsheet. Appendix B talks about viruses. Appendix C extracts key features of the Communications Decency Act of 1996. The accounting resources directory of the Rutgers Accounting Web is presented in Appendix D.

Alexander Kogan
Ephraim F. Sudit
Miklos A. Vasarhelyi

Acknowledgments

We thank the following reviewers who were kind enough to assist us in this endeavor.

    W. David Albrecht, Bowling Green State University
    Roger Collins, University College of the Cariboo
    Richard B. Hanna, Ferris State University
    Phillip A. Jones, Sr., University of Richmond
    David H. Olsen, University of Akron
    Gary P. Schneider, University of San Diego

CHAPTER

Introduction

What the Internet Is and Why It Is Important to Accounting

WHAT IS THE INTERNET?

The Internet is a superstructure interconnecting heterogeneous computer networks worldwide. It is rapidly becoming an essential communication infrastructure of modern civilization. The users of the Internet have access to a variety of services ranging from traditional electronic mail, remote login, and file transfer, to the World Wide Web (WWW or Web). The Web is the most sophisticated modern information system distributed all over the Internet. One of the most important features of WWW is its friendly graphical user interface. The development of WWW is mostly responsible for the recent explosive growth in Internet usage and popularity.

A BRIEF HISTORY OF THE INTERNET

Historically, the seed money for the development of what later became the Internet was provided by the federal government in the late sixties and early seventies for the purpose of creating an independent computer network capable of preserving connectivity after a massive nuclear attack. Designed to connect many heterogeneous networks, this network of networks evolved into a self-managing global computer supernetwork.

Early development of the Internet was supported by the Advanced Research Project Agency (ARPA) of the federal government. A big part of the Internet was then known as ARPANet, which connected most of the military supercomputer sites. Since 1985/86 the major Internet backbone in the United States was supported by the National Science Foundation. This governmental support had been phased out and ultimately terminated. Since May 1, 1995, the U.S. part of the Internet has been privately owned and operated.

The size of the Internet, measured by the number of connected computers (*Internet hosts*), has doubled in size almost every year in the last fourteen years. The number of Internet hosts reached 1,000 in 1984, 10,000 in 1987, 100,000 in 1989, 1,000,000 in 1992, and is currently more than 16,000,000 (1997)[1] (Figure 1-1). Note that many host computers connect numerous users to the Internet. However, Internet user count is much less reliable than the host count. Matrix Information and Directory Services estimates that as of October 1995 the Internet had over 26 million users worldwide. As many as 39 million users may have exchanged electronic-mail messages over the Internet and other networks in October 1995.[2] The size of the World Wide Web, measured by the number of Web servers (providers of Web materials), has been quadrupling about every six months, reaching 100,000 in January 1996.[3] With the World Wide Web being the fastest growing segment of Internet, the composition of the services used on the Internet has been changing in favor of WWW. History has shown rapid expansion of new Internet services preceding a slowdown trend at maturity.

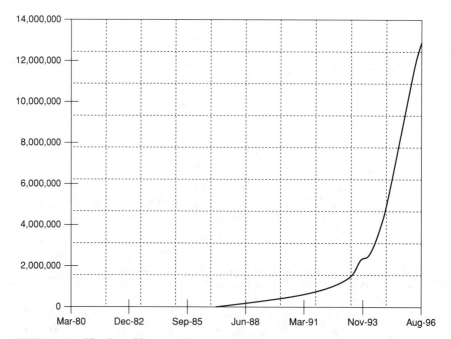

FIGURE 1-1 Number of Internet Hosts

BASIC BUILDING BLOCKS OF THE INTERNET

The basic building blocks in the Internet architecture are *local area networks* (LANs) of computers located in close proximity and physically connected to a single wire. The LANs connect to the Internet through specialized computers, called *routers,* which direct information traffic (see Figure 1-2). The routers and the dedicated long-distance wires that connect them form the structure of *wide area net-*

---

[1]http://www.nw.com/zone/host-count-history
[2]http://www2.mids.org/mn/603/ids3sum.html
[3]http://www.mit.edu/people/mkgray/growth/

works (WANs). The most important high-speed/high-bandwidth long-distance wires are collectively called the Internet backbone.

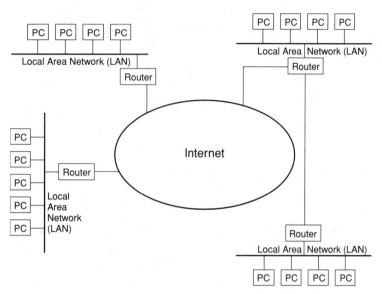

FIGURE 1-2 Routers and LANs

A recent trend of the Internet is the substantial increase in the number and scope of intranets. Intranets are localized and internal corporate computer networks with restricted access utilizing IP Internet technology.

All the computers on the Internet talk to each other using a special "language" known as the *TCP/IP* (*transmission control protocol/Internet protocol*) protocol suite. Each computer connected to the Internet is assigned its own unique address in the form of four numbers separated by dots (e.g., 128.6.10.4). These numerical addresses are called **IP addresses.** They are not easy to memorize. Therefore, Internet computers are also given symbolic names. For example, the computer with the IP address 128.6.10.4 has been given the name `andromeda.rutgers.edu.` (see Figure 1-3). This name refers to a computer called `andromeda` at Rutgers University. The component `rutgers.edu` is called a domain name, and all the computers of Rutgers University have this component in their names. The `edu` suffix is a top-level domain name that designates Rutgers as an institution of higher education. Thus, `andromeda` is analogous to a first name of a person, and `rutgers.edu` is analogous to the family name. Members of a family have different individual names, but they have the same family name.

There are relatively few top-level domain names. As mentioned above, `edu` designates institutions of higher education. Similarly, `com` designates commercial entities, `gov` designates governmental organizations, `org` designates not-for-profit organizations, etc. There are also two-letter top-level domain names designating countries (e.g., `de` for Germany, `fr` for France, `ca` for Canada).

Domain names of major organizations are usually easy to guess. For example, the Securities and Exchange Commission is known as the SEC. It is a governmental organization. Therefore, it is an educated guess that its domain name is `sec.gov.`, which happens to be correct.

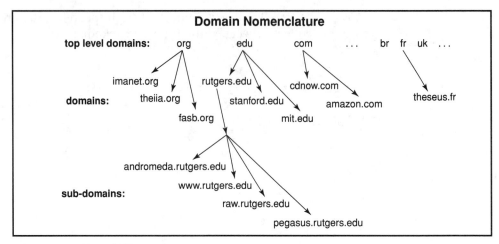

FIGURE 1-3 Domain Nomenclature

While symbolic names are convenient for humans, computers can communicate only by using IP addresses. In doing so, computers use a special Internet directory service to translate names to IP addresses. This directory service is called *Domain Name Service (DNS)*. This is in some ways analogous to communicating by telephone, which requires dialing a number rather than a name. A telephone directory can be used to match names and addresses with their corresponding telephone numbers.

When a computer is trying to find the IP of a location, it may use the network to look up several parts of the full domain name in a sequence. For example, it will first go to a DNS that knows "EDU" and finds "RUTGERS," then it goes to a Rutgers DNS and finds "ANDROMEDA," finishing by returning the full IP address to the user.

The Internet is known as a *packet-switching network.* Computers on the Internet send information to each other in **packets,** which are basic information units consisting of a header and a body. The header contains source and destination information (the IP addresses), while the body contains a portion of transmitted data. Internet packets typically range from a few bytes to more than a thousand bytes.[4] A message, to be transmitted over the Internet, is first partitioned into packets of appropriate size. Packets of each message may traverse the Internet following different routes to be reassembled at their destination point.

The paths of packets are determined by routers who read packet headers and direct them in accordance with certain algorithms.

GLOBAL INTERNET STRUCTURE

The Internet is anarchic in nature as its only central organization deals with standards and the establishment of domain names and IP numbers. Much of the administration is delegated progressively to lower and lower levels of the hierarchy. This hierarchy allows for nearly unlimited Internet growth with ensuing problems

---

[4]A **byte** is a unit of information that consists of eight binary (0 or 1) digits called **bits.**

associated with network congestion, lack of planning, lack of content control, lack of standardization, security weaknesses, etc.

The base of the Internet architecture (see "Basic Building Blocks of the Internet"[5]) is anchored to four all-purpose Network Access Points (NAP), which were originally supported by the National Science Foundation (NSF) (Figure 1-4). These NAPs are located in the vicinity of San Francisco, Chicago, New York, and Washington, D.C., and are respectively operated by Pacific Bell, Ameritech, Sprint, and MFS Datanet. For the purpose of accessing the Internet, a user must have three main resources: (1) a computer with a modem, (2) a communication line connected to a source of Internet provisioning, and (3) permission to connect to this provider. Consequently, if you have a computer and have installed the America Online (AOL) access software, you must have telephone access to AOL (often a free local telephone call) and pay AOL for connection. Larger users will have their own computers, acquire a T1 telephone line (approximately 1.5 Mbs) from the local telephone company, and buy access from a wholesalers (say, UUNet) Internet access provider. Internet access providers purchase a thick pipe of Internet access and resell this capacity as a series of thinner pipes.

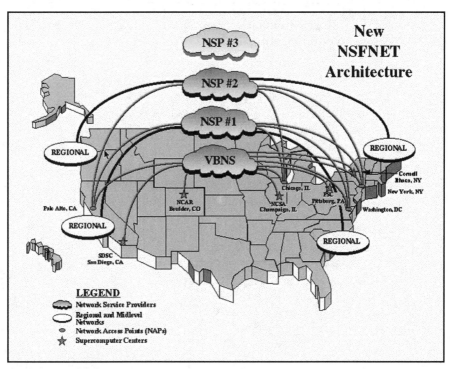

FIGURE 1-4 The Internet Architecture

The NAPs allow various computer networks within the Internet to interconnect and exchange traffic. At the top of the Internet service provider hierarchy are the Network Service Providers (NSPs). The NSPs (e.g., MCI, Sprint, ANS, UUNet, PSI) maintain their own large-scale wide area networks and, by the NSF rules, must connect to at least three of the NAPs. NSPs may also interconnect their networks directly. Most of the NSPs implement their backbone networks using very high speed lines (i.e., T3 lines with a speed of about 45 Mbs).

---

[5]http://www.cerf.net/cerfnet/about/gif/nsfnetmap.gif

Regional Network Providers (RNPs) make up the second tier of Internet service providers. The RNPs usually connect to the Internet through NSPs but may also have direct connections to NAPs. Larger organizations usually connect to the Internet through RNPs, while individual customers or small organizations typically connect to the Internet through intermediaries, the so-called Internet Access Providers (IAPs), who resell Internet access over telephone dial-up connections. Boundaries between various types of providers are not well defined.

Dial-up connections to the Internet sold by IAPs to individual users are typically slow channels (their speed now ranging from 14.4 to 33.6 Kbs). These dial-up connections use special versions of the Internet protocol called SLIP and PPP. These protocols lend the user an IP address for the duration of the session.

Any Internet host can be either a user or a provider of content on the Internet. An Internet site that provides content tends to be a constantly connected node with its own IP address. Most computers connecting to the Internet through dial-up lines do not have permanent IP addresses. They are assigned a temporary IP number for the duration of the session.

Computers without permanent IP numbers cannot be effectively used as servers to provide information on the Internet.

Figure 1-5 shows a view of various connections to the Internet. It was presented by Anthony M. Rutkowski, Executive Director of the Internet Society, in his testimony before the U.S. House of Representatives Committee on Science hearing on July 26, 1995,[6] and updated with more recent numbers.

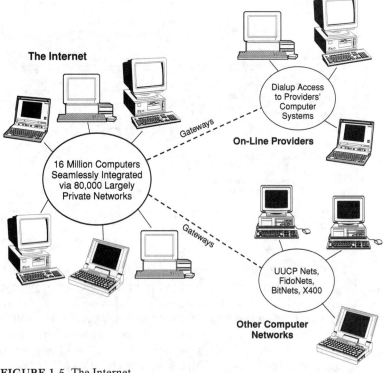

FIGURE 1-5 The Internet

[6]http://www.isoc.org/rutkowski/hr_hearing.html

INDIVIDUAL ACCESS TO THE INTERNET

**Website
Internet Access
Providers**

Many individuals have access to the Internet through their employers or organizations to which they belong. Others can access Internet services in several ways. The most typical access is through an IAP (see Figure 1-6). These providers range from local "mom-and-pop" shops to national and international telecommunications giants (e.g., Sprint, MCI, Netcom, PSI, etc.).

Internet hosts have a special software layer designed to provide Internet connectivity. The standard for this software is called windows sockets (*winsock*). This software either comes with the computer-operating system or is supplied by the IAP. Practically all IAPs now provide standard winsock connections. Most new Internet application programs (e.g., Netscape, Eudora, ws_ftp, described in this book) are winsock based. This means that any winsock-based Internet application program should work well over any standard winsock connection.

Most IAPs will supply their users with a basic Internet software package containing programs similar to those described in this book. A typical example of a basic package is the Internet in a Box, including a configuration utility, a dialer, a Web browser (AIR Mosaic), an E-mail program (AIR Mail), a telnet program (AIR Telnet), a newsreader (AIR News), and more. Modern browsers (e.g., Netscape) may contain much of this functionality already incorporated in its main body and allow for "plug-ins" for additional features.

Another Internet access option for an individual is to join one of the traditional on-line services (e.g., America Online, Prodigy, CompuServe). Initially, they used to be a completely different type of service, with their own content structure and access communication lines. In recent years they became a closer part of the Internet by providing gateways and access to the Internet (acting as quasi IAPs). In providing access to the Internet, the on-line services are evolving toward the use of standard winsock-based software tools (subsequently described in this book). In the future they may become a nearly indistinguishable part of the net.

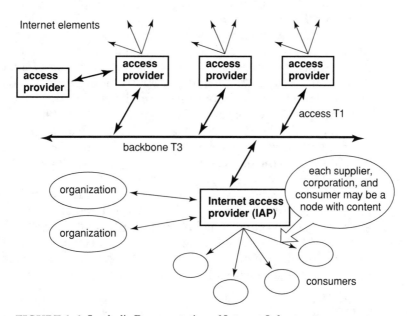

FIGURE 1-6 Symbolic Representation of Internet Infrastructure

Three distinct costs are associated with any kind of Internet access:

1. The cost of an appropriate computer
2. The cost of a communication line to an IAP
3. The Internet access fee charged by the IAP

For most users the incremental cost of connecting to the Internet is low. Users may already own an appropriate computer for other purposes. Practically all users will have a communication line in the form of a telephone connection. For users who own an appropriate computer and have access to a telephone line, the incremental cost is reduced to the Internet access fee charged by the IAP (currently about $20 per month for unlimited access). Some users enjoy "free" access to the Internet in the sense that their organizations (e.g., universities, companies) pay for it and provide it free of charge.

CONGESTION ON THE INTERNET

Since it was developed as a research project, the Internet architecture has not been geared to support its functioning in a completely privatized free-market environment. The majority of the early Internet users were academics for whom the Internet access was free. Universities and governmental organizations paid flat fees for Internet access with unlimited usage. Driven by technological developments, communication needs, and media attention, the Internet usage is exploding exponentially. As a result, sporadic delays due to Internet traffic congestion occur with increasing frequency.

Website
Internet congestion

Technically, congestion happens when the pipe is not wide enough, or the routers are overwhelmed by the number of packets they get. When Internet traffic congestion happens, end users start experiencing significant slowdowns in establishing connections with remote computers, in the speed of information flows (the number of bytes transferred per unit time), and in the most extreme cases, the unavailability of certain Internet services. These are called Internet brownouts.

Unfortunately, congestion on the Internet is becoming a household topic. Internet "brownouts" are catching newspaper headlines. Even casual users can be frustrated by occasional long waits, forced to stare impatiently for minutes, if not hours, at the "host contacted . . . waiting for reply" message on the status line of a Web browser. Doom sayers predict an Internet meltdown. The economy is reacting to these concerns. Thirty-four universities have announced a consortium they called Internet II to guarantee the availability of bandwidth among themselves. Intranets are blossoming within companies for the same purpose and benefiting from the universality and richness of the tools that use the TCP/IP protocol.

Are there serious reasons for concern? The real question is whether demand growth will outpace capacity expansion. It is impossible to tell just on the basis of anecdotal evidence. Fortunately, some traffic and congestion data are systematically collected. Matrix Information & Directory Services (MIDS) samples regularly the traffic conditions on the Internet and makes the results available on a daily basis as the so-called "Internet Weather Report" (see Figure 1-7).[7]

---

[7]http://www2.mids.org/weather/

INTER@CTIVE WEEK November 11, 1996

**ECONOMICS & THE NET:
MAKE OR BREAK?**

Ethernet inventor Bob Metcalfe earlier this year drew a lot of attention when he predicted a collapse—this year—of the Internet. He called the capacity of the Net a "house of cards" that would fall under the weight of such bandwidth-hungry uses as telephony and transmission of video images.

Now comes Pacific Telesis Enterprises Chief Executive Michael Fitzpatrick with the argument that the meltdown of the Internet is not a technical problem, but an economic one. "The financial paradigm underlying the Net is not at all sturdy," he said at WesCon/96 in Anaheim, Calif.

The person who "saves the Net," he said, will be the person who "invents a realistic pricing structure," that doesn't discourage use, that doesn't discourage investment and doesn't discourage innovation.

Without it, soaring use of the Internet threatens to swamp the local public switched telephone networks, he and other Bell company executives have been arguing before the Federal Communications Commission and elsewhere.

By Tom Steinert-Threlkeld

The Internet Weather Reports are presented as regional maps showing round-trip times from MIDS offices to approximately 4,500 domains worldwide (see Figure 1-8 for the Internet weather in the United States on April 19, 1996). Measurements are currently taken every four hours (six times a day), seven days a week. According to the company:

**Website
Internet weather
reports**

"The maps use an intuitive technique for displaying latency data. The size of a circle indicates the round trip time to a host at that location. Bigger circles indicate closer hosts (lower latency) and smaller circles indicate more distant hosts (higher latency), providing a sort of three dimensional perspective view. The upper left legend gives the latency scale, which is logarithmic. The unit is the millisecond, so 1000 indicates one second. The range displayed is from the very large circles for 100 milliseconds (1/10 second) to tiny circles for 5000 milliseconds (5 seconds). This range goes from response almost like in the same room to so slow as to be unusable.

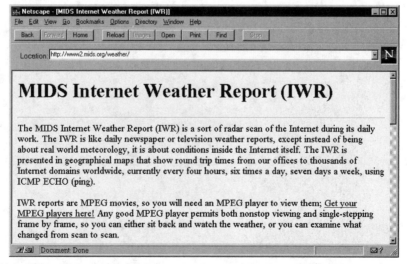

FIGURE 1-7　Internet Weather Report (Reprinted with permission by John S. Quarterman, Founder/Editor)

"Colors indicate the number of hosts at a given latency and location. The upper right legend gives the host count scale, which is also logarithmic: red for 1, orange for 2, and so on through yellow, green, and blue to violet. For some of the more densely surveyed cities, it is possible to see Bell curves in the size and colors of the icons plotted, with red (few hosts) on the outside and inside of the icon, and indigo or violet (many hosts) between. Even on a black and white display, the different latencies are visible, and some of the differences in numbers of hosts can be seen by differences in gray scale, but the maps are best seen in color." Readers should visit the MIDS site and see the value of these colors for visualization.

The Internet as we know it today has been in use for over a decade. Its architecture has been developed to support activities of the academic and military communities, and its recent explosive commercial growth has not been originally anticipated. Although some people blame the congestion problem on "greedy businessmen" and "commercial exploitation," the problem of Internet congestion is not completely new. In 1986 Internet backbone traffic was severely jammed. At that time the culprit was dramatic growth in academic use bumping against inadequate bandwidth of the backbone. The problem was remedied by a major upgrade of the Internet backbone. Internet optimists place their faith in continuous expansions of Internet capacity (bandwidth and routers). Pessimists point to prospective quantum jumps in demand fueled by a remarkable shift to continuous streams of multimedia data (audio and video) generated by desktop video teleconferencing and similar applications leading to inevitable congestion. These discontinuities in provisioning are analogous to the now-forgotten expansion of the telephone network in the 20s and 30s when universal access, capacity, and interconnectivity were not taken for granted as they are today.

During congestion, queuing is resolved on a "first-come-first-serve" basis. In the absence of usage-sensitive pricing, economic rationing of Internet traffic flows does not exist. Hence there is no differentiation between higher-valued and lower-valued packets of information. This system is economically inefficient. It is analogous to all mail deliveries handled as having the same priority with no provisions for any kind of priority mail. This method denies the users options of paying dif-

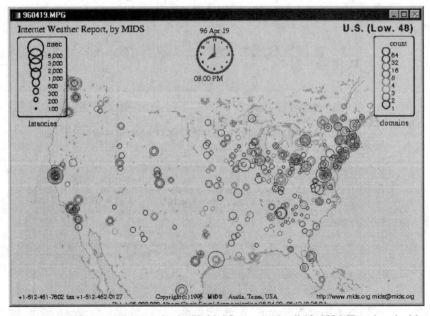

FIGURE 1-8 Internet Latency in the United States on April 19, 1996 (Reprinted with permission by John S. Quarterman, Founder/Editor)

ferent prices for different quality of service, and it prevents the providers from increasing their profits by matching prices to quality of service.

Sophisticated economic pricing mechanisms have been suggested for the Internet. However, accounting systems required to support billing based on these mechanisms have not been developed. Moreover, existing Internet instrumentation may limit the capability of accounting systems to support complex pricing mechanisms. Yet, without an efficient pricing system, investment in capacity expansion may suffer due to lower expected returns. Absence of adequate activity and cost-accounting systems precludes economically efficient allocation of costs among providers of Internet services.

All major users of the Internet are likely to be profoundly affected by the efficiency of the Internet pricing system. The more they rely on the Internet in the conduct of their business, the higher their stake is in the economic consequences of the Internet pricing system.

WHY IS THE INTERNET IMPORTANT TO ACCOUNTING?

The rapid growth of the Internet is bound to have a great effect on the accounting profession. A growing Internet provides wider, less costly, almost instantaneous access to increasing amounts of on-line business information. For the better or the worse, much of this growing body of business information will have to be collected, classified, presented, analyzed, and audited by accountants. While this fact is easily predictable, the actual paradigms of the accounting business utilization of the Internet are just emerging. Many years will pass until services, practices, and standards are mature and stable.

Website Accountants on the Internet

Consider a fully networked world, with most organizations and business enterprises connected to the net and having Web sites. Most professional accountants will access the Internet through their organizations, and their homes.

Intranets, best described as "internal organizational Webs," which use Internet technology and protocols will be available in most organizations. The use of intranets gives companies the benefits of open standards and Internet technology, while protecting their sensitive systems from risks of exposure to the global Internet.

Organizations will have a hierarchy of intranets with selective access. While these intranets will simply be part of the corporate infrastructure, their capabilities will deeply affect methods of doing work and tool capabilities. For example, full-motion video transmission over the wider bandwidth provided by intranets will allow face-to-face virtual meetings between accountants and their clients. A more-detailed discussion of the future of accounting on the Internet can be found in chapter 10.

The Impact of the Internet on Financial Disclosure

Website Disclosure on the Internet

Private accountants for companies and investors will have to design, administer, control, and audit much more complex information networks born out of a variety of Internet–Intranet fusion among businesses and their constituencies. Public accountants will have to modify their audit and certification procedures to allow for more information being disclosed with greater speed and frequency. Academic accountants will have to modify their curriculum to prepare future accountants for the challenges of the new environment.

The issue of providing on-line real-time accounting information raises great passions between managers, accountants, and regulators. A progressive tug-and-pull game will be an inseparable part of the evolution of on-line disclosure.

Many companies keep parts of the Income Statement and Balance Sheet information updated close to real-time. Banks would not be able to invest overnight if they did not have daily cash balances at the close of business, manufacturers need on-line inventory balances for JIT (just-in-time) and optimal inventory reordering, and corporate treasury needs on-line payable information to maximize the use of vendor payment discounts. Consequently, the incremental cost of some form of on-line reporting should not be drastic. On the other hand, corporations fear litigation from disclosure, managers manage their numbers prior to reporting, and investors still do not know in what ways on-line information will affect their operations.

> The likely outcome is progressive and increasingly leveraged disclosure allowing investors to "drill down" on financial records and acquire some degree of more-detailed disclosure information.

The advent of on-line reporting will pressure accountants further to on-line auditing of transactions. An entire new set of attestation may be forthcoming. The Elliott Committee of the AICPA is considering these issues, and their Web pages at the AICPA site illustrates their thinking.

The Accountant and Electronic Commerce[8]

Actual and projected exponential growth in electronic commerce on the Internet will challenge accountants to new and demanding tasks. Accountants will have to set new accounting systems to meet the needs of electronic commerce and, in the process, modify existing accounting procedures. New methods will be required to account for the effectiveness of advertising on the Internet and for billing for such advertising. On-line selling of products and services may necessitate commensurate on-line accounting entries, postings, reporting, and retrieval.

Most forecasts project more than 5 billion dollars worth of business to be processed over the Internet by the year 2000. While the current emphasis of the Internet is on personal use, the forthcoming years will shift the focus to commerce. Consequently, new commerce-related accounting duties will emerge that are different from traditional methods. For example,

- the processing and approval of e-payments
- the booking of electronic transactions
- the on-line verification of balances
- the management of electronic audit confirmations

Furthermore, the medium gives rise to an array of concerns that did not exist, or existed in limited form, in the past:

- systematic fraud[9]
- security of the hosting environment
- foreign unauthorized access
- access authorizations at many levels

---

[8]For a detailed discussion of electronic commerce, see chapter 8.
[9]For a detailed discussion of Internet security, see chapter 7.

- external access to corporate data
- data sharing arrangements due to joint reengineering (both entities reingineer their prosesses)

Some of these problems already exist. However, the dramatic change in information economics, where public and shared data are feasible, cheap, and facilitate very different processes, will cause major changes in audit risk and reporting possibilities.

CONCLUDING REMARKS

As the spread of the Internet revolutionizes access to and retrieval of information and spawns electronic commerce, it is bound to profoundly change accounting information systems and professional practices in auditing, financial reporting, management accounting, tax accounting, forensic accounting, and business intelligence and counter intelligence.

The following chapter will introduce the reader to the basic technology of the World Wide Web. This will set the stage for the accountant's Maiden Voyage through Cyberspace (in chapter 3) designed to visit some of the most remarkable accounting sites on the Web.

Problems

1. Describe the history and the evolution of the Internet. Compare it with the early years of telecommunications. Do you foresee similarities between the development patterns of telecommunications and the future development of the Internet?
2. What are intranets? How are these different from the Internet? How have they evolved? What are the reasons for their popularity? What are the prospects for intranets.
3. Explain the mechanism used in the Internet to find a particular IP site, assuming that the Web address (say, http://www.att.com) is known to the user.
4. What is the difference between an IAP and an Online Service?
5. What are the issues concerning Internet congestion, and what are the alternatives for the solution of this problem?
6. Describe the changes that, in your opinion, will happen to the traditional corporate disclosure model, due to the economics of global internetworking.
7. The concept of on-line auditing has been around for a while. What does it encompass, and how will it be facilitated by the Internet?
8. In your opinion, how will the accounting profession evolve, and are there going to be new approaches and services due to the Internet?

CHAPTER

Surfing the Web

2

This chapter provides an introduction to the World Wide Web. It explains the main features of a Web browser, shows how to browse the Web, and provides instructions on finding information resources on the Web. After reading this chapter, the reader should be able to independently surf the Web, searching and finding available information in any area of interest.

WHAT IS THE WWW?

The **World Wide Web** (WWW or Web) is an Internet-based information system that provides access to documents organized as hypertext. This access to documents allows extensive communications, logical constructs, and is the current basic platform for electronic commerce. A document is **hypertext** if it incorporates links (or pointers) to other documents. Links are parts of the document (e.g., words, sentences, images) that are distinguished from the rest of the document by some special means. These links are usually underlined and/or displayed in a different color. The user can follow the link (bring up on his or her screen the document to which the link points) by positioning the mouse pointer on the link and clicking the mouse.

While the user gets the feeling that he or she is visiting the Web site, he or she actually is requesting a file(s) from that site. These files are assembled into a page at the user's computer and displayed. Certain "objects" in this page can be highlighted and if clicked by a mouse will "link" to another file. This linking is the request for content of other files that will be assembled in the same form. Consequently, the user can navigate within a page, within a site, and between sites effortlessly, without being very aware of these adventures and migration.

Figure 2-1 illustrates the linkages among pages. These linkages contain textual pointers and links to images, data, and other sites. Hypertext systems are familiar to most computer users. For example, most MS Windows programs (e.g., word processors, spreadsheets, databases) come with on-line help. These help systems are hypertext systems; therefore, whoever uses them has been exposed to hypertext. Usually, links in help documents are displayed in green and underlined. The main difference between WWW and MS Windows help systems is that the latter can link only the documents stored on the hard drive of the user's PC, while the former can link documents stored on WWW computers anywhere on the Internet. The hypertext, by including pointers (links) to other documents, makes it possible to browse the Internet as easily as clicking a mouse.

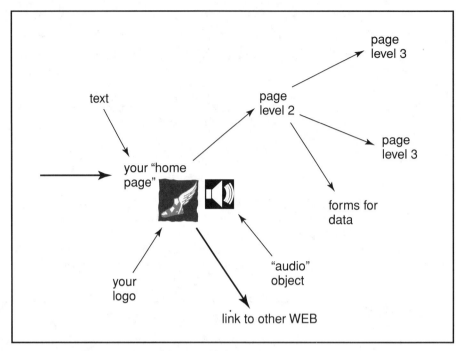

FIGURE 2-1 Hypertext-Based Content Linkage

When a user retrieves a Web document from a remote computer, his or her computer engages in a special "conversation" over the Internet with that remote computer. The two computers converse in **http (hypertext transfer protocol),** a "language" that was specifically developed for this purpose. The Internet computers that understand and speak http make up the World Wide Web.

The WWW enabled the Internet to leap almost overnight from a technologically esoteric tool to a widely usable medium. It has been the sector of largest growth of the Internet in the last two years. Its basic hypertext-oriented design made it easy to use. Web documents can incorporate not only text but also images, sound, and video. These multimedia capabilities endow the Web with color and animation and make it extremely attractive to users.

WHAT IS A WEB BROWSER?

Early development of the WWW took place at CERN[1] located near Geneva in Switzerland in the late eighties/early nineties. Initially, this new Internet system was limited to a text-only interface, and it was used primarily by scientists. The most popular text-based Web browser is called lynx. The WWW really took off when the first graphical browser for the Web (called Mosaic) was developed in 1993 at the University of Illinois National Center for Supercomputer Applications (NCSA). It was Mosaic that brought forward the multimedia glory of the Web.

Website Browsers

A **Web browser** is a special program that allows the user to browse through the contents of documents stored on the Web. In browsing, the user retrieves Web documents from remote computers and displays those documents on his or her

[1]European Laboratory for Particle Physics.

computer screen. A user can access a document on the WWW following a link from another document or, alternatively, by directly telling the browser where the document is located.

Presently, there are many Web browsers (e.g., Netscape, Microsoft Internet Explorer) on the market. Major on-line services and Internet Access Providers supply their users with Web browsers. Most Web browsers are graphical Windows-based programs. While Mosaic played a major role in the development and the popularity of the Web, it did not become one of the dominant browsers. At the present time the most frequently used Web browser is Netscape, which was developed by many members of the original Mosaic team. By some estimates Netscape currently controls more than 75 percent of the browser market. Netscape achieved its dominant market position by being the most technically advanced browser and by being distributed free for personal use.

Recently, Microsoft introduced its own Web browser—Internet Explorer. It has many of Netscape's capabilities, and it is currently completely free for personal as well as commercial use. Microsoft promises that in the future this browser will be bundled with its operating systems (Windows 95 and Windows NT). This means that when you purchase Windows 97 (maybe with a new computer) it will also come with a WWW browser that will be close to an integral part of the user interface.

In this book we will mainly use Netscape in the examples, but in some pictures the Prodigy browser, the AOL browser (progressively being replaced), and Microsoft Internet Explorer will be demonstrated. However, for basic uses, the differences between the browsers are not significant.

WHAT IS A URL?

To retrieve documents from the Web, one needs a way of specifying their location and how they can be retrieved. The Web introduced a universal approach to this problem in the form of the so-called Uniform Resource Locator (URL). Any URL consists of the following three parts:

```
protocol://computer/path
```

where the `protocol` is usually `http` (hypertext transfer protocol)[2], `computer` is a legitimate Internet computer name, for example, `www.rutgers.edu`, and the `path` is a sequence of directories and subdirectories leading to the file, for example, `Accounting/raw.htm`, which is the main page (*homepage*) of the Rutgers Accounting Web (see Figure 2-2):

```
http://www.rutgers.edu/Accounting/raw.htm
```

Some URLs do not have the path part. For example, the URL of the homepage of the Securities and Exchange Commission is `http://www.sec.gov`. The path part is missing to make this URL shorter. It is possible to omit the path part if the remote computer is configured appropriately. In this case, upon asking, the browser will automatically bring up an image like a homepage, or an index. Path omission is common for the URLs of homepages of major organizations. It is analogous, in a sense, to the use of abbreviated names.

---

[2]While http is the most common, ftp, gopher, and so forth, may also be used.

Since many computers providing Web documents have www as their first name, it is often not difficult to guess a URL of the homepage of a major organization. For example, the American Institute of Certified Public Accountants (AICPA) is a not-for-profit organization, and as such, it belongs to the org top-level domain. The domain name of this organization can, therefore, be easily guessed as aicpa.org, and the URL of its main homepage can then be figured out as http://www.aicpa.org, which happens to be true.

FEATURES OF A WEB BROWSER

The homepage shown in Figure 2-2 contains textual material, pictures, and sound. By clicking on the International Accounting Network emblem, the user makes the computer play the first sounds of the triumphal march of Radames in Verdi's *Aida*. Hypertext links usually appear in blue and are underlined. Clicking on such a link

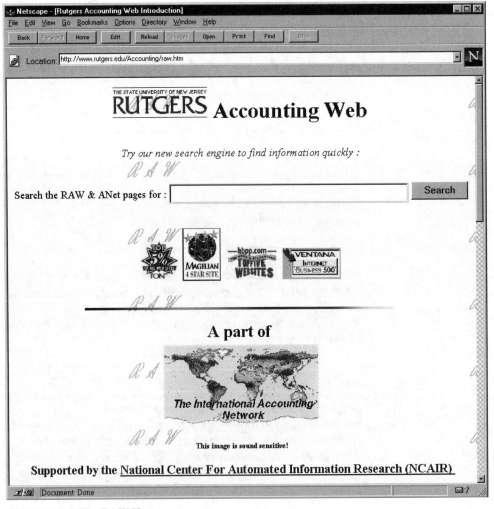

FIGURE 2-2 The RAW Homepage

will bring up a document pointed to by this link. For example, clicking on NCAIR in Figure 2-2 will have the browser request and display on the screen the RAW page describing the National Center for Automated Information Research.

The URL of the RAW is displayed in the Location field under the button bar. This URL can be edited. The user can start editing by simply clicking anywhere in the field. The first click highlights the whole existing URL. The user can then either type the new URL over the previous one or select the part of the URL to be modified and type over it. When this is complete, the user can reach the document of the newly typed URL by pressing the **Enter** key.

Several newer browsers (like Netscape or Internet Explorer) use http as the default protocol. The `protocol://` part of a URL can be omitted, and `http://` will be inserted automatically. Thus, typing in the Location field

<code>www.rutgers.edu/Accounting/raw.htm</code>

results in displaying the same homepage of the RAW as above.

> Most Web browsers display the title of a retrieved document on the title bar. If a document does not have a title, the browser will usually display the URL of the document on the title bar in addition to displaying this URL in the Location field.

The status line at the bottom of the Netscape screen displays an icon of a key. A broken key indicates that the retrieved document is not encrypted. If the key is

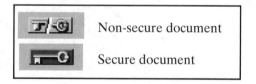

not broken, then the document is secure. The status line also shows the URL of a link in the document when the mouse pointer is placed over that link.

As most Windows programs, a Web browser has a hierarchical pull-down menu system. Commonly used menu commands (e.g., Back, Print, Open, Stop) can be accessed by clicking their corresponding buttons on the button bar under the menu.

Netscape is highly customizable using various entries under the **Options** item on the main menu. The precious screen real estate can be saved by toggling off the **Options | Show Directory Buttons** item. This leads to no loss of functionality since the user can accomplish the same tasks by choosing menu items available by pulling down the **Directory** or **Help** main menu items.

The ways of customizing the appearance and other features of a Web browser differ from one program to another. Internet Explorer is currently not as customizable as Netscape. To customize the appearance of Internet Explorer, the user should select **View** | **Options** and click on the **General** tab. The startup page and the link expiration time can be changed under the **Navigation** tab. The font size can be changed by repeatedly clicking on the **Font** button of the toolbar.

One of the most useful features of Web browsers is their capability to bookmark desired Web documents. For example, in Netscape users can add the URL of any document on their screen to their bookmark list by selecting **Bookmarks** | **Add Bookmark** from the menu. The title of the bookmarked document then appears on the **Bookmarks** menu list, and the user can easily retrieve it in the future by simply selecting this title from the list. In Figure 2-3 the AICPA homepage has just been added to the bookmark list.

Frequent Web users tend to accumulate dozens, if not hundreds, of bookmarks in their lists. Newer browsers allow bookmarks to be organized in the tree-like hierarchical system of folders and subfolders. Such a bookmark hierarchy accumulated by one of the authors is shown in Figure 2-4. Folders are identified by black arrows (triangles) next to them.

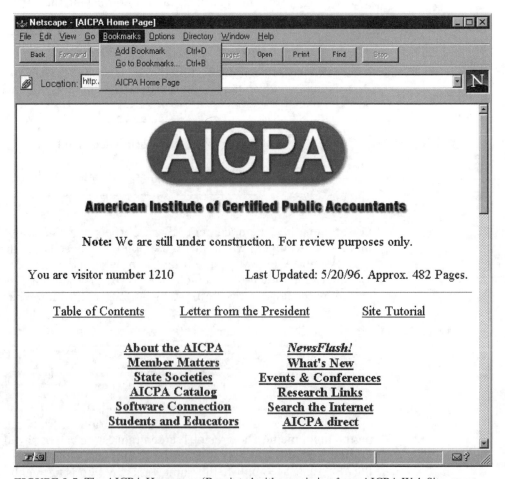

FIGURE 2-3 The AICPA Homepage (Reprinted with permission from AICPA Web Site, copyright ©1997 by the American Institute of Certified Public Accountants)

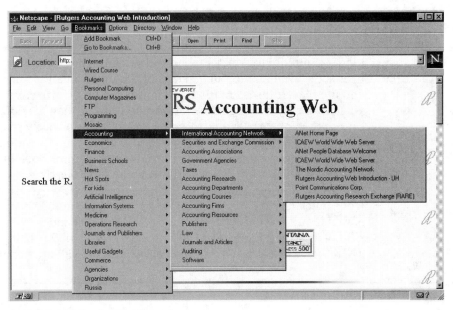

FIGURE 2-4 Bookmark Hierarchy

Web browsers other than Netscape may use different terms for bookmarks. For example, Microsoft Internet Explorer calls them favorites. However, the basic operations and features are almost identical.

SELECTING A WEB BROWSER

Web users benefit from the fact that the two major competitors in the Web browser market—Netscape Communications and Microsoft—continue to make their browsers available for free for personal use. As a result of this unbeatable pricing, combined with superior quality, their browsers—Netscape and Internet Explorer—control more than 90 percent of the market. Most commercial on-line services provide at least one of these two browsers to their users.

From the viewpoint of an average user, there is little, if any, difference between the two browsers. The current versions of Netscape and Internet Explorer are usually head to head in terms of their performance, stability, and advanced features. For many users the choice between these two browsers will be determined by their aesthetic preferences. There are, however, certain considerations that may be crucial in choosing the most appropriate browser.

If the average user connects to the Internet from several computers (say, home and office), she or he will find it imperative to synchronize the collection of bookmarks (or favorites, in the Internet Explorer terminology) in all computers. Netscape Navigator maintains all the bookmark hierarchy in a single file called `bookmark.htm`, while Internet Explorer implements the favorites hierarchy as a directory subtree in the `favorites` subdirectory of the `windows` directory. Netscape may therefore be simpler to use when several computers are involved, since it is easier to transfer its bookmarks from one computer to another [i.e., it is simpler to copy a single file (`bookmark.htm`) than a directory structure].

Some advanced users may connect to the Internet from a number of different computer platforms (PC, UNIX[3], Mac). These users should be interested in having similar browsers on every platform. Currently, only Netscape demonstrates this kind of multiplatform capability—basically the same implementation of this browser is available for all versions of Windows on a PC, various UNIX platforms, and the Mac. Internet Explorer promises multiplatform capabilities, but the 95/NT version usually has been developed much earlier than versions for other platforms (at the time of this writing, the beta version of Internet Explorer for Mac just became available, but there is still no UNIX version on the horizon).

The browser market is possibly the most dynamic one in the whole computer history, with the new versions following the previous ones several times a year. According to various estimates, at the time of this writing, Netscape continues to control a much larger share of the browser market. But the share of Internet Explorer is rapidly increasing. Microsoft is promising to seamlessly integrate the next version of Internet Explorer (4.0) with the Windows 95 shell—Windows Explorer. Therefore, a prudent user should periodically reevaluate her or his browser choice.

MULTIMEDIA

What makes the Web especially attractive is the capability of Web browsers to display graphics and other multimedia objects. In addition to pictures, the Web provides easy access to other types of multimedia—sound and video files. A Web document may have a link to such a multimedia file, and clicking on this link will make the browser download[4] the file and start a program that can play that file. Some simple sound players may come bundled with a Web browser, but in most cases installation of additional programs would be required to view multimedia documents. Many freeware or shareware multimedia viewers can be found on the Internet.

Website Multimedia

Multimedia can greatly enhance the Web-browsing experience. For example, by visiting the site

```
http://www.hal.com/~nathan/Sumo/
```

a Web user can view and download pictures of Sumo wrestlers, the results of recent tournaments, or a QuickTime video of a particularly exciting contest. It will probably take more than 10 minutes to download 40 seconds of QuickTime footage, depending, of course, on the speed of the net connection.

Audio, graphical, and video versatility, however attractive, exact a price. Multimedia files are typically very long. With a slow Internet connection over a telephone line, or with Internet traffic congestion, the download time of multimedia files may be intolerable. To alleviate slowdowns most Web browsers give the user an option to turn off the downloading of pictures embedded in Web documents. In Netscape it can be done by toggling off the **Auto Load Images** item in the **Options** menu. In Internet Explorer the user has to check off the **Show pictures** option in the **Appearance** folder of the **View | Options** box. As a result, the embedded pictures will not be shown automatically in a Web document. It is possible, however, to instruct the browser to download them. In Netscape it can be done by simply clicking on the Images button on the main button bar, or by selecting **View | Load Images.** In Internet Explorer the user has to click the right mouse but-

---

[3]A computer operating system developed at Bell Labs in the early seventies.
[4]**Downloading** means transferring files from a remote computer to a local one.

ton on the box serving as a picture placeholder and then choose from the menu that pops up the item called **Show Picture.**

In both Netscape and Internet Explorer the user can easily save as a graphic file on the hard disk any picture shown on the window. In both programs one should right-click on the picture and choose from the menu that pops up—**Save this Image as** (in Netscape) or **Save Picture as** (in Internet Explorer). In a similar way, one can save on the hard disk any file (audio, movie, etc.) pointed to by a Web link by right-clicking on that link and choosing **Save link as** (in Netscape) or **Save Target As** (in Internet Explorer).

SEARCHING THE WEB

A Web document of interest to the user often can be found on the Web by guessing correctly the URL of the homepage of the Web site and subsequently following the hierarchy of hypertext links from the homepage. If this does not work, the user may have to resort to a more systematic search. This requires the use of special Internet search engines or Internet directories. Major browsers now include in their menus an item pointing to a Web page with an Internet search engine and directory links. For example, in Netscape it can be found as **Directory | Internet Search,** while in Microsoft Internet Explorer it is **Go | Search the Internet.**

Internet search engines are based on large, automatically collected databases of WWW documents. Developers of search engines have their programs continuously scan the Web for new documents and/or updates. Internet directories provide hierarchical systems of Web links classified by subject. Directories usually contain fewer documents than search engines, but their hierarchical structure is often better developed. They are also more selective in the sense that they usually list just one or two documents (main homepages only) from the same Web site. The boundaries between Internet search engines and directories are becoming increasingly blurred as major search engines start adding subject hierarchies to their sites.

There are more than a dozen different main Internet search engines. Here we will briefly discuss the three we consider to be the most powerful, the oldest of which is called **Lycos.** The two others are **AltaVista,** developed by the Digital Equipment Corporation, and **Excite.** These search engines can be found at the following locations:

- `http://www.lycos.com`
- `http://altavista.digital.com/`
- `http://www.excite.com/`

**Website
Search engines**

Each search engine homepage provides the user with a field (rectangular box) in which to type the key words describing the search object. The engine then retrieves from its database the list of documents that contain the key words. Most search engines assign to each link in the list a numerical measure of how close it is to the target (*in the engine's opinion*). The links are sorted according to their proximity to the target.

A successful search requires some practice. Let us consider as an example our attempt to find the homepage of the Institute of Management Accountants (IMA) using Lycos. In the first attempt we type the acronym IMA. The engine returns a long list of documents. The first link in the list points to the Institute of Mathematics and Its Applications at the University of Minnesota, and the second one points to the Interactive Multimedia Association (IMA). Our search object, the Institute of Management Accountants, is listed as number three.

This particular search may be considered a success since the very first page on the screen gives us the link we are looking for. In most search cases, however, the user has to refine the specifications several times to get to the target. When we type in the full name, Institute of Management Accountants, most of the links listed (starting with the second link) point to our target, which can be found at

`http://www.rutgers.edu/accounting/raw/ima/ima.htm`

Many search engines are capable of an advanced search that gives the user more options in using key words. It is possible to use the standard Boolean connectives AND, OR, and NOT to specify the conditions for the search. For example, the search string

`(FASB OR SEC) AND "stock options"`

prompts Excite to return a list of links, the beginning of which is shown in Figure 2-5. This search string describes the documents that contain the phrase "stock options" and either FASB or SEC or both. The objective of this search is to locate documents that deal with the controversy spawned by a recent FASB exposure draft on Accounting for Stock Compensation, which requires recognition, beginning in 1997, of accounting expense for stock options based on the "fair value" of the options at the time of grant, and/or the SEC position on the subject.

Note that the **Find** button on the button bar of Netscape is not related to the Internet search described above. This button simply enables the user to find a word or phrase in the document displayed in the Netscape window. A similar feature is available in Internet Explorer as a menu item—**Edit | Find (on this page).**

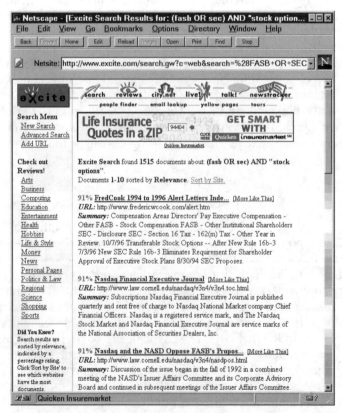

FIGURE 2-5 Advanced Search (Reprinted with permission by Excite, Inc.)

GOPHER

Most of the WWW browsers can give users access not only to the WWW but also to some other Internet services. One important example is gopher, which can be described as an early generation Internet information browsing system. This system allows browsing through either simple menu screens or plain text documents. An example of a URL of a gopher site is

```
gopher://gopher.financenet.gov/
```

Nowadays gopher is almost extinct, and the last gopher sites will soon join the ranks of the dinosaurs of the WWW age of the Internet, which is barely three years old.

CONCLUDING REMARKS

This chapter provided a basic introduction to the World Wide Web. We introduced the basic concepts on how to surf the Web, the nature of interlinked pages, the usage of a browser, and the characteristics of search engines. In later chapters we will take our reader on a "maiden voyage" through Cyberspace to show the richness and the variety of the Web accounting resources. We will also discuss how our reader can become not only a Web surfer but also a "personal Web publisher" by preparing his or her own materials for the Web.

Problems

1. Browse the Internet daily for general news, as well as news items in which you are particularly interested. Evaluate the effectiveness of obtaining news from the Internet, as compared with other media.
2. Plan your next vacation on the Internet. Compare the amenities of alternative vacation destinations, prices of lodging, cost of transportation, and so forth.
3. Organize your bookmarks in a hierarchical system of folders and subfolders. Add at least five new sites to your bookmark archives every week.
4. Discuss the features of two different browsers. Define a way you would choose among them and pick your choice. Read an article from a computer magazine (say *PC World*) that compares browsers and evaluate your method.
5. Visit two different search engines, search for the same key words, and compare the results.
6. For your hobby or an area of interest, identify interesting sites, bulletin boards, and newsgroups. Mark them with bookmarks. Visit these sources regularly. Modify and expand your portfolio.
7. Modify the default visited link expiration time to a value suitable to you.
8. Compare the speed of browsing the Web when the downloading of pictures is turned on to when it is turned off.
9. Save as a picture file on your hard disk the International Accounting Network logo from the RAW homepage.
10. Go to the list of the FASB statements at

```
http://www.rutgers.edu/Accounting/raw/fasb/st/stpg.htm
```

and use search to find all the statements dealing with accounting for futures contracts.

CHAPTER

Accountant's Journey through Cyberspace

INVITATION FOR YOUR MAIDEN VOYAGE

Accounting is catching on (at least on the Internet) with other information disciplines. Join us on the exciting Cyberspace journey to sample some of accounting's hottest sites on the World Wide Web. This chapter illustrates the wealth and diversity of accounting information to be found on the Internet. You can participate in this voyage by surfing the Web and exploring the sites on your own screen, or you can glance over this material at your reading pleasure and return to this chapter later on when you are ready to dive into the Internet.

Rutgers Accounting Web—The Accounting Travel Guide

Barely two years old, the Rutgers Accounting Web (RAW) can be considered the granddaddy of Web accounting sites. It has been recognized as one of the most important Internet sites by several rating services. The RAW has become an indispensable Internet resource for accounting scholars, practitioners, and students alike. It is now getting more than 300,000 hits a week and is growing rapidly.

The RAW provides a variety of accounting and auditing materials including Accounting Education Change Commission projects, the complete text and database of the Jenkins Report of the AICPA, numerous lectures, and outlines in systems, auditing, and accounting. The RAW also hosts the Web sites of important accounting and auditing organizations such as the Financial Accounting Standards Board, the Institute of Internal Auditors, the Institute of Management Accountants, the Association of Government Accountants, and the American Accounting Association. The RAW site can be found at

```
http://www.rutgers.edu/accounting
```

(see Figure 3-1). The RAW is part of the International Accounting Network (IAN) with five partners around the world. It concentrates on U.S. accounting, while other nodes of the IAN have British, Australian, Hawaiian, Japanese, and Finnish orientations.

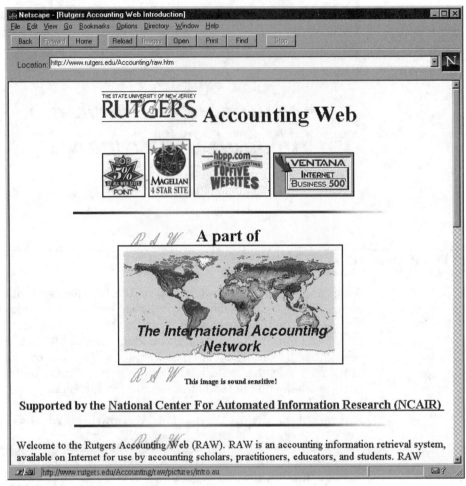

FIGURE 3-1 Rutgers Accounting Web

The RAW develops and maintains an information resource of great value called "**Accounting Resources on the Internet.**" There you can find a comprehensive directory of pointers to the Internet accounting and auditing sites including CPA firms, the FASB, publishing houses, accounting software and courseware, and more. The RAW strives to maintain the standing of this resource as the central directory of Internet accounting information.

FINANCIAL INFORMATION, REPORTING, AND DISCLOSURE

Financial Accounting Standards Board (FASB)

The homepage of the Financial Accounting Standards Board is hosted on the Rutgers Accounting Web at

```
http://www.rutgers.edu/accounting/raw/fasb
```

(see Figure 3-2), while a connection to this site can also be made through the FASB Web server at

http://www.fasb.org

The RAW has been providing some FASB materials for quite a while, although those materials were primarily limited to press releases. In the summer of 1996 a full-fledged FASB Web site was developed on the RAW. It contains detailed information about the structure and functions of the board. The site also provides the summaries and the status of all the released Statements of Financial Accounting Standards (125 as of July 1996). On an experimental basis, the full text of a number of recent exposure drafts is made available for viewing on-line (in HTML) and downloading (in MS Word).

Website FASB

The FASB site provides on-line the content of the current issue and the archive of past issues of the FASB weekly newspaper, *Action Alert.* The full text of FASB press releases starting from January 1996 is also available, as well as the information and ordering instructions for FASB publications. Among those publications is *The FASB Cases on Recognition and Measurement* authored by L. Todd Johnson, FASB Research Manager, and Kimberley R. Petrone, FASB Project Manager, and published through John Wiley & Sons, Inc. Five of the cases are available on-line. Finally, the site describes the current Board Agenda Projects, Emerging Issues Task Force, and other issues under consideration (from FASB newsletter *Status Report*).

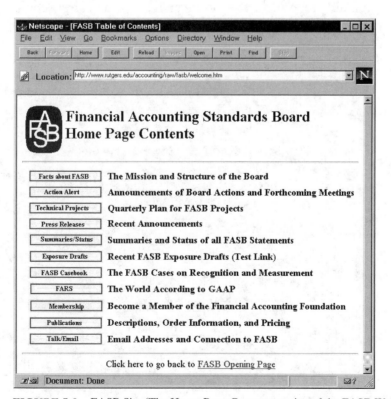

FIGURE 3-2   FASB Site (The Home Page Contents section of the FASB Web site is reprinted with the permission of the Financial Accounting Standards Board, 401 Merritt 7, P.O. Box 5116, Norwalk, Connecticut 06856-5116)

Jenkins Report (AICPA): AICPA Special Committee on Financial Reporting, Database of Materials on Users' Needs for Information

A very significant recent development in the accounting profession was the Jenkins Report by the Special Committee on Financial Reporting of the American Institute of Certified Public Accountants. This committee was formed in 1991 to "address concerns about the relevance and usefulness of business reporting." The committee was charged with the task of recommending "(1) the nature of information that should be made available to others by management and (2) the extent to which auditors should report on the various elements of that information."

The committee studied the use of financial information by professional investors and creditors and their advisors by meeting with groups of users and analyzing users' documents as well as business and investment models. On the basis of these studies the committee formed a set of recommendations that were tested by conducting a survey of approximately 1,200 users.

The committee recommended changes in four areas: "improving the types of information in business reporting, improving financial statements, improving auditors' involvement with business reporting, and facilitating change." Among the important recommendations of the committee, we can list the following: improve disclosure of business segment information; address the disclosures and accounting for innovative financial instruments; improve disclosures of off-balance-sheet financing arrangements; report separately the effects of core and noncore activities and events, and measure at fair value noncore assets and liabilities; and improve quarterly reporting by reporting on the fourth quarter separately.

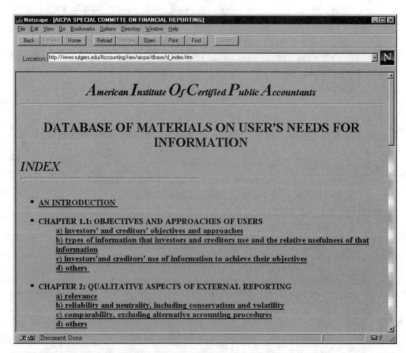

FIGURE 3-3 Jenkins Report (AICPA) (Reprinted with permission from AICPA Web site, copyright 1997 by the American Institute of Certified Public Accountants)

When the committee completed its work in September 1994, it published a comprehensive 200-page report and a 1600-page database of materials supporting its findings. With help from the AICPA, the Rutgers Accounting Web team put the full text of the report and the supporting database on-line. Anyone can freely access these materials on the Internet at

```
http://www.rutgers.edu/Accounting/raw/aicpa/index.htm
```

(see Figure 3-3).

EDGAR Database of Corporate Information

Effective January 1, 1994, the Securities and Exchange Commission made it possible for publicly traded companies to opt for an electronic filing of their statements with the SEC. At the same time a project, called Edgar, was sponsored to make the emerging electronic database of corporate filings publicly available on the Internet. This project was sponsored in 1994 and 1995 by the National Science Foundation and implemented by New York University (NYU) in conjunction with the Internet Multicasting Service. In October 1995 the Securities and Exchange Commission opened its own Web site, thereby replacing the Edgar site of the Internet Multicasting Service. New York University retained its Edgar site, which provides additional advanced services (e.g., more convenient and powerful searches of the Edgar database).

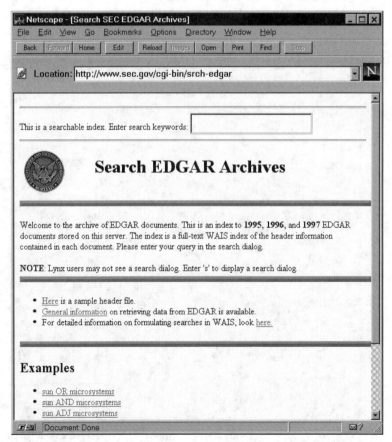

FIGURE 3-4 EDGAR Database of Corporate Information (Reprinted with permission by the United States Securities and Exchange Commission)

As of May 1996 all publicly traded companies are required to file most of their financial documents with the SEC electronically. For foreign companies electronic filing is optional. An increasing number of foreign companies voluntarily choose to file electronically. The SEC Edgar site can be found at

```
http://www.sec.gov/edgarhp.htm
```

(see Figure 3-4), whereas the NYU Edgar site is at

```
http://edgar.stern.nyu.edu/
```

The NYU Edgar site also has an important pointer to the R. R. Donnelley Library of SEC Materials including the links to the on-line versions of the Securities Act of 1933 and the Exchange Act of 1934. The Edgar electronic database includes quarterly and annual filings of Forms 10-Q and 10-K. Users have immediate on-line access to financial statements through an efficient search engine, which permits retrieval of all electronic company filings. Figure 3-5 shows the 1994 annual report (on Form 10-K) of AT&T found on Edgar.

> The convenience of finding an annual report at a well-known central location (Edgar) is partly offset by its cumbersome and unattractive format (a very long single plain text file). Fortunately, there is an alternative in the case of many companies: direct retrieval of the report from the company's own Web site. Those reports are usually well organized in an attractive hypertext form.

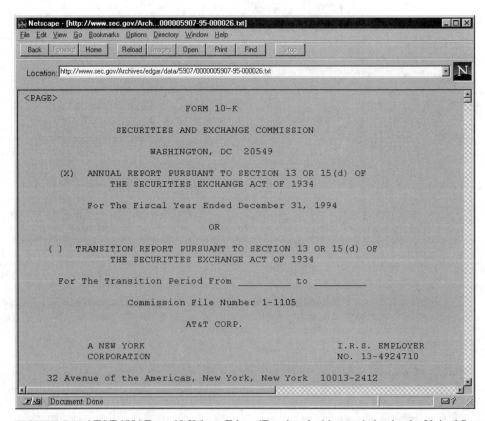

FIGURE 3-5 AT&T 1994 Form 10-K from Edgar (Reprinted with permission by the United States Securities and Exchange Commission)

The same financial information (1994 AT&T annual report) can be found in the AT&T Web site at

`http://www.att.com/ar-1994/htm13/index.html`

(see Figure 3-6). As a service to investors, many companies nowadays provide their annual (and even quarterly) reports on their Web sites.

It is much easier to work with financial statements that are accessible electronically. Financial data from those statements can be imported directly into electronic spreadsheets without any retyping.[1]

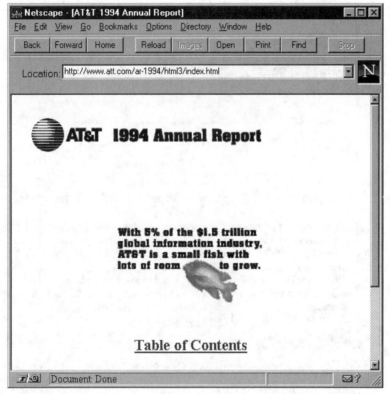

FIGURE 3-6 1994 AT&T Annual Report (Used with permission. © 1995. AT&T.)

Governmental Accounting Standards Board (GASB)

Website GASB

The federal government has been very active in providing valuable resources on the Internet. The General Accounting Office (the investigative arm of Congress charged with examining matters relating to the receipt and disbursement of public funds, and performing audits and evaluations of government programs and activities) has its annual report and other important documents available from its Web site at

`http://www.gao.gov`

An impressive collection of government-provided financial information is organized as the FinanceNet. One of the important accounting resources provided by

---

[1]For a detailed discussion of how to do this, see Appendix A.

the FinanceNet is the homepage of the Governmental Accounting Standards Board (GASB) found at

```
http://www.financenet.gov/gasb.htm
```

(see Figure 3-7).

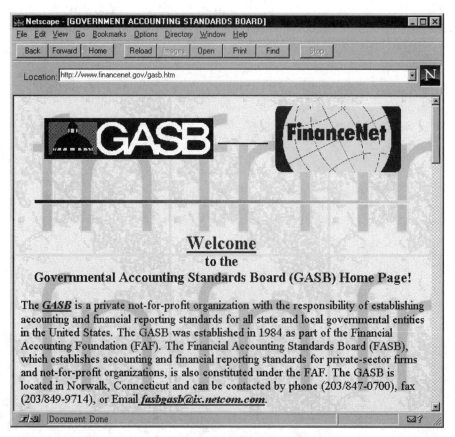

FIGURE 3-7 Governmental Accounting Standards Board (GASB) (The GASB "Welcome" page from the GASB Web site is reprinted with the permission of the Governmental Accounting Standards Board, 401 Merritt 7, P.O. Box 5116, Norwalk, Connecticut 06856-5116)

The GASB was organized in 1984 by the Financial Accounting Foundation to establish standards of financial accounting and reporting for state and local governmental entities. The GASB homepage provides access to GASB publications including standards, concept statements, and research reports. It also provides recent news, press releases, and announcements.

Stock Market Information from GALT Technologies

The Internet provides a great variety of stock market information ranging from the latest news about individual companies and mutual funds to nearly real-time (fifteen minute delay) stock quotes. One of the most impressive stock market quote servers was developed by GALT Technologies, and it can be found at

```
http://quotes.galt.com/
```

The information is available for securities traded on American and Canadian stock exchanges, and it provides both "immediate" (fifteen-minute delay) stock quotes and graphs of historical performance (currently going back almost seven years). A twenty-day chart displaying the performance of the IBM stock obtained from this server is shown in Figure 3-8.

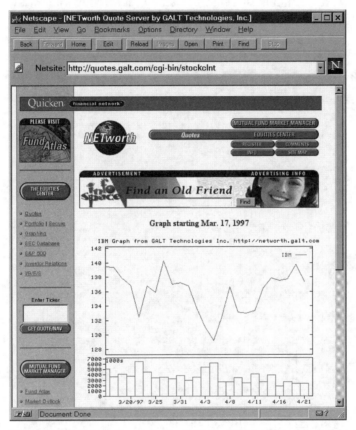

FIGURE 3-8 GALT Technologies IBM Stock Chart (Reprinted with permission by GALT Technologies, Inc.)

ACCOUNTING AND AUDITING METHODOLOGIES AND COURSEWARE

Momentum Accounting and Triple-Entry Bookkeeping by Yuji Ijiri
STUDIES IN ACCOUNTING RESEARCH #31

The American Accounting Association publishes a series of research monographs under the general title "Studies in Accounting Research." The book *Momentum Accounting and Triple-Entry Bookkeeping: Exploring the Dynamic Structure of Accounting Measurements* by Professor Yuji Ijiri of Carnegie Mellon University has been published in this series. The full text of this work is available in hypertext form from the Rutgers Accounting Web at

```
http://www.rutgers.edu/accounting/raw/aaa/resea/yich.htm
```

(see Figure 3-9). This demonstrates how frontiers of accounting research are made instantly accessible to accounting scholars and students all over the world. The hypertext form makes it easier to study research works by allowing readers to bring up simultaneously on the screen (in separate windows) different parts of the work.

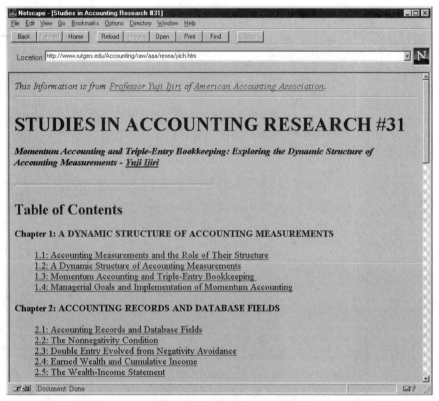

FIGURE 3-9 *Momentum Accounting and Triple-Entry Bookkeeping* (Reprinted with permission by American Accounting Association)

Activity Based Risk Evaluation Model of Auditing (ABREMA)

One of the more interesting auditing resources on the Internet is ABREMA—the Activity Based Risk Evaluation Model of Auditing developed by Howard Holmes from Macquarie University in Australia. It can be found at

```
http://www.efs.mq.edu.au/accg/resources/abrema/
```

(see Figure 3-10). ABREMA is "a prescriptive model of financial statement auditing . . . which primarily relates to the independent audit of the financial statements of a corporate entity."

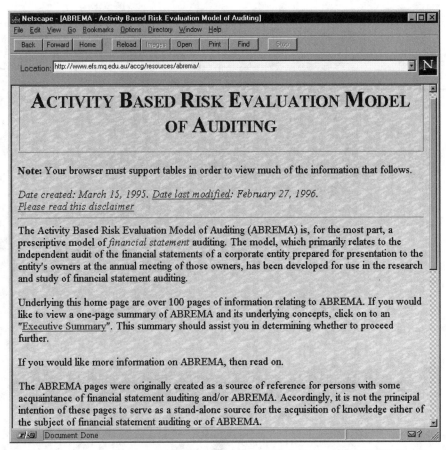

FIGURE 3-10 Activity Based Risk Evaluation Model Of Auditing (ABREMA) (Reprinted with permission by Howard Holmes, MacQuarie University)

The model is presented in an unabridged form containing more than 100 pages of information based on Holmes's monograph "Auditing: An Activity Based Risk Evaluation Methodology." The presentation of ABREMA is organized for three levels of users: novice, intermediate, and advanced. The site contains a comprehensive on-line glossary of auditing concepts and terms. This site is distinguished by its sophisticated multidimensional structure providing an effective demonstration of the potential inherent in the Internet medium for new forms of exposition.

Free Exchange of Accounting Knowledge

Free exchange of information is an honored tradition of the Internet. In that spirit many authors made software and written documents freely available on-line (known as *freeware*). This practice has been spreading to educational materials. A growing number of accounting scholars put on-line free-of-charge materials they have prepared for their teaching. The Web technology makes it increasingly easy for educators to prepare hypertext educational materials and for students to retrieve them. With the advent of electronic publishing, we will see more work in progress and experimental teaching materials posted on the Web, taking advantage of low costs of publication and the worldwide exposure.

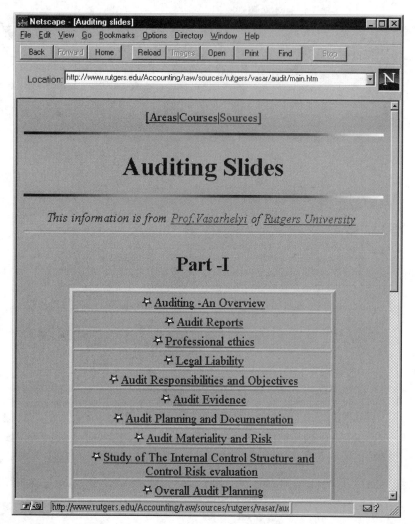

FIGURE 3-11 Professor Vasarhelyi's Auditing Slides

It is popular to post copies of slide shows on the Web as standard pictures. Figure 3-11 shows the list of slides prepared by Prof. Vasarhelyi for his auditing course to be used in conjunction with the textbook *Auditing* by A. Arens and J. Loebbecke.[2] These slides are available on the Internet at

```
http://www.rutgers.edu/accounting/raw/sources/rutgers/vasar/audit/main.htm
```

The slides presented as standard pictures are accessible through any standard Web browser. It is impossible, however, to conveniently and fully edit those slides by using standard presentation software (e.g., PowerPoint or Freelance). To allow for easy editing it is possible to keep on-line a copy of the slides in their native presentation software format. Such slides, however, cannot be viewed using standard Web browsers. The users who have the proper software can download such slides and use them.

---

[2]Prentice Hall, 1995.

Accounting Publishers

Website
Accounting texts

Most accounting publishers have established Web sites. Prentice Hall is a good example to consider, which is located at

http://www.prenhall.com

This site provides convenient on-line access to the company's offerings in various disciplines. The accounting books are classified by subject matter.

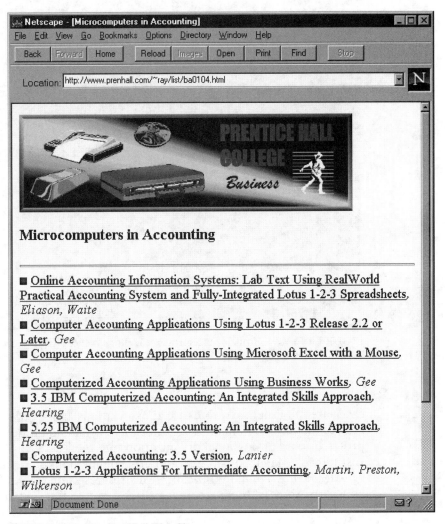

FIGURE 3-12 Prentice Hall Web Site

Figure 3-12 shows the Internet page listing Prentice Hall titles in the area of "Microcomputers in Accounting." Under the title of each book there is a description of its main features and a detailed table of contents. Information about ordering procedures for individual users and college faculty is provided as well. The Prentice Hall Web site also has search capability, allowing the user to find individual titles matching user-chosen key words.

THE ACCOUNTING PROFESSION
AND ACCOUNTING PRACTICE

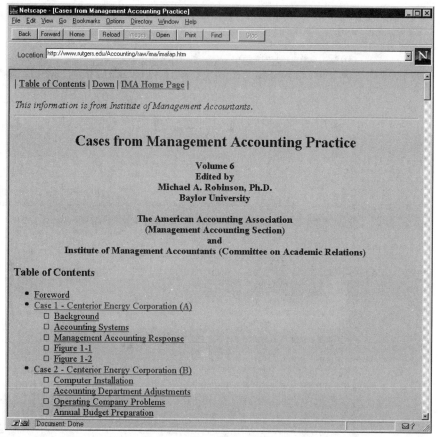

FIGURE 3-13 Cases from Management Accounting Practice (Reprinted with permission by the Institute of Management Accountants)

Cases are very important resources for accounting education. Various accounting cases are published by professional associations, universities, and major publishers. An increasing number of cases become available on the WWW as individual professors and professional organizations put their cases on-line. For example, the Institute of Management Accountants commissions and publishes *Cases from Management Accounting Practice*. It distributes them free of charge to interested educators. Some of them are now available on the Internet at

        http://www.rutgers.edu/Accounting/raw/ima/imafap.htm

(see Figure 3-13).

What Corporate America Wants
in Entry-Level Accountants:

A Joint Research Project of the Institute of Management Accountants and the Financial Executives Institute, August 1994, Gary Siegel and James E. Sorensen
    The Institute of Management Accountants and the Financial Executives Institute recently commissioned an important research study to determine the educa-

tional needs of entry-level management accountants from the point of view of Corporate America. The results of this study were obtained by analyzing about eight hundred responses to a mail survey of U.S. accounting and financial executives. The study revealed that Corporate America thinks that universities are doing a less-than-adequate job of preparing people for entry-level work in management accounting. The graduates lack practical experience and have little understanding of the "big picture" or how the "real world" works. Their communication and social skills are poor, and they are insufficiently prepared in manufacturing accounting. The broad accounting knowledge and skills areas considered as the most important for management accountants are budgeting, working capital management, product costing, strategic cost management, asset management, control and performance evaluation, consolidated statements, and information system design.

The majority of respondents thought that there was a difference in skills and knowledge required by entry-level positions in corporate accounting and their counterparts in public accounting. They also thought that universities overemphasized public accounting at the expense of management accounting. The vast majority of respondents preferred graduates with a bachelor's degree in accounting over graduates with a master's or associate degree. The surveyed executives attributed greater importance to the content of the accounting courses than to their sheer number. The complete text of this study can be found in the IMA section of the RAW at

```
http://www.rutgers.edu/Accounting/raw/ima/entry/entry1.htm
```

(see Figure 3-14).

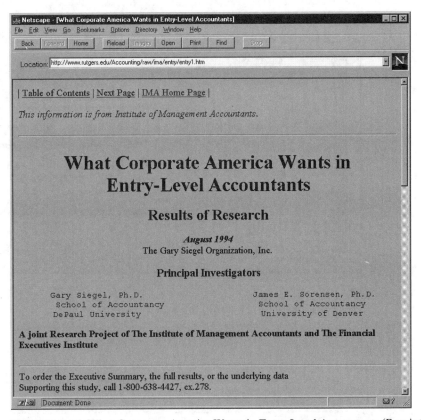

FIGURE 3-14 What Corporate America Wants in Entry-Level Accountants (Reprinted with permission by the Institute of Management Accountants)

Professional Magazines On-line

An increasing number of professional publications deem it necessary to establish Web sites. *Controller Magazine*'s Web site is a very interesting example of such a site created by a professional accounting publication. This site can be found at

$$\texttt{http://www.controllermag.com}$$

(see Figure 3-15).

The site provides all the standard information about the publication, including general description, staff, editorial and subscription information, as well as a convenient interface to communicate with the magazine (send an E-mail message to the editors, submit an idea for a new article, etc.). The most interesting and useful feature of this site is the on-line archive, which contains hypertext versions of many articles that appeared in print. This is of great value to subscribers and nonsubscribers alike because a hypertext version of an article linking and cross-referencing it with other materials is in many respects superior to a printed version. The *Controller Magazine*'s site maintains an on-line listing of upcoming conferences and professional trade shows. The visitors to the site can find the editorial plan of the magazine extending as far as nine months into the future. The site also maintains a list of links to some of the accounting resources on the Internet.

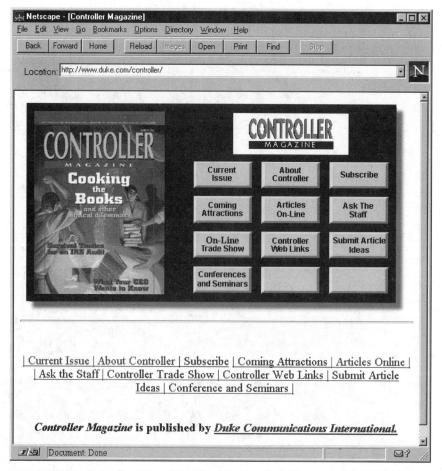

FIGURE 3-15 *Controller Magazine*'s Web (Reprinted with permission by Duke Communications)

Deloitte & Touche 1996 Industry Forecasts

Industry forecasts are instrumental in predicting earnings per share. One of the Big 6 accounting firms (Deloitte & Touche) started providing analyses of prospects and strategies as well as forecasts for thirteen major industries and the public sector on the Internet:

```
http://www.dtcg.com/publications/public01.html
```

(see Figure 3-16).

The industries analyzed include aerospace and defense, automotive, chemicals, consumer intensive businesses, energy and utilities, financial services, health care, high technology, manufacturing, pharmaceutical/medical devices, telecommunications, and trade. These industry surveys provide general background, describe major trends, and analyze problems and prospects for the main players in the field.

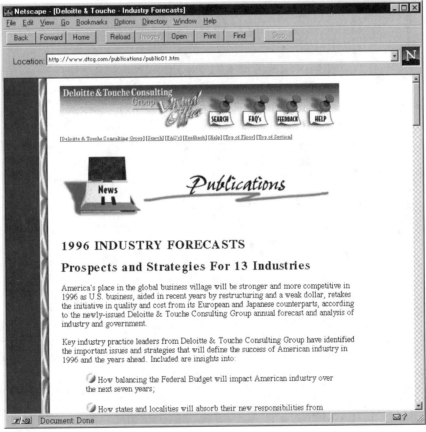

FIGURE 3-16 Deloitte & Touche 1996 Industry Forecasts (Reprinted with permission of Deloitte & Touche Consulting Group LLC. Copyright © 1997 by Deloitte & Touche Consulting Group LLC.)

Accounting Software Vendors

Most, if not all, accounting software companies have a presence on-line. Peachtree Software, one of the oldest developers of entry-level integrated accounting packages, provides a typical example of such a site. It is found at

```
http://www.peach.com
```

(see Figure 3-17). The Peachtree Web site contains information about the company and a detailed description of all the products, including evaluation versions of some products available for downloading. The site also provides extensive technical support for the company's products, including an interesting set of on-line usage tips.

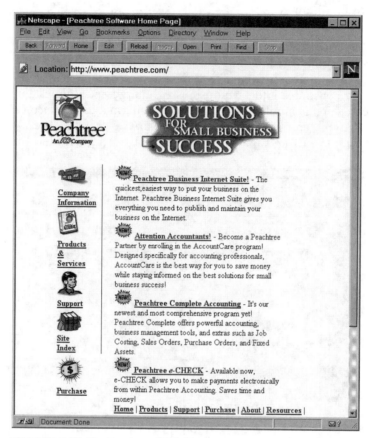

FIGURE 3-17 The Peachtree Web (Reprinted with permission by Peachtree Software)

This is typical of software companies who find on-line Internet technical support to be the cheapest, the easiest, and the most convenient mode of customer support. Under the title "Peachtree University," the company provides detailed information about its user training programs.

TAXES, TAXES, TAXES . . .

Internal Revenue Service

Website
Taxes

The federal government is very active on the information superhighway. It is not surprising that the Internal Revenue Service has had its own Web site for quite a while. Recently, it underwent a major facelift to become one of the prettiest sites for an accountant to encounter on his or her professional Internet journey. The site can be found at

```
http://www.irs.ustreas.gov/prod/cover.html
```

(see Figure 3-18).

FIGURE 3-18 Internal Revenue Service

The IRS site provides answers to frequently asked tax questions, gives up-to-date information on changes in the tax law, and also allows taxpayers to download any and all IRS tax forms and instructions. Any form can be downloaded in several-page description formats that can be printed out by various printers or through special programs to produce a standard-looking form. Tax professionals can be very interested in the immediate access to all recently released IRS regulations (currently available regulations include all those released since August 1, 1995). The IRS site also provides tax forms and tax preparation instructions for businesses.

Tax Code On-line

The Internet is home to important tax-related information. The full text of the U.S. Tax Code (current up to January 24, 1994) is available on-line at

```
http://www.fourmilab.ch/ustax/www/contents.html
```

(Figure 3-19). The U.S. Tax Code was obtained from the U.S. Congress gopher, and then it was automatically converted into a hypertext format. This resource provides an example of the advantages of the hypertext form by cross-referencing various sections of this complex document.

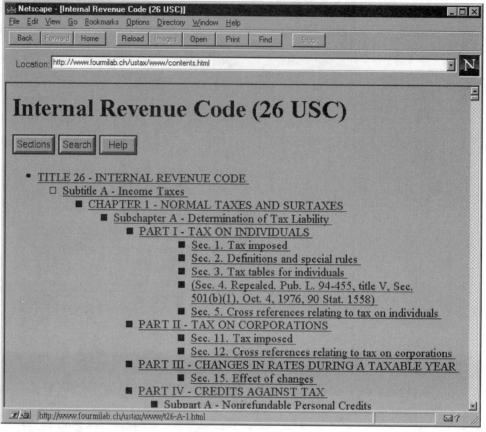

FIGURE 3-19 U.S. Tax Code On-line

Another Web site that contains a hypertext version of the U.S. Tax Code on-line is

```
http://www.tns.lcs.mit.edu/uscode/
```

developed by the Telemedia, Networks and Systems Group at the MIT Laboratory for Computer Science. Both sites have search engines to facilitate the location of needed information.

International Taxes (World Tax from Ernst & Young)

One of the manifestations of the global nature of the Internet in accounting is the abundance of on-line international accounting materials. These materials range from international accounting E-mailing lists maintained by the ANet in Australia to financial statements for listed Finnish companies provided by the Nordic Accounting Network. One of the richest on-line international accounting resources is the World Tax from Ernst & Young.

This resource can be found at

```
http://www.eyi.com/itax
```

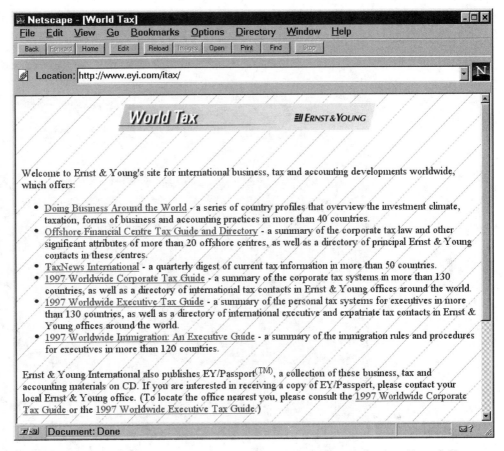

FIGURE 3-20 World Tax from Ernst & Young (Reprinted with permission from Ernst & Young International, Ltd.)

Website International taxes

(see Figure 3-20), and it currently includes a series of country profiles that overviews the investment climate, taxation, forms of business, and accounting practices in more than 30 countries (*Doing Business Around the World*), a summary of the corporate tax systems in more than 130 countries (*Worldwide Corporate Tax Guide and Directory, 1997 Edition*), a quarterly digest of current tax information in more than 50 countries (*TaxNews International*), and other materials.

This comprehensive database allows all accounting practitioners and scholars to be informed about the most significant developments in tax law and tax accounting all over the world.

ACCOUNTING JOKES

Accounting has an unchallenged reputation for being a very serious (if not boring) subject. No wonder that the profession and its practitioners have been the subject of many jokes. Some of those jokes now find their home on-line. Anytime entries and ledgers start dancing before your weary eyes, and you see quadruple entries instead of double ones, you may want to visit the pages like the "Two Fun Guys and an Accountant" shown in Figure 3-21 and located at

```
http://www.execpc.com/~thorsten/JOKE.HTML
```

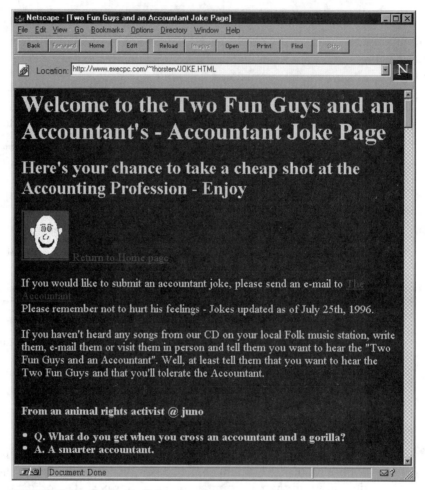

FIGURE 3-21 Accounting Jokes

Another place to visit to relieve some of your accrued (and not yet amortized) accounting stress is the "Keyu and Gizmo's Home for Neurotically Challenged Accountants" at

```
http://uts.cc.utexas.edu/~gizmo/main.html
```

CONCLUSIONS

Our maiden voyage into Cyberspace has come to its end. What you have seen so far is only the tip of the iceberg of accounting knowledge and information available on the Internet. With new accounting materials coming on-line, this iceberg is growing at an ever-increasing rate. The purpose of our Cyberspace journey is to give you a feeling for the wide scope and comprehensiveness of the Web accounting resources. A compendium of the complete set of accounting resources on the Internet known to us is given in the appendix to this book. We hope that this journey and the other information in this book will get you started and help you become a seasoned traveler in accounting Cyberspace.

Problems

1. Visit the Rutgers Accounting Web. Go to "Accounting Resources on the Internet." Identify what are to you the ten most important accounting resources. Place them in your bookmark hierarchy.

2. Retrieve the financial reports of companies you either invest in or are most interested in from their SEC filings or directly from their Web sites. Also retrieve their stock market quotes and historical records of their market performance. Find any additional information on-line you can about those companies and construct their "Internet profiles." Keep updating your information.

3. Depending on your level of study of auditing, read the novice, intermediate, or advanced presentations of ABREMA. Identify important learning opportunities for students interested in the study of auditing risks, as well as materials that can serve as useful supplements for introductory and/or advanced courses in auditing. Build a course syllabus that integrates these on-line materials.

4. Surf the Web and identify locations of accounting cases.

5. Surf the Web and find the homepages of several accounting associations.

6. Find Web sites containing educational materials for the accounting courses you are currently studying. Visit these sites regularly to enrich your learning experience.

7. Locate Web sites of CPA firms in your area. Compare the coverage and the presentation of materials these sites provide.

8. Find and visit the Web site of the developers of accounting software you are using. Check to see if it provides any patches, upgrades, or information about new versions of the software.

9. Visit the IRS Web site, and find, download, and print out at least one tax form.

10. Find and visit the Web sites of the publishers of your accounting textbooks. Look for any materials the sites may provide to supplement your textbooks.

CHAPTER

Basic Internet Services

4

INTRODUCTION

So far the discussion has focused mainly on surfing and browsing. The purpose of this chapter is to introduce the reader to the many other important services for which the Internet is famous. These services range from the simple exchange of messages (E-mail) to more sophisticated tools of information retrieval. After reading this chapter, the reader should be able to move information around the Internet, use Internet electronic mail, and gain a degree of access to and control over remote computers on the net.

MOVING THINGS AROUND (FTP)

Website
ftp

The file transfer protocol (ftp) was the first Internet service that allowed users to move information (files) over the Internet. In ftp the user connects to a remote computer, navigates the file system, and locates and transfers desired files back and forth between the local computer and the remote one. Certain file transfers can be done using standard Web browsers. Other transfers require special ftp programs. Web browsers can download files from publicly accessible areas on some Internet hosts. Ftp is particularly useful in downloading programs. Unlike documents that can be viewed in a browser window, programs have to be executed (run) on a local computer. For that purpose, a program has to be first downloaded (copied) to the local computer using ftp.

To point a Web browser to an ftp site, a URL has to use ftp as the protocol and specify a path to a publicly accessible ftp file or directory on the remote computer. For example, the URL of the public ftp area of the Rutgers Accounting Web is

```
ftp://www.rutgers.edu/pub/accounting
```

and the resulting directory listing is shown in Figure 4-1. The list consists of files and directories. Netscape shows directories as folders and files as sheets with special sheet icons for certain file types. Each item on the list is a link. Clicking a directory link instructs the browser to change to that directory and display its contents on the screen. Clicking a file link instructs the browser to display that file on the screen whenever possible.

Text, hypertext, or standard image files can be readily displayed on the screen. Programs (.exe) or compressed (.zip) files cannot be properly displayed on the screen, and the browser will give the user the option to save them on the local hard disk. Consider the example of downloading a special ftp program (called ws ftp) from the Web site of this book. This program is located in the following directory:

ftp://www.rutgers.edu/pub/accounting/book/software/

and the name of the file is wsftp32z.exe. Going to that directory and clicking on that file's link will make Netscape display the Unknown File Type dialog box shown in Figure 4-2. Clicking on the **Save** button will produce the standard Save As . . . dialog box, in which the user can choose the directory to save that file.

The wsftp32z.exe file is a compressed self-extracting file containing all the files of the ws_ftp application. If the user runs it, it uncompresses itself, extracting

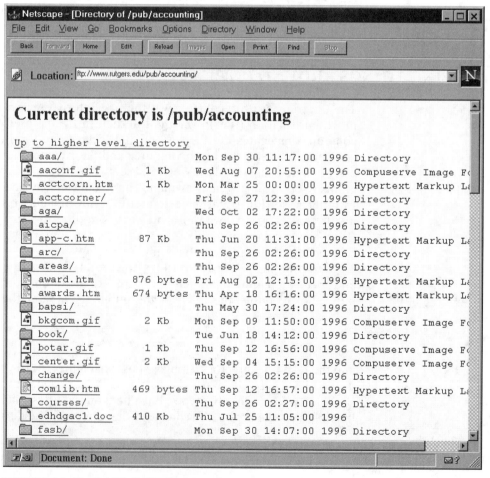

FIGURE 4-1 The RAW's Public ftp Area

all the program files in the directory where it is. Hence, it is advisable to put this file in an empty directory. The program requires no special installation. Therefore, the directory may be the actual directory created to keep this program.

This ftp program is to be used under MS Windows 95 or Windows NT. The name of the file to run is `ws_ftp32.exe`. While Web browsers can handle some ftp tasks, special ftp programs are needed for uploading files and transferring files that are not in the public domain. These are tasks that many Web browsers cannot do. For example, a user may have an account on a UNIX computer at a university or local IAP. Files in that account are protected by a user ID and a password and are, therefore, accessible to that user only. Special ftp programs have the capability to specify the user ID and password to get access to the account and transfer files between that account and the user's PC. Some Web browsers, like Netscape, are capable of accessing protected information. It requires the addition of the user ID in the URL and entering the account password when prompted by the browser.

Consider the following example. One of the authors of this book has an account on the computer `andromeda.rutgers.edu`. The user ID is `kogan`. The password is not disclosed for security concerns. Let us first discuss how to access files in this account using Netscape.

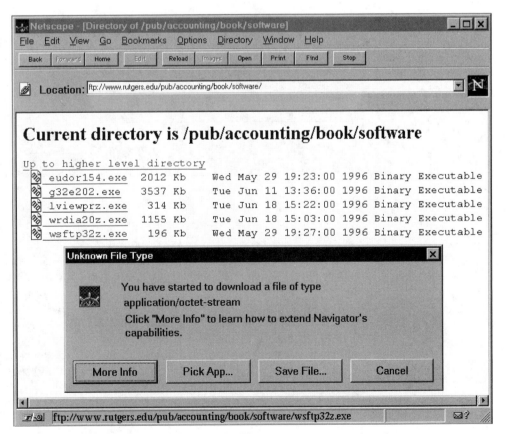

FIGURE 4-2 Download from This Book's ftp Site

Since this account is protected, the URL should contain its user ID. The general structure of such URLs is the following:

`ftp://user@computer/path`

Since the home directory of `kogan` is `/fac/kogan`, the URL to open is

`ftp://kogan@andromeda.rutgers.edu/fac/kogan`

When Netscape tries to open this URL, it prompts for the account password as shown in Figure 4-3. Unfortunately, not all the Web browsers support this password prompting. For example, Microsoft Internet Explorer for Windows 95 version 3.0[1] does not. Consequently, attempting to open the URL above results in an error message saying that the password "was not allowed." To solve this problem one can enter the password as a part of the URL. It is possible to access protected user accounts by entering URL of the following form:

`ftp://user:password@computer/path`

It is the authors' opinion that this method should not be used since it compromises security because the password part of the URL is not encrypted and is shown by the browser in the location field. As a result, the password can be seen easily by any person who happens to take a look at the computer screen during this procedure.

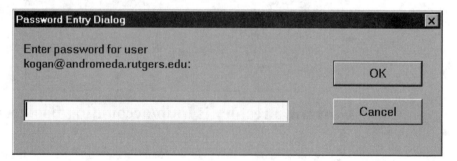

FIGURE 4-3 Ftp Password Prompt

After entering the correct password, Netscape displays the content of the directory. Now the user can browse this protected directory tree and download any files in exactly the same way as above. In some situations the user may want to transfer files in the opposite direction—to upload them from her or his PC to the protected account. Unfortunately, very few Web browsers support the uploading of local files. In fact, even early versions of Netscape did not support it; newer versions of Netscape (2.0 and up) do. To upload a local file, the user should change first to the remote directory where the file should be uploaded, and then select **File** | **Upload File** (see Figure 4-4).

---

[1]The newest version at the time of this writing.

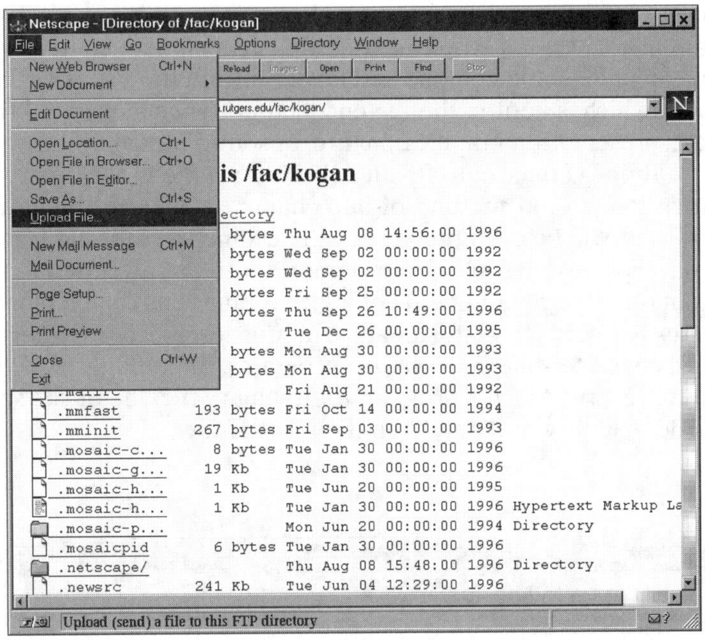

FIGURE 4-4   Uploading a File by ftp

Although newer advanced Web browsers gradually become capable of taking on most ftp tasks, dedicated ftp programs, like ws_ftp, for the time being remain the most convenient and versatile option. When ws_ftp starts up, it produces the Session Profile dialog box (see Figure 4-5) in which the user is to provide the information required for establishing an ftp connection: the computer name, the user ID, and the password. The Session Profile shown at the startup is the last session profile used by the program.

Clicking on the **New** button allows the user to specify a new session profile. To save a new session profile permanently, the user should click on the Save button. When the program is running, the user accesses the Session Profile box by clicking on the **Connect** button in the program window. The **Profile Name** field has a drop-down list giving the user choices from all the session profiles saved in the program. The program establishes the connection after the user clicks on the **OK** button.

When the ftp connection is established, the user can browse both the local and the remote directory structures by double-clicking directory names shown in the upper parts of the window (see Figure 4-6). To transfer a file, the user highlights that file by clicking on it and then clicks on the center arrow that points in the direction of this transfer.

Ftp transfers can be done in two different modes: binary and ASCII (or text). It has to do with the basic distinction between ASCII files and binary files. The acronym ASCII stands for the American Standard Code for Information Interchange. This is a way of encoding characters as a sequence of 0's and 1's. ASCII (or text) files are all those files that contain regular text only, that is, standard printable characters (alphabet, decimal digits, punctuation signs). All the other files are called binary. For example, all executable files (**.EXE** or **.COM**) are binary files. It is more surprising that a word-processing document (such as an MS Word file) or an electronic spreadsheet (such as Lotus 1-2-3 **.WK1** or MS Excel **.XLS** file) are binary files. Even if a Word file looks like a document containing plain text only, it in fact includes some complicated layout information such as fonts, their size, and so forth, which is kept in the file encoded in a special way. All the spreadsheet, database, presentation graphics, picture, or sound files are binary.

It does no harm to ftp an ASCII (text) file in the binary mode (it just takes a notch longer and the end-of-line characters will not be adjusted). A binary file, however, will be corrupted (i.e., will become unusable) if transferred in the ASCII mode. For this reason it is very important to pay attention to the mode the ftp program is in. The default mode of ws_ftp is binary, as can be seen in Figure 4-6 (binary status is selected). Unfortunately, in most early ftp programs, particularly in standard character-based UNIX ftp programs, the default mode is ASCII. If the user has to resort to such a program to ftp binary files, he or she should first change the mode to binary, and only then transfer the files.

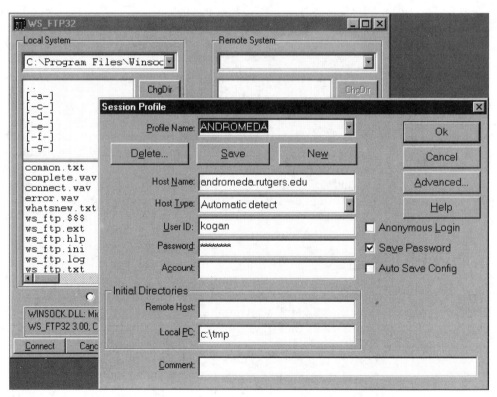

FIGURE 4-5 Starting an ftp Session in ws_ftp

It goes without saying that special ftp programs (like ws_ftp) can be used for downloading files from public ftp areas. The user should log in as `anonymous` and use `ident` or his or her E-mail address as a password. After logging in, the user either immediately gets access to the public ftp area or should go to that area by changing to the `pub` subdirectory. These sites are called anonymous ftp sites, and many of them serve as huge repositories of freeware and shareware programs.

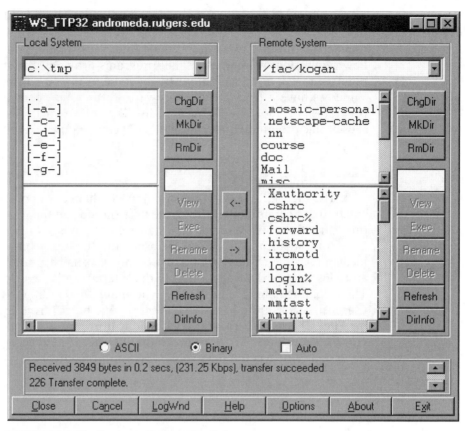

FIGURE 4-6 Ftp Session in Progress (ws_ftp)

INTERNET ELECTRONIC MAIL

Website
E-mail

An early and strong motivating force in the development of the Internet was a societal need to provide an independent universal communication medium. Electronic mail has always been one of most important and widely used Internet services. Most proprietary electronic-mail systems operated by major on-line services and telecommunication companies have become increasingly integrated with the Internet E-mail that became the standard.

Basic electronic mail provides for exchanges of text messages between Internet users. To use Internet E-mail, a person has to establish an account on one of the *Internet hosts,* that is, computers that are directly connected to the Internet and have their own Internet address, the so-called IP address. Symbolic names of Internet hosts are universally used to represent IP addresses because they are much easier to memorize. The user login and the computer constitute the Internet E-mail address for that user. For example, the Internet address of the user `sudit` of the computer `andromeda.rutgers.edu` is `sudit@andromeda.rutgers.edu`, which is much easier to remember than `sudit@128.6.10.4`. It is also much more informative because it shows that sudit resides at Rutgers, which is an institution of higher education (signified by `edu`).

Most early Internet hosts were UNIX computers, and for that reason most of the early Internet E-mail programs were UNIX based. Lately, an increasing number of Internet users do all their Internet E-mailing on a PC or a Mac. The new generation of Internet E-mail programs provides a friendly Windows-based point-and-click interface. Interestingly, some of the best E-mail programs for MS Windows have a freeware or shareware status. One of the most popular E-mail programs is Eudora by QUALCOMM. The self-extracting file containing all the files of this program (Eudora Light 1.5.4) can be downloaded from the book's ftp site at

> `http://www.rutgers.edu/Accounting/raw/book/software/eudor154.exe`

The file `eudor154.exe` should be put in a blank temporary directory and executed to extract its content. Then the user should run the `setup.exe` file and follow the instructions on the screen to install the program.

Although Eudora runs on the user's PC, the user's Internet mailbox remains located on a UNIX computer. This computer, usually located at a university or at an IAP site, is hard-wired directly to the Internet and is operated around the clock. The incoming E-mail messages keep accumulating in the UNIX mailbox until the user instructs Eudora to retrieve them (in one batch) from the mailbox by choosing **File** | **Check Mail.** This retrieval is done using the so-called *Post Office Protocol (POP).* Therefore, Eudora refers to the Internet E-mail account on a UNIX computer as a POP account (see **Tools** | **Options** in Figure 4-7).

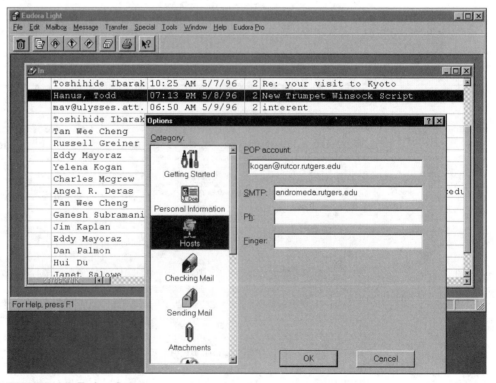

FIGURE 4-7 Eudora Setup

The main protocol of Internet E-mail is called *Simple Mail Transfer Protocol* (SMTP). UNIX computers exchanging E-mail messages over the Internet use SMTP all the time (both when sending and when receiving messages). When Eudora sends a message out, it also uses SMTP (as opposed to POP used for E-mail retrieval). Therefore, Eudora requires the user to specify an SMTP server—usually a UNIX computer that will receive messages from a PC program and deliver them to their destinations over the Internet (see **Tools | Options Hosts**). In many cases the SMTP server and the computer of the POP account are the same.

When Eudora retrieves messages, they are usually removed from the UNIX mailbox but remain available in the Eudora's mailbox. If the user works with his or her E-mail on several PCs (say, home/office), then the messages that were transferred into the Eudora's mailbox of one of the computers will not be reachable from the other one. Most PC-based E-mail programs have the same problem.

Figure 4-8 shows an E-mail message in Eudora addressed to the RAW webmaster `kogan@andromeda.rutgers.edu`.

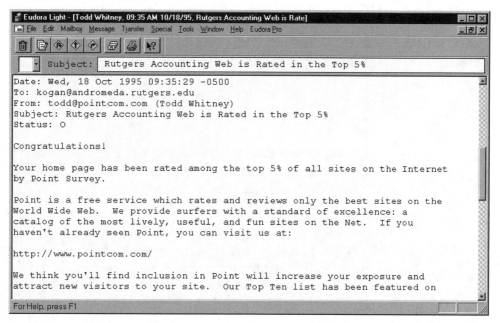

FIGURE 4-8 Incoming E-mail Message in Eudora

After reading a message, the user can use the **Message** menu to reply to the message or forward the message. The user can also save the message in a file using **File | Save As.**

A new message can be composed in Eudora after choosing **Message | New Message.** Eudora's new message window is shown in Figure 4-9. A typical Internet E-mail message consists of two parts: the head and the body. The head contains information about the recipient of the message (To:), the sender of the message (From:), the subject (Subject:), and so forth. The body of the message may contain any text.

Standard Internet E-mail can transmit textual information only. Newer E-mail programs (such as Eudora) make it possible to send by E-mail various nontextual information such as images, sound, movies, and computer programs by encoding them as text and *attaching* them to a regular E-mail message. As was discussed above in the ftp section, all the word-processing documents, electronic spreadsheets, databases, or presentation graphics files are binary files and therefore can be E-mailed only if properly encoded (i.e., attached to the message).

In Eudora, a binary file can be attached to an outgoing message using **Message | Attach File.** The path to the attached file is displayed in the **Attachments:** field, indicating that the file will accompany the message.

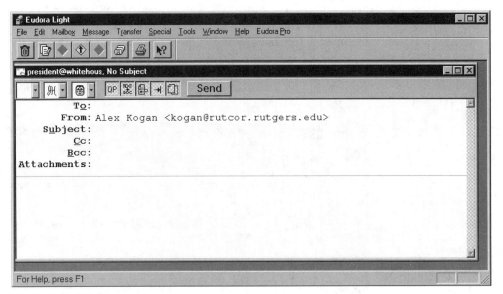

FIGURE 4-9 Composing a New Message in Eudora

For historical reasons, different methods of encoding attachments were used by different communities. Most UNIX mailers used the so-called uuencode, whereas Macintosh mailers used BinHex. These encoding methods are not compatible, and a mailer using one method may not be able to decode a message encoded using the other one. To mitigate this situation, a standard for encoding binary files called **Multipurpose Internet Mail Extensions** (MIME) has been developed. Most newer E-mail programs (like Eudora) support this standard and can exchange attachments encoded using MIME. Eudora Light can also encode and decode BinHex but cannot use uuencode. Eudora Light, therefore, will not be able to decode attachments created by some older UNIX mailers that do not use MIME.

It is possible to simultaneously send or forward the same message to numerous recipients. These very important features are provided by all E-mail programs. To send a message to several recipients, it is sufficient to put their E-mail addresses separated by commas in the **To:** or **Cc:** fields. A convenient feature of Eudora allows the user to create the so-called nicknames (see **Tools | Nicknames**). A nickname can be a shortcut for a single E-mail address or even a list of E-mail addresses. When the user sends a message to a nickname, Eudora distributes it to all the addresses on the list.

So far we have been discussing local mailing lists maintained by Eudora on the local PC for its user who is the only one that can send messages to the list (nickname). By contrast, special mailing list programs can run on an Internet host and distribute messages from anyone to their subscribers. The three most popular E-mailing list programs are LISTSERV, ListProc, and Majordomo. Users communicate with these programs by sending E-mail messages to them (e.g., subscribe, unsubscribe, get help, access archives, etc.). E-mailing lists can be moderated or unmoderated. The former distribute to their subscribers only messages that are approved by their moderators, and the latter will directly distribute any messages to their subscribers.

Many E-mail list sites now maintain Web front-ends to their E-mailing lists. These front-ends usually include a Web-based access to hypertext versions of the list archives. The comprehensive collection of accounting mailing lists maintained by ANet is a good example, see Figure 4-10 and the following URL:

```
http://www.rutgers.edu/accounting/anet/lists/index.html
```

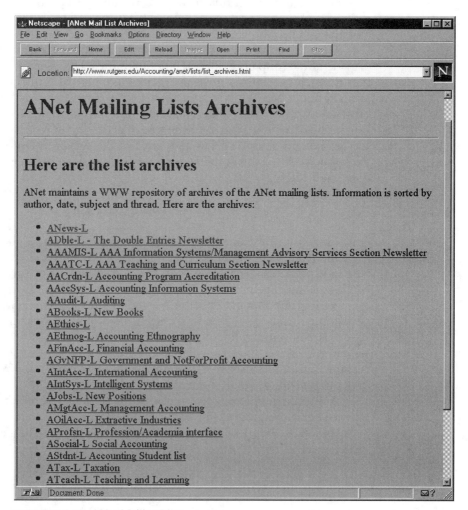

FIGURE 4-10 ANet Mailing Lists

All E-mail systems inform the sender of delivery failure. Some E-mail systems support confirmations of receipt. Sophisticated E-mail programs can filter the incoming messages by size, origin, and so forth. Most E-mail programs have cataloging capabilities, making it possible for users to save incoming and outgoing messages in various folders.

There is now a trend of integrating Internet E-mail in the Web browsers. Starting with version 2.0, Netscape Navigator supports both sending E-mail messages using SMTP and retrieving E-mail messages using POP. At present, however, stand-alone E-mail programs like Eudora are far superior to their browser counterparts in features and capabilities.

INTERNET BULLETIN BOARDS (NEWSGROUPS)

**Website
Newsgroups**

Internet bulletin boards serve exactly the same purpose as regular bulletin boards: Users can post messages on the boards and read the postings of other users. The system of Internet bulletin boards is called Usenet (or netnews), and individual bulletin boards are called newsgroups. Newsgroups are hierarchically classified by topic, and their distribution ranges from local to regional and global.

Many large Internet sites (e.g., major universities) maintain news servers that provide newsgroup access to their communities. The user can read newsgroups either through specialized news programs (like nn or tin under UNIX, or Agent or WinVN under MS Windows) or through news-reading capabilities in newer Web browsers. Web browsers like Netscape generally provide adequate news-reading capabilities. To make Netscape capable of accessing newsgroups from a local news server, the user should specify the name of the server in **Options | Mail and News Preferences.** After this setup is done, newsgroups can be accessed simply by specifying their URL as

```
news:newsgroupname
```

Consider, for example, a global newsgroup `biz.comp.accounting` available from the Rutgers news server. Opening the URL `news:biz.comp.accounting` makes Netscape pop up a special news window and show the newsgroup hierarchy in that window. A message posted to this newsgroup is shown in Figure 4-11.

Newsgroup names reflect newsgroup hierarchy. The general category of this newsgroup (`biz.comp.accounting`) is business newsgroups (`biz`), the subcategory (`comp`) is computer related, and the sub-sub-category is accounting. Most news servers will carry this newsgroup. There are, however, specialized newsgroups that are not distributed globally. They are usually available only from the news server of the organization maintaining them.

A good example of local newsgroups is provided by FinanceNet. To access FinanceNet Newsgroups, the name of their server (`news.financenet.org`) should be included as a part of the URL, that is, the URL of the newsgroup `fnet.fin-reporting` is

```
news://news.financenet.gov/fnet.fin-reporting
```

and an article from that newsgroup is shown in Figure 4-12.

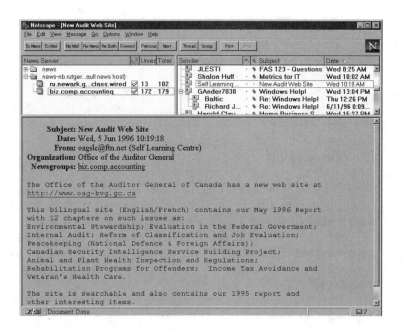

FIGURE 4-11
A Newsgroup Article
in Netscape

Opening the URL `news://news.financenet.gov` allows the user to browse the whole FinanceNet newsgroup hierarchy.

A user can post a message to the newsgroup either by clicking on the **To: News** button in the Netscape News window or by selecting **File | New News Message** from the main menu. Some news servers will accept postings from authorized users only. If this is the case, the server will prompt for the user name and password. The structure of a newsgroup message looks identical to the structure of a regular E-mail message, although the distribution mechanisms differ significantly.

Some newsgroups will accept posting from anybody. Other newsgroups are moderated (i.e., to be posted, a message has to be approved by the moderator). To avoid flame wars and heated discussions, some newsgroups prefer to be moderated.

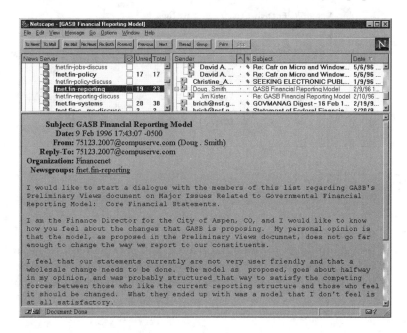

FIGURE 4-12
An Article from
fnet.fin-reporting

INTERNET REMOTE CONTROLS (TELNET)

Website
Telnet

The telnet and rlogin protocols allow users to access and control remote computers without having a direct physical connection to them. For example, it is possible to connect to the Internet through dial-ups of Columbia University in New York City and run programs on one of the University of Illinois Supercomputer Center machines. Most organizations require proper clearance for remote access to their computers. Some public organizations, however, allow any anonymous users to access their computers for certain well-defined purposes. For example, the New York Public Library permits anonymous users to access its on-line catalogs using `telnet` to `nyplgate.nypl.org` and logging in as `nypl`. Figure 4-13 shows this telnet session established using the telnet program `telnet.exe` available in the standard distribution of MS Windows 95 (in `c:\WINDOWS`).

When a user establishes a telnet connection, he or she has to specify the computer name and the type of the terminal (using **Connect | Remote System**). The terminal type most commonly used in connecting to UNIX computers over the Internet is VT100.

The example above illustrates the use of telnet for getting access to a remote database (NYPL catalogs). This use of telnet is being replaced by Web-based access (e.g., NYPL Research Library Catalog is already available through the Web, while the Branch Library Catalogs are reachable through telnet only). However, telnet will retain its importance in providing distributed access to computing power to enhance limited computing capabilities of desktop machines.

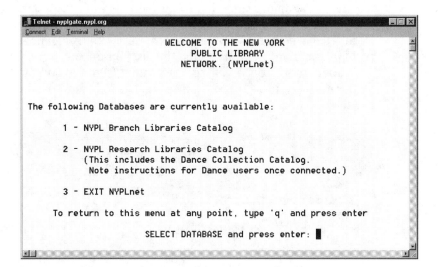

FIGURE 4-13
Telnet to the New
York Public Library

INTERNET RELAY CHAT

Website
Internet relay chat

The Internet Relay Chat (IRC) provides a way for real-time communications over the net. Chat rooms are tremendously popular on on-line services as a forum for special interests, for meeting people, and for sheer entertainment. Chat rooms provide a live medium for exchanging opinions without the delays associated with E-mail. Chat is being progressively used in intranets to replace expensive conference calling and to keep records of group meetings. Figure 4-14 illustrates a chat session of a Prodigy finance room exploring investment alternatives.

SYSTEM Greeter:	You are now in room "Investing in Stocks"
SYSTEM Greeter:	You have READ/WRITE Access
rawmaster:	hi: this seems to be a quiet day
quesswork:	hi rawmaster
The Big Tuna:	sure guess see another 1/2 down on rates
quesswork:	when was the last time rates were that low?
rawmaster:	what do you think of the astronomical rates that Netscape is still selling?
The Big Tuna:	so another few months then what? short it
quesswork:	Sell off in the late fall
Kopella:	My guess is - after elections - more borrowing will be needed nationally and internationally - to finance all government deficits and definitely rates will have to surge increasing inflation
The Big Tuna:	so guess if rates keep it going another few months then what?
rawmaster:	i agree. the Microsoft free (so so) hosting offer will hurt them. why late fall?
The Big Tuna:	I prefer to buy quality when prices and pe's are low and wait it out
quesswork:	the Firms will have most of their clients in a profit situation, and the sell off will begin...They will tell clients the top is near and should sell for that profit for a number of reasons...
rawmaster:	all pe's are crazed at this point
The Big Tuna:	not semi-conductors
The Big Tuna:	the stock is down over 120 pts since its peak
quesswork:	Tuna, why do you like the PE of Semi's Companies
The Big Tuna:	there are some excellent companies selling pretty cheap
quesswork:	and their profit growth potential?
rawmaster:	is there overcapacity in semi-conductor plants??? or maybe some major technological change? sims have been kept artificially high for many years. is it possible that an adjustment is coming?
The Big Tuna:	coming? its come and gone
rawmaster:	the market was at 2700 in 87 now is at 5600. this is not an adjustment
The Big Tuna:	MU 94 to 30 I would say that is a correction
quesswork:	Everyone would like to be in the next Micro-soft or Intel, But the bottom line is always can they make money, Remember when MU was at 93 were is it how and why?
The Big Tuna:	at 9 times earnings its cheap even if earnings expectations are too high
rawmaster:	sorry about my ignorance MU????
The Big Tuna:	micron technology
quesswork:	Micron Tech
Kopella:	What's your annual average return on your investments?
SYSTEM Greeter:	*USAirJB* has entered the room
rawmaster:	thanks. they are having manufacturing quality problems.
The Big Tuna:	maybe semis wont grow 30-50% this year or next but 20 is realistic now and long term this situation is good
quesswork:	Tuna, i agree. you have a little room for gain in Mu, but keep a watchful eye on it
USAirJB:	Guys I'm new in this computing system..
The Big Tuna:	I have a watchful eye on everything guess
USAirJB:	please need on where to invest some money
USAirJB:	stocks or mutual funds?
The Big Tuna:	Air what is your knowledge of the markets inexperienced-expert?

FIGURE 4-14   Prodigy Chat Room

CONCLUDING REMARKS

The review of important Internet services in this chapter following the previous discussion of surfing and browsing should have convinced readers that the Internet is here to stay and grow. It will substantially change our professional lives. For accounting, the discipline that deals with financial information and its use for decision support, the Internet is of particular importance. It should also be realized that the Internet is still in its infancy. Many additional services and capabilities are likely to emerge. Some of the Internet future prospects are discussed later in chapter 10.

Problems

1. Use a Web browser to connect to this book's Internet site at

   `ftp://www.rutgers.edu/pub/accounting/book/software`

   and download the ws_ftp program (wsftp32z.exe). Install this program on your computer.
2. Create and save the ws_ftp profile for the public ftp software site of this book given in the previous question.
3. Use ws_ftp to download from this book's Internet site the E-mail program Eudora. Install and configure Eudora on your computer.
4. Use Eudora to send an E-mail message to an acquaintance of yours describing your experience with basic Internet services.
5. Create a nickname including the E-mail addresses of several classmates of yours who form together with you a team in one of your projects. Use this nickname to send an E-mail message to all the members of the team.
6. Prepare a document in one of common word-processing formats and E-mail it to an acquaintance of yours by attaching it to the message.
7. Subscribe to one of the Anet mailing lists that is of most interest to you. Become an active participant in the list's discussions.
8. Find a newsgroup not mentioned in this book that you would consider useful to read regularly for your professional development.

CHAPTER

Personal Publishing on the Web

INTRODUCTION

Web technology has reduced the cost of publishing dramatically. As a result, exciting publishing opportunities are there for almost everyone to use. Publishing becomes a readily available personal option. Like in the Hyde Park corner, one can talk to all those in the vicinity who would listen. Except that in the case of the Internet the vicinity is global, and the potential global Internet audience grows by leaps and bounds.

In this chapter the reader is introduced to the growing personal publishing opportunities on the Internet. Ways to set one's own personal homepage on the Internet are discussed. The reader is shown how to use the HTML markup language to put his or her own material on the Web, cross-reference it, and link it to other pertinent materials.

WHAT IS WEB PUBLISHING?

The advent of Web technology has brought about a second global revolution in publishing. The first global publishing revolution was made possible by the invention of the printing press. Printing made it feasible to circulate materials in large enough quantities to make them widely available to the public (i.e., to publish). However, publication of printed material entails significant costs. As a result, it is contingent on adequate sales or sufficient financing. The Web technology permits a very low cost production and distribution of materials over the Internet. Consequently, almost everybody can publish materials on the Internet. Hence, publishing becomes personal. Our objective in this chapter is to familiarize the reader with the basics of personal publishing on the Web, that is, how to prepare materials for the Web.

In browsing the Web, the reader has probably encountered many URLs that include file names having extensions `.html` or `.htm`. These extensions indicate that Web documents are written in a special language called *Hypertext Markup Language (HTML)*. HTML is the common language of the Web. All Web documents must be prepared in HTML.

Once a Web document is created in HTML, it can be "published" by being made available on the World Wide Web. This is accomplished by placing the document on a so-called ***Web server.*** A Web server is a computer permanently connected to the Internet that runs a special Web server program. When a user opens a URL in a Web browser, the browser contacts the Web server whose name is given in the URL and requests the document specified by the URL. Web servers are constantly watching out for Web document requests. When a request comes in, the server responds to it by sending the document to the browser.

As a publishing language, HTML has limited capabilities. It provides tools for the description of the basic structure of a document and major formatting elements. However, it does not give the publisher full control over how the document will be presented to the reader. It is up to a Web browser to interpret HTML commands and create the final layout of the document on the browser's window. For this reason, the same Web document may be displayed in slightly different ways by different Web browsers. The problem is further complicated by the fact that HTML is still an evolving standard. HTML extensions have been introduced periodically by the developers of Web browsers, with Netscape taking the lead. As a result, some newer HTML features are supported by a very limited number of Web browsers. If a Web browser encounters an HTML element that it cannot interpret, it ignores that element in creating the layout of the document. The result may be less than satisfactory from the publisher's point of view. To prevent this from happening, some Web sites include a warning in their homepage saying, for example, that the site is "Netscape (or Internet Explorer) enhanced."

Web publishing is different from Web browsing. For browsing it is sufficient to have access to the Internet. To publish documents on the Web, the publisher has to arrange for some space on a Web server. Most Internet access providers are currently selling such space for a modest fee. Many organizations provide some of their constituencies with such space free of charge. For example, it is now available to students at most major universities.

BASICS OF HTML

The basic feature of HTML is that it is a markup language. This means that any document written in this language is a plain text (ASCII) document; that is, it contains only standard printable characters. All of the nontextual information (e.g., fonts, bold face, italics, page layout) are described in the body of the document using special HTML commands. These HTML commands are textual "tags" shown in angle brackets (e.g., `<tag>`). For example, the HTML tag `<HR>` makes Web browsers display a horizontal line. The case of the tags is not important; that is, `<Hr>`, `<hR>`, and `<hr>` will produce the same effect as `<HR>`. It is, however, customary to use capital letters in HTML tags to make them more distinguishable from the rest of the document.

Since any HTML file is a plain text (ASCII) file, it can be created using any text editor, for example, Notepad—a simple editor available in the standard distribution of MS Windows. The reader can follow the presentation in this chapter by creating simple HTML files in Notepad.

Most HTML tags come in pairs—the opening tag and the closing tag. Each HTML document should open with the tag `<HTML>` and close with the tag `</HTML>`. The closing tags always have a slash. The beginning of a Web document is a header that provides Web browsers with some information about displaying the document. The most common header element is the title of the document specified between `<TITLE>` and `</TITLE>` tags. This title will not be displayed in the browser window. Newer browsers such as Netscape or MS Internet Explorer display titles of documents on their title bars. The main content (body) of a Web document should be delimited with `<BODY>` and `</BODY>` tags.

Consider the following personal publishing project: creating a resume for the Web. The general structure of John Doe's resume is the following:

```
<HTML>

<TITLE>
John Doe's Resume
</TITLE>

<BODY>
Content of the resume
</BODY>
</HTML>
```

Content of the resume usually starts with the name and address of the person. It then specifies the objective. Special HTML tags can be used to format this information. If a phrase has to be displayed in bold letters, it should be delimited by (enclosed in) `<B>` and `</B>` tags. Letters can be displayed in different sizes. HTML uses `<H1>` to `<H6>` tags to specify six headings of progressively smaller size. These heading tags can also be used to logically organize a Web document into section-subsection structure.

A Web browser will display single spaces only and ignore multiple spaces and line breaks in an HTML file. A special HTML tag `<BR>` has to be used to denote the line break. This tag has no closing counterpart. Similarly, the `<P>` tag denotes a new paragraph. The tag pair `<CENTER>` `</CENTER>` instructs Web browsers to center whatever is enclosed by the pair. This tag was introduced as an extension of the original HTML. For that reason some older Web browsers do not understand it and will simply ignore it.

Using the above tags, the beginning of John Doe's resume in HTML language will look like the following:

```
<HTML>

<TITLE>
John Doe's Resume
</TITLE>

<BODY>

<CENTER>
<H1>John Doe</H1>
<H3>
123 Main Street<BR>
Anytown, NJ 07100<BR>
(201) 555-1234
</H3>
<HR>
</CENTER>

<B>OBJECTIVE:</B><BR>
A challenging entry-level position in accounting.

</BODY>

</HTML>
```

All the Web browsers are capable of viewing local files. In Netscape Gold, choose **File | Open File in Browser.** Figure 5-1 shows how this HTML file is displayed by Netscape.

Lists are very important elements of documents. HTML provides some basic tools to build them. The <UL> </UL> tag pair delimits a bulleted list, with list items beginning with the <LI> tag, which has no closing counterpart. An example of a bulleted list in Doe's resume lists his computer skills:

```
<B>COMPUTER SKILLS:</B>

<UL>
<LI> MS DOS, MS Windows, MS Windows 95
<LI> MS Excel, MS Word, MS PowerPoint
<LI> PeachTree Accounting for MS Windows
</UL>
```

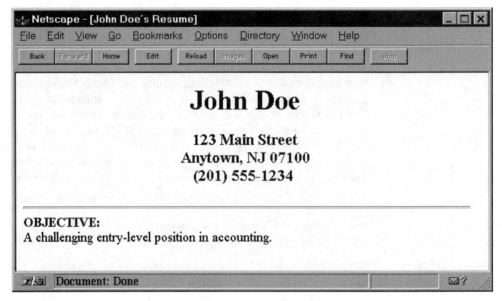

FIGURE 5-1 Doe's Resume: Just the Title

Figure 5-2 shows how the extended resume containing this list is displayed by Netscape. Numbered lists can be created in the same way as bulleted lists with the <OL> </OL> tag pair used instead of <UL> </UL>.

HYPERTEXT LINKS

The most important feature of HTML is hypertext links. A hypertext link is created by the <A> </A> tag pair. What is delimited by this pair will be indicated by the browser to be a link (e.g., shown in blue and underlined). To point to the destination of the link, the URL of the destination has to be specified. This is accomplished by using a special attribute, HREF, in the opening tag <A>.

Here is how MBA in Professional Accounting is made into a hyperlink to the Rutgers Professional Accounting Web site:

```
<A HREF="http://www.rutgers.edu/accounting/raw/ru_pa"><B>MBA in Professional
Accounting</B></A> (1996),<BR>
```

Note that the URL of the destination is entered in quotes (following HREF=). Similarly, a link to the homepage of the Rutgers Graduate School of Management is added as follows:

```
<A HREF="http://www.rutgers.edu/accounting/raw/gsm">Graduate School of
Management</A>, Rutgers University, Newark, NJ.<P>
```

Some other HTML tags also admit attributes. For example, an insertion of an image on a Web page requires a special image tag <IMG> with the image location given by the value of the SRC attribute. Images are not parts of HTML documents and are kept in separate graphics files. HTML documents are plain text documents (ASCII), while images are binary files. The most common image format understood by all the Web browsers is GIF. Newer browsers like Netscape or Internet Explorer are also capable of displaying images in JPG (JPEG) format.

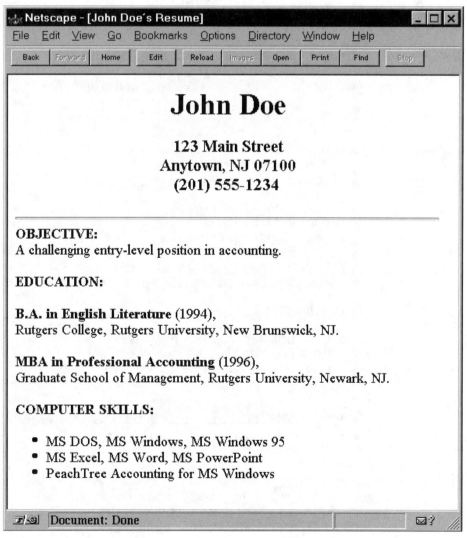

FIGURE 5-2 Doe's Resume: Lists

Consider John Doe placing his picture at the top of his resume. The drawing is in the `doe.gif` file. The HTML coding specifying the insertion of this picture is

```
<H1><IMG SRC="doe.gif" ALIGN="BOTTOM"> John Doe</H1>
```

In addition to the `SRC`, the `<IMG>` tag above has another attribute `ALIGN`, describing the alignment of the text following the image. The values of this attribute can be `TOP`, `MIDDLE`, or `BOTTOM`, indicating respectively that the text following the image should be aligned with the top, middle, or bottom of the image. Figure 5-3 shows how John Doe's picture and the hypertext links are displayed by Netscape in the resume.

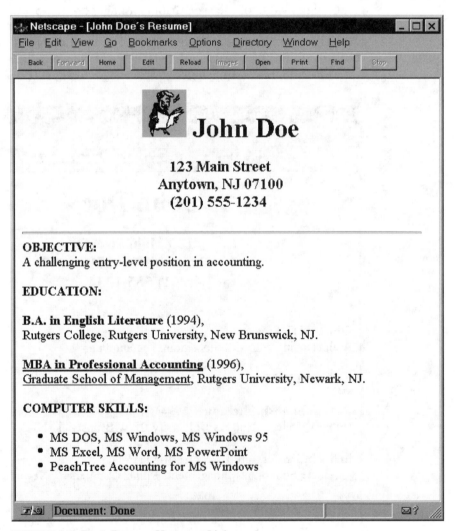

FIGURE 5-3 Doe's Resume: Hypertext Links

The value of the `SRC` attribute in the `<IMG>` tag can be any valid URL, making it possible for a Web page to display images that are physically located elsewhere on the Web. Let us now compare the values of the `HREF` and `SRC` attributes above. The `SRC` attribute does not include the protocol and the computer name parts of a standard URL. Moreover, the path part is just a file name. This is an example of the so-called *relative reference*. It means that the protocol, the computer, and the path are the same as the protocol, the computer, and the path of the document containing this reference. By contrast, in *absolute references* all the parts of the URLs are specified explicitly (as in the values of the HREF attributes above).

The use of relative references for cross-linking a set of documents and images makes this document structure portable. It will work both on the local computer where it is developed and on any Web computer it is placed on. Therefore, the use of relative references makes it possible to develop a system of Web pages locally on a PC and upload these pages to a Web server, once all the cross-links work properly.

GRAPHICS FOR THE WEB

One of the benefits of the Web are images that greatly enhance viewing experience. Personal publishing on the Web is all but unthinkable without using images. Numerous graphic file formats are in common use. As mentioned above, the formats to be used on the Web are GIF and JPG (JPEG). Any picture file in another format (e.g., BMP, TIFF, PCX, etc.) has to be converted to one of these two. Many programs are capable of such conversions. One of the best is a shareware program called LView.

LView understands (can read and write) many graphic formats. The conversion simply entails opening the original file in LView and saving it as GIF or JPG. LView also provides basic image editing capabilities. A copy of LView can be downloaded from this book's on-line site at the following URL:

```
ftp://www.rutgers.edu/pub/accounting/book/software/lviewprz.exe
```

The file is a self-extracting archive to be run in the directory where the reader would like to put LView files.

The choice between GIF and JPG depends on whether the graphic file is a photograph or a drawing. JPG is usually preferable for photographs, while GIF may be better for drawings. JPG is better than GIF at compressing images, but it loses some details in the process. By contrast, GIF compression loses no details. GIF is limited to 256 colors, while the number of colors in JPG is practically unlimited (more than 16 million).

WEB EDITORS

So far, we explained how to create HTML files using no special programs, just a plain text editor (Notepad). There are, however, some tools available to facilitate the process of Web authoring. These tools fall under two general categories: word processor add-ons and dedicated HTML editors.

The word processor add-on most commonly used for Web authoring is Microsoft Internet Assistant for Word 95. This program can be freely downloaded from the Microsoft Web site (http://www.microsoft.com) or from this book's site at

```
ftp://www.rutgers.edu/pub/accounting/book/software/wrdia20z.exe
```

Microsoft Word, of course, has to be available on the computer before installing this add-on. Running this program will add some functionality to Word, allowing us to use Word as a basic Web editor and browser.

Once this add-on program is installed, MS Word can be used either to create HTML documents from scratch or to convert standard Word documents into HTML files. To start from scratch, one has to go to Word, choose **File | New** and double-click in dialog box the HTML.DOT template icon. This will give a new HTML document window and produce special HTML tool bar and menus. With the basic knowledge of HTML, figuring out how to use them is relatively easy. It may be even easier for an experienced Word user to create a standard Word document first. Then this document can be saved as HTML by choosing **File | Save As,** and then selecting HTML Document type in the "Save as type" drop-down list. Thus, John Doe can type his resume in Word and then switch to the HTML mode (see Figure 5-4).

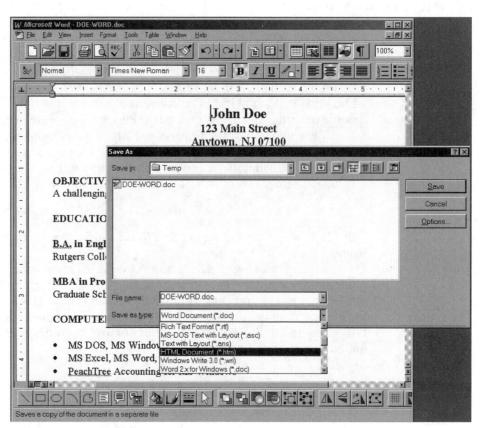

FIGURE 5-4 Doe's Resume in Word

Once in the HTML mode, standard **Insert | Picture** can be used to add an image to the Web page. The file name of the picture should either be typed in or be found by browsing. Then this file name will be kept as the value of the src attribute in the underlying HTML source.

If the picture file is selected by browsing, then capital letters may be used by Word to record this name in the HTML code. This will make no difference when viewing this Web document on a PC, but it may become a problem when the HTML document and the picture file are uploaded to a UNIX Web server. As opposed to MS DOS, UNIX is case sensitive, and many Web servers are UNIX based. Therefore, `DOE.GIF` and `doe.gif` (or even `Doe.gif`) refer to the same file under MS DOS but refer to different files under UNIX. For the image to be displayed on the page when retrieved from the Web server, both the actual file and the value of the `SRC` attribute should use letters in the same case.

To add a hyper link to the document in the HTML mode, one has to highlight the text to be linked, choose **Insert | HyperLink,** and type into the dialog box the URL of the link (see Figure 5-5).

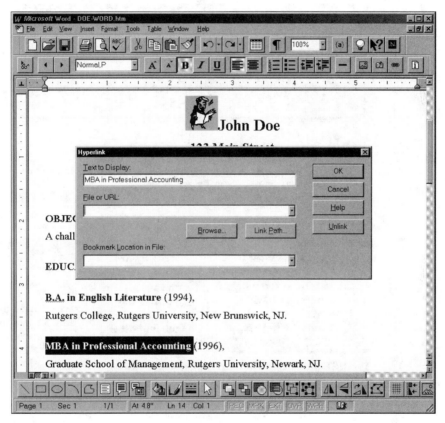

FIGURE 5-5 Link in Doe's Resume in Word

Web publishing of ordinary resumes is relatively simple, and the HTML features described above are normally adequate for the task. Intricate types of publishing require more sophisticated features of HTML. One of the best ways to learn advanced forms of Web publishing is to analyze existing Web documents. Fortunately, most Web browsers allow users to view the underlying HTML source of a Web document.

Consider, for example, a fairly advanced Web page "Rutgers Accounting Web's Accounting Resources on the Internet" shown in Figure 5-6. To make Netscape display the HTML source of this page, one should choose **View | Document Source.**

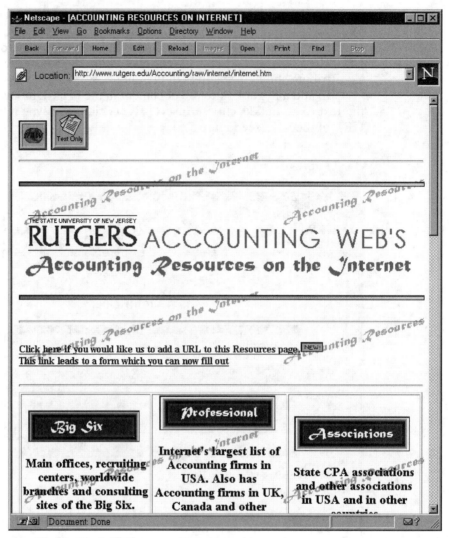

FIGURE 5-6 The RAW's Accounting Resources

Netscape 2 will pop up a separate window with the source, as shown in Figure 5-7. Note the new HTML features in this source. The BACKGROUND attribute in the <BODY> tag creates a "wallpaper" for the document. The ALT attribute in the <IMG> tag provides the text to substitute for the image in character-based Web browsers. Finally, the very last part of the picture shows the beginning of the HTML source that creates a table structure in the document (the <TABLE> tag and what follows it).

Tables are delimited with the <TABLE> </TABLE> tag pair. The optional attribute BORDER, which can be seen in the figure, specifies that the border lines around the table and between the cells of the table should be displayed. By default (when the attribute is missing), tables are displayed without border lines. HTML tables are composed of rows. Each row is delimited with the <TR> </TR> tag pair. The ALIGN attribute shown in the figure specifies the horizontal alignment of the elements in the row. The default value (when the attribute is missing) is LEFT. Other possible values are RIGHT and CENTER.

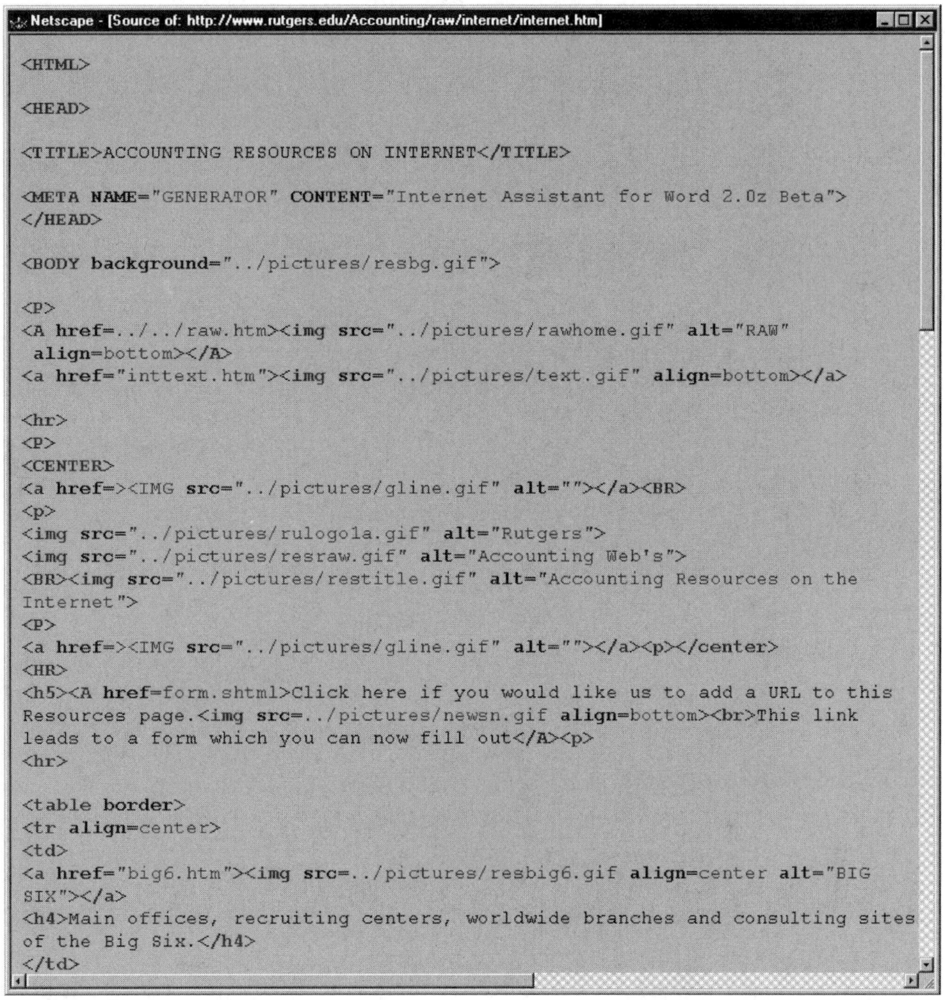

```
Netscape - [Source of: http://www.rutgers.edu/Accounting/raw/internet/internet.htm]        _ □ ×

<HTML>

<HEAD>

<TITLE>ACCOUNTING RESOURCES ON INTERNET</TITLE>

<META NAME="GENERATOR" CONTENT="Internet Assistant for Word 2.0z Beta">
</HEAD>

<BODY background="../pictures/resbg.gif">

<P>
<A href=../../raw.htm><img src="../pictures/rawhome.gif" alt="RAW"
 align=bottom></A>
<a href="inttext.htm"><img src="../pictures/text.gif" align=bottom></a>

<hr>
<P>
<CENTER>
<a href=><IMG src="../pictures/gline.gif" alt=""></a><BR>
<p>
<img src="../pictures/rulogo1a.gif" alt="Rutgers">
<img src="../pictures/resraw.gif" alt="Accounting Web's">
<BR><img src="../pictures/restitle.gif" alt="Accounting Resources on the
Internet">
<P>
<a href=><IMG src="../pictures/gline.gif" alt=""></a><p></center>
<HR>
<h5><A href=form.shtml>Click here if you would like us to add a URL to this
Resources page.<img src=../pictures/newsn.gif align=bottom><br>This link
leads to a form which you can now fill out</A><p>
<hr>

<table border>
<tr align=center>
<td>
<a href="big6.htm"><img src=../pictures/resbig6.gif align=center alt="BIG
SIX"></a>
<h4>Main offices, recruiting centers, worldwide branches and consulting sites
of the Big Six.</h4>
</td>
```

FIGURE 5-7 Source of Figure 5-6

Rows of HTML tables consist of elements that can be either data elements delimited with the <TD> </TD> tag pair or heading elements delimited with the <TH> </TH> tag pair. These tags also accept the ALIGN attribute whose value will override the value of the ALIGN attribute in the corresponding <TR> tag. The <TH> tag is usually used for column and row headings (if any), whereas the <TD> tag is used for all the other purposes.

Finally, the caption of a table (if any) is delimited with the <CAPTION> </CAPTION> tag pair and can be placed anywhere in the table. This tag also accepts the ALIGN attribute whose value (TOP , BOTTOM , LEFT , or RIGHT) determines where the caption will be displayed.

Tables are particularly important in representing spreadsheets, which are commonly used in financial statements. Additionally, tables may be used as a convenient formatting tool to improve the presentation of information that at the first glance seems to be inappropriate for a tabular form. For example, the formatting of John Doe's resume shown in Figure 5-3 can be made more elegant by representing section names and section content as columns of an HTML table:

```
<TABLE>
<TR>
<TH ALIGN="LEFT">OBJECTIVE:</TH><TD></TD>
</TR>
<TR>
<TD></TD>
<TD>A challenging entry-level position in accounting.</TD>
</TR>
<TR>
<TH ALIGN="LEFT">EDUCATION:</TH><TD></TD>
</TR>
<TR>
<TD></TD>
<TD><B>B.A. in English Literature</B> (1994),<BR> Rutgers College, Rutgers
University, New Brunswick, NJ.<P>
</TD>
</TR>
<TR>
<TD></TD>
<TD><A HREF="http://www.rutgers.edu/accounting/raw/ru_pa"><B>MBA in
Professional Accounting</B></A> (1996),<BR>
<A HREF="http://www.rutgers.edu/accounting/raw/gsm">Graduate School of
Management</A>, Rutgers University, Newark, NJ.</TD>
</TR>
<TR></TR>
<TR>
<TH ALIGN="LEFT">COMPUTER SKILLS:</TH><TD></TD>
</TR>
<TR>
<TD></TD>
<TD>
<UL>
<LI> MS DOS, MS Windows, MS Windows 95
<LI> MS Excel, MS Word, MS PowerPoint
<LI> PeachTree Accounting for MS Windows
</UL></TD>
</TR>
</TABLE>
```

The resulting improved format of the resume is shown in Figure 5-8. Note that in the HTML source above the names of sections are not formatted as bold face. Nevertheless, Figure 5-8 shows them displayed in bold, since they are defined in the table as heading elements (TH).

It is noteworthy to observe that there exists a version of Netscape called Netscape Gold that adds a graphical Web editor to the browser. This version allows users to open HTML documents for editing by choosing **File | Open File in Editor.** Its HTML capabilities are superior to those of Microsoft Internet Assistant for Word, while its word processing capabilities are basic. Netscape Gold also allows an easy switching from browsing a document to its editing by choosing **File | Edit Document.**

Unfortunately, the HTML capabilities of this built-in Netscape HTML editor are still limited. For example, in spite of the fact that the TABLE tag was introduced in HTML by Netscape, the editor does not support tables. Therefore, the version of John Doe's resume shown in Figure 5-8 cannot be worked on using the Netscape Gold editor. Figure 5-9 shows John Doe's resume (the version of Figure 5-3) opened in Netscape Gold editor.

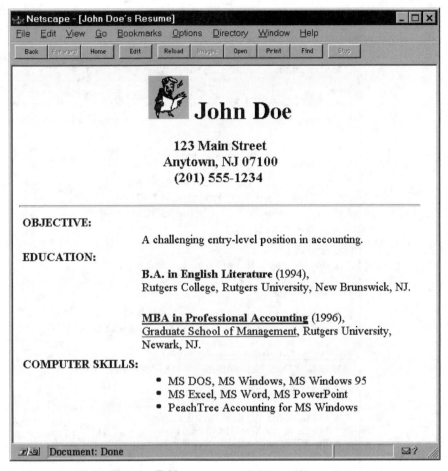

FIGURE 5-8 Doe's Resume: Table

HTML ON-LINE REFERENCES

Being the language of on-line publishing, HTML is well supported by on-line reference materials. This is especially important since it makes it easy to consult with an authoritative source while being in the process of Web content development. On-line documents were the only source of early Web developers (including the developers of the Rutgers Accounting Web) since at that time (early 1994) no conventionally published documents about HTML were available. One of the most popular documents of those ancient days was "*A Beginner's Guide to HTML*" provided by the National Center for Supercomputer Applications (NCSA) at the University of Illinois at Urbana-Champaign (the birthplace of the first graphical Web browser—Mosaic). An updated version of this document still remains one of the most popular starting points for HTML beginners. It can be found at

`http://www.ncsa.uiuc.edu/General/Internet/WWW/HTMLPrimer.html`

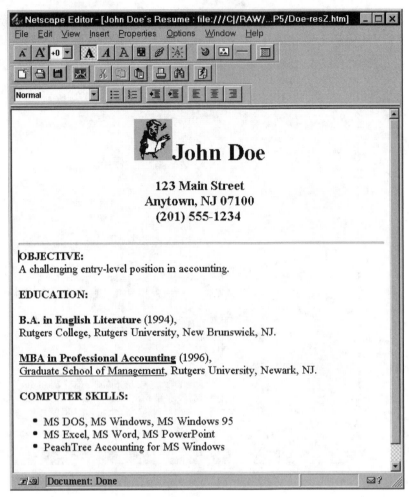

FIGURE 5-9 Doe's Resume in Netscape Editor

Another popular very short introduction into HTML called "Crash Course on Writing Documents for the Web" is available from *PC Week* Web site at

```
http://www.pcweek.com/eamonn/crash_course.html
```

The HTML on-line reference source considered among the most useful by many advanced Web developers is "*Introduction to HTML*" by Ian S. Graham at the University of Toronto (see Figure 5-10). It is located at

```
http://www.utoronto.ca/webdocs/HTMLdocs/NewHTML/htmlindex.html
```

This material is a derivative of an HTML book published by Graham and is extremely thorough, succinct, and convenient to use.

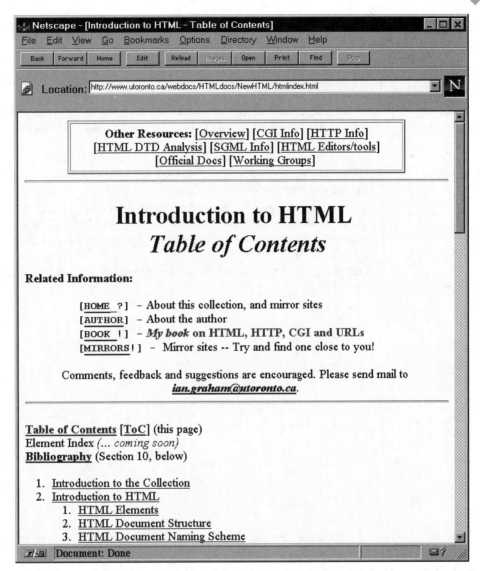

FIGURE 5-10 Homepage of Graham's *Introduction to HTML* (Reprinted with permission by Ian S. Graham)

CONCLUDING REMARKS

By now, the reader knows how to surf and browse the Internet to search, retrieve, and bookmark materials of interest; to use other Internet basic services such as electronic mail, file transfers, and remote access; and to publish his or her own material on the Internet. The reader has also gained some appreciation of the richness and diversity of accounting materials available on-line. The stage has been set for a more thorough and systematic review of the accounting resources on the Internet as presented in chapter 6 below.

Problems

1. Prepare your resume in HTML including information about your education, skills, and experience implemented as HTML lists.

2. Improve the look of your resume by implementing the information in the previous question as an HTML table.

3. Install Microsoft Internet Assistant for Word, recreate your resume as a Word document, and then convert to HTML. Compare the look of the resulting resume with the version that was manually created in HTML.

4. Repeat the previous experiment using Netscape Gold editor.

5. Search the Internet for the Web sites of the institutions of higher education you attended and companies you worked for.

6. Link in your resume the names of the institutions of higher education you attended and companies you worked for to their Web sites (if they exist).

7. Include in your resume your recent photograph. Make sure that the link to the picture file is a relative reference.

8. Compile a bookmark folder with the links to Web sites providing useful information about HTML.

CHAPTER

Accounting Resources on the Internet

6

INTRODUCTION

In our maiden voyage through Cyberspace we visited several impressive accounting Web sites. In this chapter we present a systematic survey of the accounting resources currently available on the Internet. The reader should keep in mind that this survey represents a snapshot of accounting materials that existed in the summer of 1996. The Internet medium keeps developing at an astonishing speed, and the situation will undoubtedly change. We do hope, however, that the framework presented here will prove useful in discerning structure in the unstructured ocean of accounting materials on the Internet.

A casual Internet user may infer that it is relatively easy to find an existing accounting resource on the Internet by using standard search engines (e.g., Lycos, Alta Vista, or Excite). Unfortunately, Internet search engines provide sporadic and ill-structured accounting information. Locating a specific accounting resource through them may be a daunting task. This explains the need for a well-organized directory of accounting resources on the Internet.

ACCOUNTING DIRECTORIES

Yahoo (http://www.yahoo.com) is the most famous Internet directory. Although Yahoo remains the single most useful directory, its accounting resources are not well organized. They are spread over several categories such as

Social Science:Economics:Accounting and Auditing

Economy:Companies:Computers:Software:Financial:Accounting

Business and Economy:Companies:Financial Services:Accounting

Business and Economy:Companies:Financial Services:Taxes

While certain categories (such as lists of accounting firms) are very well represented, the coverage of many other categories (such as accounting associations or accounting departments) is poor.

The inadequate coverage of accounting in general-purpose Internet directories is mitigated by the existence of dedicated accounting directories. One of the oldest and the most comprehensive ones is the directory of accounting resources on the Internet constructed and maintained by the Rutgers Accounting Web, which can be found at

```
http://www.rutgers.edu/Accounting/raw/internet/internet.htm
```

(see Figure 6-1).

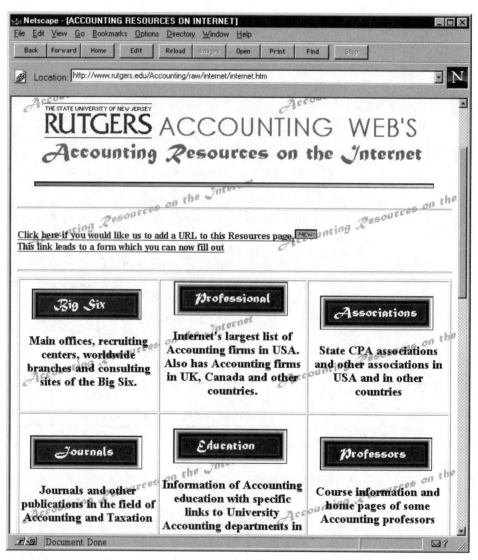

FIGURE 6-1 RAW's Accounting Resources Page

This directory classifies the Internet accounting resources primarily by their sources of origin. For example, it provides a table pointing to main Web pages of the Big 6 accounting firms (see Figure 6-2).

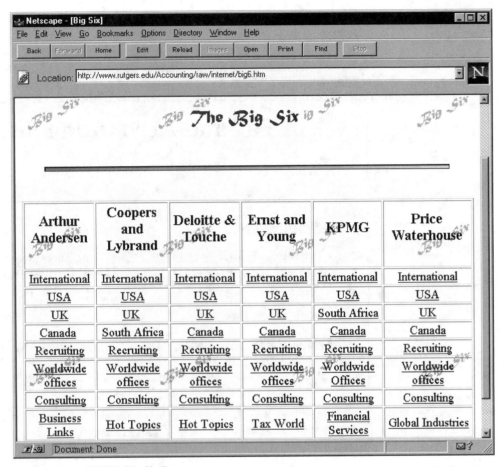

FIGURE 6-2 RAW's Big Six Page

The Web page in Figure 6-2 includes pointers to the international headquarters of the "Big 6", to their main national offices (USA, UK, Canada), to extensive Web information on recruitment, and to some of the most interesting online materials provided by the firms.

The RAW team continuously updates this directory by scanning the Internet for new accounting resources and soliciting information from the accounting community about new developments. In addition to the RAW's directory, there are a number of other dedicated accounting directories on the Internet. Most of them include cross-references to each other. Therefore, if searching one of them does not provide the desired results, it is easy to switch to other ones. Among such directories, we mention the one developed and maintained by Professor Dennis Schmidt from the University of Northern Iowa. This directory can by found at

```
http://www.uni.edu/schmidt/bookmark.html
```

(see Figure 6-3).

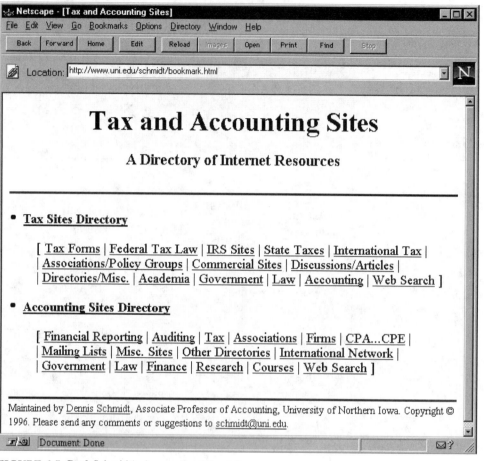

FIGURE 6-3 Prof. Schmidt's Accounting Directory

Over the last two years there has been a great increase in accounting-related sites. It now can be seen that there is a noticeable increase in non-US accounting sites, adding to the scope and flavor of accounting offerings.

An interesting collection of European accounting links is provided by the Accountancy in Europe page, located at

http://www.cybco.be/acc/

Another important Internet directory with the primary focus on auditing is the AuditNet developed and maintained by Jim Kaplan. It can be found at

http://users.aol.com/auditnet/karlhome.htm

(see Figure 6-4). One of the most important parts of AuditNet is Kaplan's AuditNet Resource List (KARL), the distinctive feature of which is the distribution over E-mail. Another interesting AuditNet resource is its Accounting/Audit/Finance E-Mail Directory at

http://www.cowan.edu.au/mra/home.htm

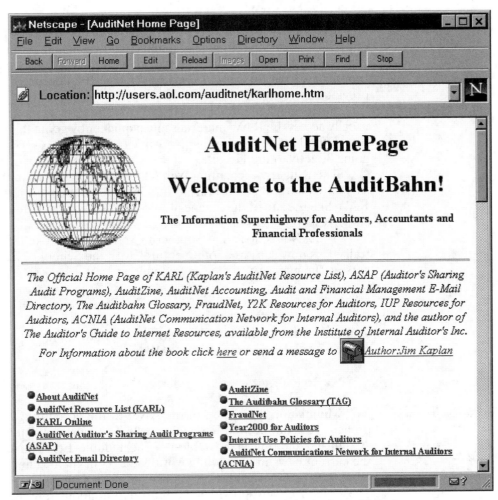

FIGURE 6-4 Kaplan's AuditNet (Reprinted with permission by James Kaplan)

It has many E-mail addresses of auditing practitioners, while its coverage of accounting academics is sporadic (for the best resource in that area, see the ANet's People Database below).

INTERNATIONAL ACCOUNTING NETWORK (IAN)

The single largest resource of accounting information on the Internet is provided by the International Accounting Network (IAN). This is an association of major accounting Web sites around the world. It was established in the summer of 1994 during the annual meeting of the American Accounting Association in New York City. The founding members of the IAN were the three major accounting Internet sites that started their active development around that time: RAW in the United States, ANet in Australia, and Summa in the United Kingdom. The IAN keeps growing as additional accounting sites around the world join in.

An important part of the IAN cooperation is the mutual mirroring agreement. Sites participating in the IAN establish mirror copies of all the materials in other IAN sites. Mirroring is accomplished by using an automated procedure that connects to another site on a regular basis (typically, every night) and uses ftp to transfer over the Internet information changes that occurred on that site since the previous mirroring.

Mirroring facilitates access to the IAN sites. For example, European users can usually access the RAW materials much quicker by going to the Finnish RAW mirror on the Nordic Accounting Network (`http://www.nan.shh.fi/raw.htm`) than by going directly to the U.S. site.

The Rutgers Accounting Web (RAW) was discussed in the previous chapter, as well as several important accounting sites and materials maintained by the RAW, like the site of the Financial Accounting Standards Board (FASB) located at `http://www.rutgers.edu/accounting/raw/fasb`.

The ANet is hosted at Southern Cross University in New South Wales, Australia. It is now run "as a joint venture" with the School of Business at Bond University. The main ANet site can be found at

```
http://anet.scu.edu.au/ANetHomePage.html
```

whereas for the users in the Western hemisphere, it may be faster to get the ANet materials from its mirror on the RAW at

```
http://www.rutgers.edu/Accounting/anet/ANetHomePage.html
```

The main contribution of the ANet to the accounting community is a comprehensive set of accounting mailing lists. The most populated and active lists are AAudit-L–Auditing and ADble-L—The Double Entries Newsletter devoted to the current news in accounting worldwide. As of the beginning of 1996, ANet had more than twenty such lists, totaling over more than eight thousand subscriptions. The ANet Web site provides the information about subscriptions, as well as the complete archive of all the E-mails sent to the lists (see Figure 6-5).

When a user subscribes to a mailing list, he or she communicates with a special program. In the case of the ANet lists, that program is called `listproc`. A single-line subscription message is sent to `listproc@scu.edu.au`. This message includes the word "subscribe," the name of the list, and the name of the user who is subscribing. For example, one of the authors of this book subscribed to the Double Entries Newsletter by sending to `listproc@scu.edu.au` the following line:

```
subscribe ADble-L Alex Kogan
```

For more information on how to communicate with the ANet mailing lists, send an e-mail with the single word "help" to the above address.

The third founding partner of the IAN is the Summa project in University of Exeter in the United Kingdom (see Figure 6-6) that can be found at

```
http://summa.org.UK
```

This project is sponsored by the Institute of Chartered Accountants in England and Wales (ICAEW), and its primary focus is on European (in particular, British)

accounting materials. The Summa site provides extensive information about the ICAEW, the British Accounting Association, as well as an extensive listing of international accounting firms (with especially rich representation of British firms).

Another European partner in the IAN is the Nordic Accounting Network (NAN) hosted at the Swedish School of Economics and Business Administration in Helsinki, Finland, and found at

http://www.nan.shh.fi/

NAN focuses on the Scandinavian accounting materials. Its pages are available not only in English but in Swedish and Finnish as well. It maintains the NAN Regional Archives that include a growing list of discussion groups.

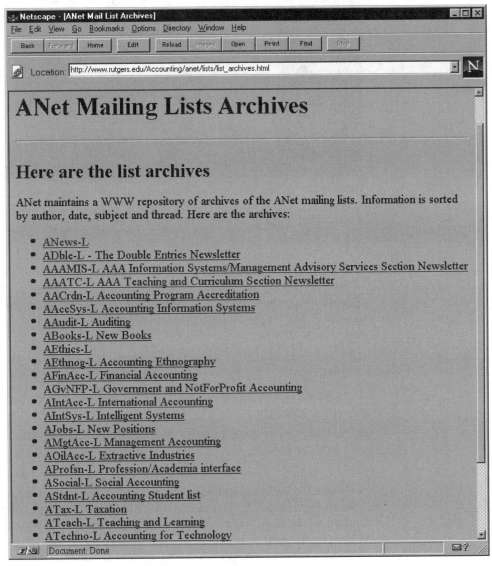

FIGURE 6-5 ANet's Mailing Lists

FIGURE 6-6 Summa's Homepage (Reprinted with permission by the Summa project)

ACCOUNTING INDUSTRY

Website
Accounting firms

The accounting industry was slow to embrace the Web in its early days. By now, however, it is unthinkable for big accounting companies not to have a Web presence. For example, all Big 6 accounting firms are on the Web. Many smaller firms have their Web sites as well. The following lists the URLs of the main Web homepages of the Big 6:

- Arthur Andersen   `http://www.arthurandersen.com/`
- Coopers and Lybrand   `http://www.colybrand.com/`
- Deloitte & Touche   `http://www.dttus.com/`
- Ernst & Young   `http://www.ey.com/`
- KPMG   `http://www.kpmg.com/`
- Price Waterhouse   `http://www.pw.com/`

As seen in Figure 6-2, all Big 6 firms have international Web sites. Their Web sites provide information about the services rendered by their U.S. offices and by many offices abroad. All the Web sites give extensive recruiting information as well as the information about their consulting units. The Big 6 are still very much in the beginning of the process of developing their Web sites. This may be a reason why the content of their sites in many areas has not yet advanced much beyond straight advertising for their services. There are, however, a few examples of very interesting information materials found in the Big 6 Web sites. There are two such examples in the Maiden Voyage chapter showing Deloitte & Touche 1996 Industry Forecasts and World Tax from Ernst & Young. Additionally, we found the following amusing pieces on-line:

- Arthur Andresen's "A Brief History of Accounting" can be found at
  `http://www.arthurandersen.com/firmwide/about_aa/history/bridge.htm`
  It lists some milestones in the development of accounting beginning with the Babylonian tablets and ending with Andersen's own founding event in 1913.

- The Coopers & Lybrand's "Trendsetter Barometer" can be found at
  `http://www.colybrand.com/eas/trendset/`
  It provides results of quarterly interviews with over 400 CEOs of companies identified as the fastest-growing U.S. businesses over the last five years. Survey topics include companies' views about the U.S. economy, bank-borrowing activity, plans for major new business investments, and more.

- KPMG's Virtual Library can be found at
  `http://www.kpmg.com/library/`
  It provides full texts of KPMG studies in the areas as diverse as the Internet's potential and performance for retailers, airline fraud, or the worldwide impact of ethnic Chinese entrepreneurs.

Price Waterhouse's National Venture Capital Survey can be found at

`http://www.pw.com/vc`

The introduction to the results of the first quarter of the 1996 Survey is shown and described in Figure 6-7.

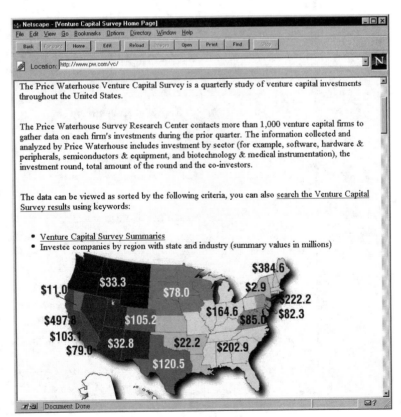

FIGURE 6-7 Price Waterhouse's Venture Capital Survey (Reproduced by permission of Price Waterhouse LLP. Copyright © 1996 Price Waterhouse LLP.)

Grant Thornton—the seventh largest U.S. accounting and management consulting firm—has a Web site at

http://www.grantthornton.com/

Its Web is comparable with the Web sites of the Big 6. Among its most interesting features is Grant Thornton Online found at

http://www.grantthornton.com/gtonline/homeonl.html

It provides on-line versions of articles from various newsletters, reports, and research studies that Grant Thornton sponsors. These articles are grouped in the following four areas: Assurance & Governance, Industries, Tax & Benefits, and Technology. A recent example is an article describing Grant Thornton's national study on banking on the Internet, which can be found at

http://www.grantthorton.com/gtonline/xsum.html

An increasing number of smaller CPA firms find it useful to have a Web presence. The Internet directories listing these sites are described earlier in this chapter. In most cases the Web sites simply advertise the services provided by the companies. Some firms even try to sell certain services over the Internet. For example, DeLellis & Company, a CPA firm in California (http://www.vcnet.com/DeLellis/) has an offering called Net Tax—the on-line tax preparation service. The engagement letter is shown in Figure 6-8. All the tax-related information is entered through a Web-form–based intuitive interface.

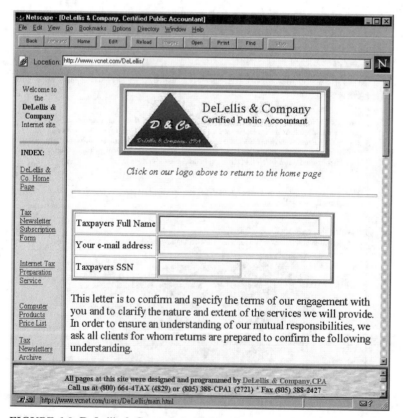

FIGURE 6-8 DeLellis & Company's On-Line Letter of Engagement (Reprinted with permission by Robert DeLellis)

Some smaller CPA firms have very well done Web sites with some useful information. For example, Blackburn, Childers & Steagall, PLC, a CPA firm in Tennessee, provides a "New Business Kit" (see Figure 6-9) on its Web site (`http://www.bcscpa.com/`). This kit provides the basic information needed for setting up a small business.

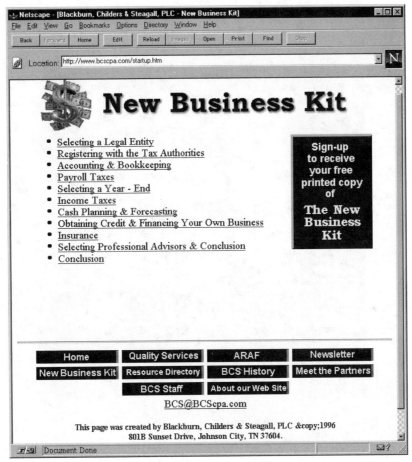

FIGURE 6-9 Blackburn, Childers & Steagall's New Business Kit (Reprinted with permission by Blackburn, Childers & Steagull, PLC)

In the above description of the accounting industry's Web presence, we focused on CPA firms. Many other segments of the industry also have on-line sites. The largest U.S. tax preparation company—H&R Block—can be found at

`http://www.handrblock.com/tax/`

The second largest tax preparation company in the United States—Jackson Hewitt Tax Service—also has an on-line site at

`http://www.infi.net/~jhewitt/`

In addition to extensive information about the company, the site provides several useful fact sheets such as "Fifty of the Most Overlooked Tax Savings" (see Figure 6-10).

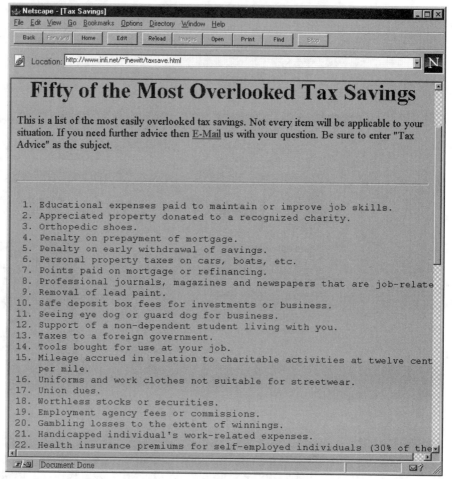

FIGURE 6-10   Jackson Hewitt's Tax Savings Tips (Reprinted with permission by Jackson Hewitt Tax Service)

ACCOUNTING EMPLOYMENT AGENCIES

Information about employment opportunities is of utmost importance for every accounting professional. The Web offers a wealth of resources in this area. Many accounting employment agencies have established on-line sites. Most accounting directories provide links to these sites. Yahoo cites them under **Business and Economy:Companies:Employment Services:Recruiting and Placement:Accounting.**

One of the largest U.S. accounting placement agencies is "accountants on call," which is located at

http://www.aocnet.com/aoc/

Website Accounting employment

The national Web site provides access to the agency's database of open positions, as well as to the database of professionals looking for jobs. After providing some basic personal information, a job seeker can retrieve a listing of positions in his or her geographic area of choice (an example of such listing for the New York city area retrieved on July 16, 1996, is shown in Figure 6-11). Among other attractions offered at the site is a form to fill out to receive a complimentary copy of the company's national accounting salary guide. The site also provides some tips on finding and keeping a job.

An alternative to using a specialized accounting employment agency is going to a general-purpose employment agency. There are numerous Web sites devoted to job search. A representative listing of such sites can be found in Yahoo under **Business and Economy:Employment.** Another impressive listing of on-line job search sites is provided by the AT&T College Network at

`http://www.att.com/college/joblinks.html`

The following lists some of the most important sites in on-line job search:

- `http://www.careermosaic.com/`—CareerMosaic, one of the older and richer on-line sites in this area.

- `http://www.careerpath.com/`—CareerPath.com, providing on-line employment ads from the seventeen major newspapers including the *New York Times,* the *Washington Post,* and the *Chicago Tribune.*

- `http://www.ajb.dni.us/`—America's Job Bank, a service of the U.S. Department of Labor and state public Employment Service Agencies containing information on approximately 250,000 jobs.

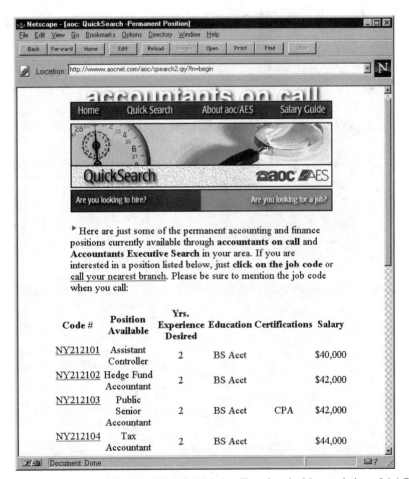

FIGURE 6-11 AOC's New York Job Listing (Reprinted with permission of AAOC)

ACCOUNTING SOFTWARE

The accounting software industry is a multibillion-dollar business with hundreds of companies competing for the market share. It is only natural that most of these companies have Web site pointers to which can be found in accounting directories or in Yahoo under

Business and Economy:Companies:Computers:Software:Financial:Accounting

Website
Accounting software

One of the best-known software companies specializing in accounting software, Great Plains Software, has a nicely designed Web site at http://www.gps.com/. In addition to the standard information about the company's products and services (including the extensive coverage of the flagship product—Great Plains Dynamics), corporate profile, and corporate news, the site provides some interesting articles for accounting professionals as a part of its Wayne's Web (Wayne Harding is the company's vice president of Accountant Relations). An example of such an article is the description of the AICPA'S top fifteen technologies that will impact the accounting profession in 1996 that were produced by the joint committees of the AICPA Information Technology at the University of Arizona "group decision support lab" (see Figure 6-12).

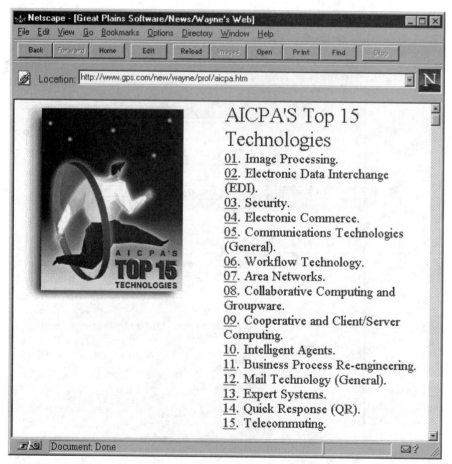

FIGURE 6-12 Great Plains Dynamics Wayne's Web (Reprinted with permission by Great Plains Software)

Among other important accounting software (developing software for companies of all sizes) sites, we mention the following:[1]

- `http://www.platsoft.com/`—Platinum Software Corporation, developer of Platinum SQL NT and Platinum for Windows.

- `http://www.solomon.com/`—Solomon Software, developer of Solomon IV™ for Windows®, and Solomon III® for Btrieve®.

- `http://www.cai.com/`—Computer Associates International, Inc., developer of CA-Masterpiece® (see Figure 6-13), as well as ACCPAC® Plus™ Accounting for DOS, CA-Accpac®/2000, CA-Simply Accounting, etc.

- `http://www.dbsoftware.com/`—Dun & Bradstreet Software, developer of SmartStream Financials, SmartStream Budget, SmartStream Procurement, etc.

- `http://www.sbt.com/`—SBT Accounting Systems, Inc., developer of Pro Series 3.01, VisionPoint 2000, VisionPoint 8.0.

- `http://www.intuit.com`—Intuit, Inc., developer of QuickBooks Pro (see Figure 6-14), Quickbooks, Quicken (the most popular personal finance software), TurboTax, etc. An interesting feature of the Intuit's site is its QuickBooks Small Business Online.

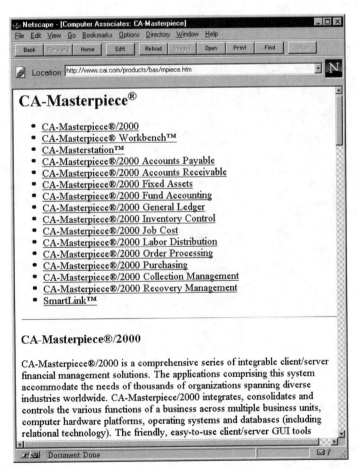

FIGURE 6-13 Computer Associates' Product Information (Reprinted with permission by Computer Associates International, Inc.)

---

[1]The site of Peachtree (`http://www.peach.com`) was described in chapter 3.

FIGURE 6-14 Intuit's QuickBooks Web Site (Reprinted with permission by Intuit, Inc.)

GOVERNMENTAL ACCOUNTING BODIES

Several very important governmental Web sites were covered in Chapter 3. They include the sites of the Securities and Exchange Commission (`http://www.sec.gov`), the General Accounting Office (GAO) (`http://www.gao.gov`), and the Internal Revenue Service (`http://www.irs.ustreas.gov`). The only part of the SEC site that was described is the EDGAR database. The site keeps growing, and many important materials are being added. One example is the selected Staff Accounting Bulletins, found at

```
http://www.sec.gov/rules/acctindx.htm
```

These bulletins reflect the Commission staff's views regarding accounting-related disclosure practices.

Website Government accounting

The federal government is actively putting much information on the Web. Many materials may be of direct interest to accountants. Management accountants will undoubtedly be interested in quality management and quality standards. The National Institute of Standards and Technology (NIST) of the Department of Commerce provides extensive information about the Malcolm Baldrige National Quality Award framework at

    http://www.nist.gov/director/quality_program/

(see Figure 6-15). This annual award was established in 1987 to promote "awareness of quality excellence, to recognize quality achievements of U.S. companies, and to publicize successful quality strategies."

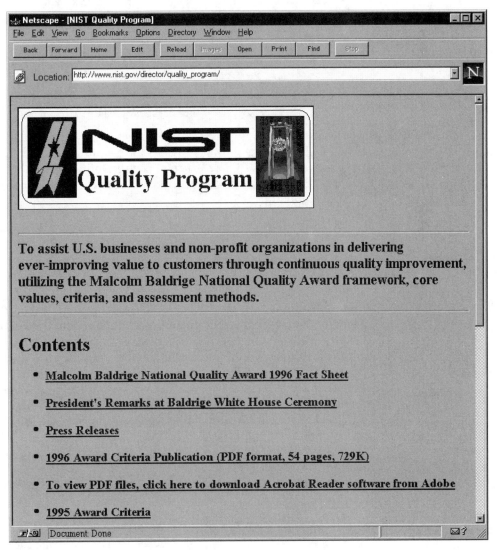

FIGURE 6-15 National Institute of Standards and Technology[2]

---

[2]Reprinted with permission of the National Institute of Standards and Technology (NIST). "NIST ®" and "Malcolm Baldrige National Quality Award,®" including their logos, are registered trademarks of NIST.

FINANCIAL INSTITUTIONS AND FINANCIAL MARKETS

The amount of financial information on the Internet is mind-boggling. In Chapter 3, we discussed one of the best stock market quote servers by Galt Technologies (http://quotes.galt.com). In fact, most major U.S. stock exchanges and many international stock exchanges have Web sites. Useful directories of domestic and international stock exchanges on-line can be respectively found at

- http://www.wsdinc.com/pgs_idx/ic181.shtml
- http://www.wsdinc.com/pgs_idx/ic182.shtml

Here is a list of the most important Web sites of the U.S. financial markets:

- http://www.nyse.com/—the New York Stock Exchange
- http://www.nasdaq.com/—the Nasdaq Stock Market
- http://www.amex.com/—the American Stock Exchange
- http://www.phlx.com/—the Philadelphia Stock Exchange
- http://www.cbot.com/—the Chicago Board of Trade
- http://www.cboe.com/—the Chicago Board Options Exchange
- http://www.cme.com/—the Chicago Mercantile Exchange

The exchanges position their Web pages as informational and educational resources. The Nasdaq market provides the graphs of its activities right on the homepage (see Figure 6-16). The Chicago Board Options Exchange provides on-line the full text of its document "Characteristics and Risks of Standardized Options" that can be found at

http://www.cboe.com/options/contents.html

The New York Stock Exchange Web site provides summaries of some research articles and some aggregate historical data. The site of the Chicago Board of Trade (CBOT) is especially impressive. It provides a wealth of information about its activities including free quotes on all CBOT contracts, financial calendar of events, liquidity data bank, market profile, market commentaries, settlement prices, daily reports, and links to government reports from the U.S. Department of Agriculture. Business students can find especially interesting the Introduction to Financial Futures (see http://www.cbot.com/introfut.htm) and the Introduction to Options on Financial Futures (see http://www.cbot.com/opintro.htm). In addition to free information, the site sells some premium information on-line, including CHART-WATCH technical research, Hollander & Feuerhaken Cash Prices for eight major grain markets.

Among the major foreign stock exchanges having on-line presence, we mention

- http://www.bourse-de-paris.fr/bourse/sbf/homesbf-gb.htlm—the Paris Stock Exchange
- http://www.stockex.co.uk/aim/index.htm—the London Stock Exchange (AIM)
- http://www.liffe.com/—the London International Financial Futures and Options Exchange (LIFFE)
- http://www.exchange.de/—the Frankfurt Stock Exchange and the Germany's Options and Futures Exchange

- http://www.tase.co.il/—the Tel Aviv Stock Exchange
- http://www.jse.co.za/welcome.htm—the Johannesburg Stock Exchange
- http://www.asx.com.au/—the Australian Stock Exchange (ASX)
- http://www.financeweb.ase.nl/cgi-bin/sh206.exe/Lang=en&ID=?cgi-bin/beursdata/default.ini—the Amsterdam Stock Exchange

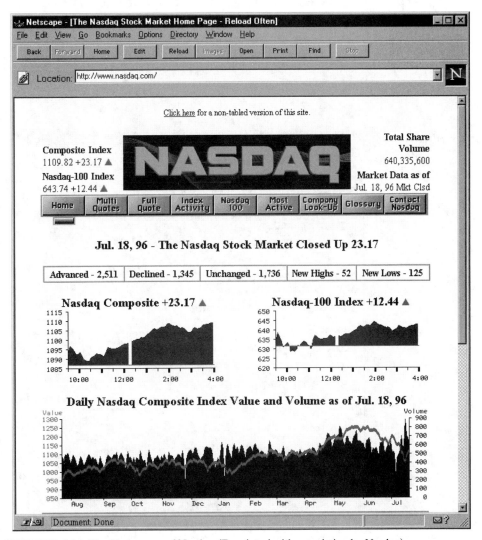

FIGURE 6-16 The Homepage of Nasdaq (Reprinted with permission by Nasdaq)

The major financial services companies actively develop their Web presence. The following is a partial listing of the most-developed sites:

- http://www.fid-inv.com/—the Fidelity Investments Online Investor Center
- http://www.ml.com/—Merrill Lynch
- http://www.ms.com/—Morgan Stanley
- http://www.gs.com/—Goldman Sachs

- `http://www.salomon.com/`—Salomon Brothers
- `http://www.schwab.com/`—Charles Schwab

The sites provide company and market information of varying depth. The most interesting part of the Fidelity Investments site is their @82DEV program that covers "a wide range of investor news, data and information—every business day." Several brokerages give their customers the option to trade electronically. A good example is Charles Schwab's *eSchwab* found at `http://www.eschwab.com/`. A demo example of buying 100 shares of IBM stock through SchwabOnline is shown in Figure 6-17. Among the smaller companies competing in this emerging area of on-line trades, one of the best known is eBroker (`http://www.ebroker.com`). Smaller companies offer the least-expensive way of trading on-line in exchange for "bare bones" services.

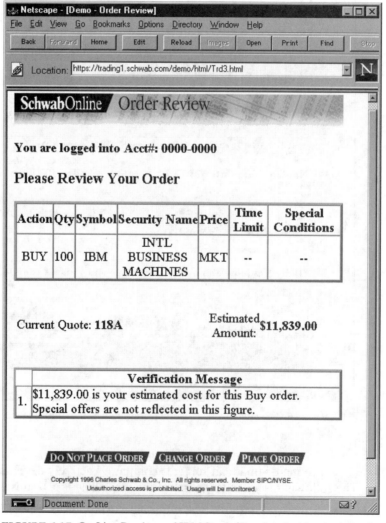

FIGURE 6-17 On-Line Purchase of IBM Stock (Reprinted with permission by Charles Schwab & Co.)

Stock quote servers are extremely popular on the Internet, and there are quite a few free delayed quote servers to choose from. The stock market quote server by GALT Technologies was already mentioned in chapter 3 (`http://quotes.galt.com/`). The Charles Schwab Web site provides an excellent quote server (stocks, options, mutual funds) at

`http://www.schwab.com/schwabNOW/SNLibrary/SNLi6068/SN068StocksSePRes.html`

The server is extremely fast, and the delay of trade quotes is very low. Another excellent quote server is Security APL's QuoteServer found at

`http://www.secapl.com/cgi-bin/qs`

Finally, it is noteworthy that the quote server StockMaster was the first stock service on the web and was formerly hosted at the MIT AI Lab. It provides free stock and mutual funds quotes and can be found at

`http://www.stockmaster.com/`

ACCOUNTING ASSOCIATIONS

All major U.S. accounting associations have established their Web presence. The screen shot of the homepage of the AICPA (`http://www.aicpa.org`) was shown in chapter 2. The site provides some basic information about the structure and the operations of the institute and the uniform CPA examination. It maintains on-line an interesting "Glossary of Terms, Acronyms, and Abbreviations" found at

`http://www.aicpa.org/members/glossary/a.htm`

Another important part of the AICPA on-line site worth visiting frequently is its news section at

`http://www.aicpa.org/news/index.htm`

The AICPA maintains a page with the pointers to the on-line site of the state societies of CPAs at

`http://www.aicpa.org/states/index.htm`

(see Figure 6-18). The map in the figure is clickable: Clicking on a state pops up a page with the addresses and telephone numbers of the State Board of Accountancy and the State Society of CPAs, as well as a link to the homepage of the State Society (if it exists).

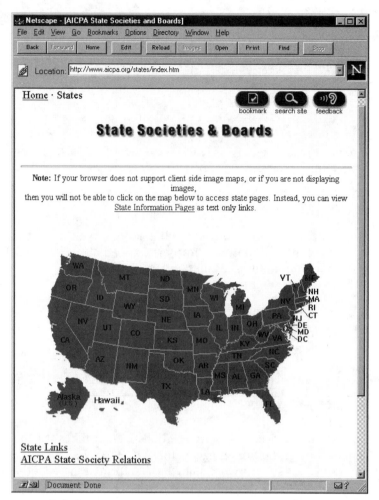

FIGURE 6-18 AICPA's States Page (Reprinted with permission from AICPA Web site, Copyright © 1997 by the American Institute of Certified Public Accountants)

Several associations are hosted on the Rutgers Accounting Web. The American Accounting Association (AAA) whose membership includes most U.S. accounting academics was the first association to establish its Web presence. The AAA homepage can be found at

http://www.AAA-GDV.org

(see Figure 6-19). The site provides extensive information about the organization of the AAA and its activities. It gives pointers to the Web sites of individual sections and regions. Yuji Ijiri's AAA monograph "Momentum Accounting and Triple-Entry Bookkeeping" was discussed in chapter 3. The site is to be checked frequently around the national meetings time as it provides the meeting information as well as some important meeting materials.

One of the largest accounting associations in the world is the Institute of Management Accountants (IMA) with approximately 84,000 members, more than three hundred local chapters, and several international affiliates. The IMA site is hosted on the RAW at http://www.rutgers.edu/accounting/raw/ima/

The site provides comprehensive information about the structure and activities of the institute, as well as a detailed description of the Certified Management Accountant (CMA) Program including the requirements and the examination dates. The site has an on-line annotated bibliography of all the IMA publications starting from 1919. A recent addition to the IMA on-line materials is the full text of the new study "The Practice Analysis of Management Accounting." Several IMA on-line materials were described in chapter 3.

The Institute of Internal Auditors is also hosted on the Rutgers Accounting Web, and it can be found at

http://www.rutgers.edu/accounting/raw/iia/

The site provides the description of the institute, its publications and activities, and the Certified Internal Auditor (CIA) program.

The newest addition to the professional societies hosting on the Rutgers Accounting Web is the Association of Government Accountants located at

http://www.rutgers.edu/Accounting/raw/aga/

The site provides information about the association and the Certified Government Financial Manager (CGFM) program. "Beginning in 1997, it is expected that CGFM candidates will be required to pass a government financial management proficiency examination."

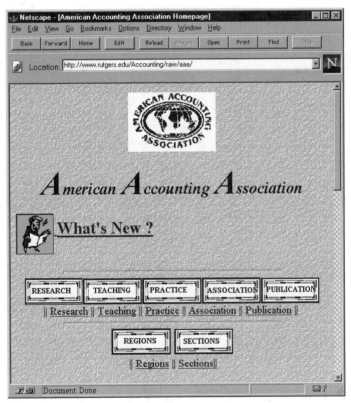

FIGURE 6-19 The AAA Homepage on the RAW (Reprinted with permission by the American Accounting Association)

Many professional associations are now in the process of establishing their Web presence. The homepage of the Financial Executives Institute is under construction at

http://www.fei.org.

In addition to national associations, a growing number of local associations have been establishing Web sites. For example, Associated Regional Accounting Firms (ARAF) has a homepage at

http://www.homecom.com/araf/home.html

The national scholastic and professional accounting fraternity Beta Alpha Psi has on-line presence both at the national level and at the level of many local chapters. The homepage of the national headquarters is located at

http://www.ECNet.Net/users/miactg/wiu/bap/bap.htm

The site provides detailed information about the fraternity and links to the Web pages of local chapters.

U.S. TAX ASSOCIATIONS

One of the major U.S. tax professional societies is the National Tax Association housed at the Arizona State University at

http://www.cob.asu.edu/nta/

**Website
Tax**

The site provides the abstracts of papers published in the *National Tax Journal* as well as some other information about the association. The American Taxation Association (ATA) at the time of this writing had a homepage at

http://omer.actg.vic.edu.8001/ata.html

The site was planning to move to a new address that was not known yet.

The materials of the Section of Taxation of the American Bar Association (ABA) can be found at

http://www.abanet.org/tax/

The National Association of Enrolled Agents has a Web site at

http://www.naea.org/

The site provides electronic filing resources, top tax news, an interesting selection of answers to frequently asked tax questions, a useful list of links to tax materials on the Internet, and the membership directory to locate on-line the nearest enrolled agent.

INTERNATIONAL ACCOUNTING ASSOCIATIONS

A number of major professional accounting associations around the world have Web sites. The most active on-line presence is provided by the associations in Canada, the United Kingdom, and Australia. The Canadian Institute of Chartered Accountants (CICA) has a Web site at

http://www.cica.ca/

This is one of the most impressive accounting sites on the Internet. It presents a rich variety of important materials, including the full text (in English and French) of the CICA exposure drafts in accounting standards (see Figure 6-20), auditing standards, and public accounting and auditing standards. The site provides on-line the content of the *CAmagazine* (a monthly magazine of CICA) starting from June/July 1995. The Institute started providing on-line the content of *The Canadian Account*—a quarterly publication of CICA.

The Certified General Accountants' Association of Canada (CGA Canada) has a Web site at

`http://www.cga-canada.org/`

The Society of Management Accountants of Canada (SMAC) has a Web site at

`http://www.cma-canada.org/`

The site provides on-line some materials from *CMA Magazine* starting from December 1995 and discusses in detail the certification requirements, the organization of the society, and various membership information.

The Institute of Chartered Accountants in England and Wales (ICAEW) has a Web site within the framework of the Summa project (see Figure 6-6). It has its own domain name, and it can be found at

`http://www.icaew.org.uk/`

The site provides interesting information about the services of the Institute to the public and to the members in business and in practice.

The Chartered Institute of Management Accountants (CIMA) in the United Kingdom has a Web site at

`http://www.demon.co.uk/cima/`

The site provides information about the institute and its activities, some materials from the PASS magazine, and two case studies from the CIMA's Business Management Competitions (1994—Change the World and 1995—Conquer Europe).

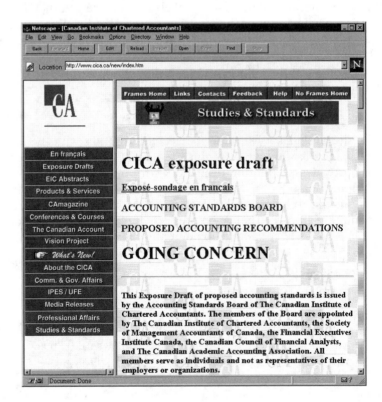

FIGURE 6-20 The Canadian Institute of Chartered Accountants

The homepage of the European Accounting Association (EAA) is located at

```
http://www.bham.ac.uk/EAA/homepage.htm
```

The most important information provided by this site is the abstracts of papers presented at the Annual Congresses of the EAA.

The Australian Society of Certified Practising Accountants has an impressive Web site at

```
http://www.cpaonline.com.au/
```

At the moment of this writing, access to many materials on the site was restricted (requiring the user ID and password). In the public domain, the site provides full content of its Australian Accountant magazine starting from February 1996, standard materials about the structure and activities of the society, and some other information.

The international accounting bodies are represented on the Internet by the Web site of the International Federation of Accountants (IFAC) with the homepage at

```
http://www.ifac.org/
```

The site provides detailed information about the structure and activities of the federation. "IFAC membership consists of more than 119 professional accountancy bodies from 86 countries."

ACCOUNTING PUBLISHERS AND PUBLICATIONS

Major College Publishers

**Website
Accounting texts**

Most accounting publishers have Web sites on the Internet. A good list of pointers to them can be found in the publishers section of RAW's Accounting Resources on the Internet. The example of Prentice Hall's accounting Web pages was shown in chapter 3.

An interesting accounting site has been developed by the South-Western College Publishing and is located at

```
http://www.thomson.com/swcp/acct/accounting.html
```

The site provides a list of all the accounting titles with the tables of contents. An uncommon useful feature of this site is its "Great Ideas for Teaching Accounting," that provides accounting professors with an opportunity to share their creative teaching ideas.

In the following is a selective list of some major publishers of college accounting textbooks. Their Web sites provide on-line information about the titles including tables of contents, supplementary materials, and so forth.

- http://www.aw.com/he/BE/BECategories/ac.html—Addison-Wesley Business & Economics
- http://www.irwin.com/catalogs/account.html—Richard D. Irwin Accounting Catalog
- http://www.mhcollege.com/business/account.html—McGraw-Hill Accounting
- http://www.prenhall.com/list/accounld.html—Prentice Hall Accounting
- http://www.wiley.com/Guides/Accounting/Accounting.html—Wiley College/University Accounting

Research Journals

Very few accounting research journals have any presence on-line. Among the exceptions is the *International Journal of Intelligent Systems in Accounting, Finance and Management,* having a Web site at

```
http://www.bus.orst.edu/faculty/brownc/isafm/isafhome.htm
```

The site provides abstracts of all the papers published in the journal since its foundation in 1992.

Another accounting journal with an on-line site is the annual publication *Behavioral Research in Accounting* by the Accounting, Behavior and Organizations Section of the American Accounting Association. It can be found at

```
http://hsb.baylor.edu/html/davisc/abo/bria/briahome.htm
```

The site provides abstracts of all the papers published in the journal since its foundation in 1989.

Professional Publishers

Most major professional accounting publishers have Web sites. Several of them are very well developed. One of the best sites is produced by Harcourt Brace Professional Publishing, located at

```
http://www.hbpp.com/
```

In addition to the extensive on-line catalog of the publisher's products, the site provides several other interesting materials. The most popular one must be "The CPA's Weekly News Update" that provides selected digests from many publisher's newsletters like *Accountant's Tax Weekly, CPA Technology Advisor, Nonprofit Tax Letter,* and others. The URL of this resource is

```
http://www.hbpp.com/weekup/weekup.html
```

Another interesting feature of the site is its "The Week's Accounting Top Five Web Sites," located at

```
http://www.hbpp.com/topfive/topfive.html
```

Every week the publisher selects the top five accounting Web sites among those that have not been previously selected. It provides a badge to recognize the winners' achievements and maintains an archive of past winners, thus compiling a directory of impressive accounting sites.

Among the most-developed accounting sites of professional accounting publishers, we mention the following:

- http://www.bisk.com/—Bisk Publishing Company providing on-line CPA exam preparation resources (such as "Practical Advice for CPA Exam Preparation") and resources for continuing professional education (CPE)

- http://www.gleim.com/accounting.html—Gleim's Accounting Books and Software providing on-line some useful exam preparation tips

- http://www.cch.com/—CCH Incorporated with its Tax Legislation Hot Link

- http://www.beckercpa.com/—The Becker CPA Review providing on-line some interesting career-related materials

ACADEMIC EDUCATION IN ACCOUNTING

Many accounting departments around the world have on-line presence. Many more are in the process of establishing it. A convenient on-line resource for accounting academics is "Accounting Scholars Page" (see Figure 6-21) maintained by the Department of Accounting & MIS (AMIS) of the Ohio State University's Fisher College of Business, which is located at

http://www.cob.ohio-state.edu/~acctmis/papers/locate.html

This site provides links to the homepage of academic accounting departments and individual homepages of accounting scholars. The on-line site of the host of this resource is one of the most impressive academic accounting Web sites (see Figure 6-22). The site provides exceptionally complete information about the department. Among other things, it keeps on-line current research papers of its faculty members. One of the remarkable features of this site is "The Accounting Hall of Fame," which was established at The Ohio State University in 1950 "for the purpose of honoring accountants who have made or are making significant contributions to the advancement of accounting since the twentieth century." The URL of this page is

http://www.cob.ohio-state.edu/~acctmis/hof/hall.html

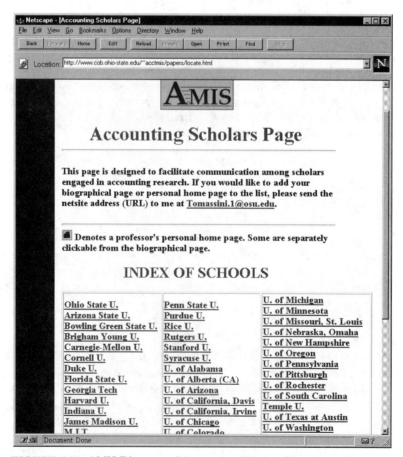

FIGURE 6-21 AMIS Directory of Accounting Scholars (Reprinted with permission by the author, Larry Tomassini)

Some accounting departments provide on-line a variety of teaching materials. In many cases the on-line content consists primarily of courses' syllabi. A more extensive on-line site can provide lecture notes, feedback forms, supplemental reading list, and so forth. A good example is the site of the Introduction to Managerial Accounting course at the College of Business Administration of the University of Iowa maintained by Professor Joyce Berg at

http://www.biz.uiowa.edu/class/6A002/notes/index.html

The page with links to the lecture notes for this course is shown in Figure 6-23. The site also provides a page with useful accounting links, the frequently asked questions (FAQ) pages, and some other materials.

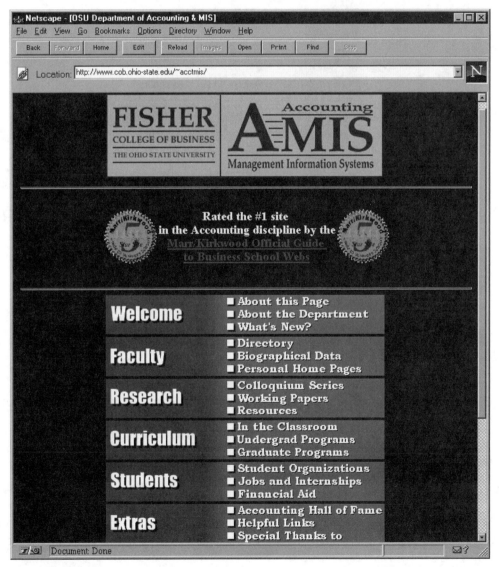

FIGURE 6-22 The Homepage of AMIS (Reprinted with permission by the author, Larry Tomassini)

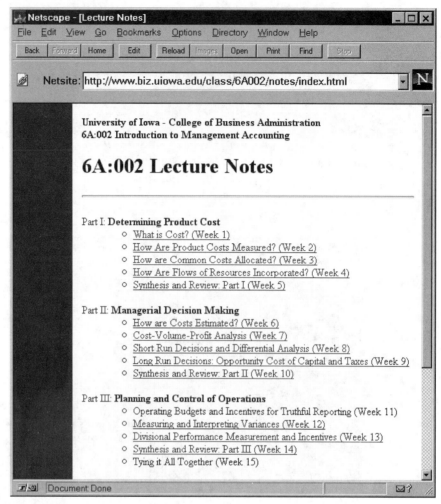

FIGURE 6-23 Prof. Berg's Management Accounting Lecture Notes (Reprinted with permission by Professor Joyce Berg, University of Iowa)

CONCLUDING REMARKS

The reader should keep in mind that the World Wide Web is in its infancy. Many more accounting resources will come on-line in the near future. What was presented in this chapter is only the beginning. Given the spectacular growth prospects, it will become increasingly important for accountants to sift the diamonds from the rough. This will require both solid knowledge of and long experience with managing accounting resources on the Internet.

Problems

1. Develop your own bookmark hierarchy of Internet accounting resources.
2. Visit the accounting resources described in this chapter, and add them to your bookmarks.
3. Each week find at least three new important accounting resources that are worth adding to your bookmarks.

CHAPTER

Security on the Internet

7

INTRODUCTION

The proliferation of Internet services increases communicative abilities by leaps and bounds. At the same time, this gives rise to increased concerns about the confidentiality of the information exchanged over the Internet. Most, if not all, communicators prefer to have complete control over third-party access to their information.

When information is transmitted over the Internet, there are many opportunities for breaches of security. Consider the analogy with conventional mail correspondence. Suppose that Alice sends a letter to Bob in a sealed envelope. The letter may not contain any secrets or sensitive information. Still, neither Alice nor Bob may want to share its content with others. If the letter does contain confidential information, then Alice and Bob want to make sure that nobody else accesses it. Although tampering with the U.S. mail is a federal crime, there is never a foolproof guarantee of confidentiality. Someone with an access to the mailbox where Alice dropped the letter can open and read it. The same is true for the letter carriers who deliver the letter to the local post office or to Bob. Sorters and handlers can open and read the letter at all the post offices through which the letter travels. Anybody having a key to Bob's mailbox can open and read the letter before Bob gets it. When Bob throws away the letter, it may still be possible for interested parties to retrieve and reassemble the pieces.

Similar breaches of security can occur when Alice E-mails a message to Bob over the Internet. Third parties can break into Alice's or Bob's computers or to their respective E-mail servers and copy the message there. These constitute breaches in the security of on-line sites. The message can be also intercepted along the way over the Internet. This is a breach of the security of on-line information flows. Internet information flows include, among other things, all the electronic financial transactions (payments, fund transfers, etc.). It is important to distinguish between problems associated with the security of on-line sites and those related to the security of on-line information flows.

SECURITY RISKS OF ON-LINE INFORMATION FLOWS

As was discussed in chapter 1 (see Basic Building Blocks of the Internet), information on the Internet flows in packets. Packets traverse the Internet hop by hop from one router to another. Since different parts of the Internet infrastructure are privately owned and operated, it is very difficult, if not impossible, to know in advance through which routes and routers the packets will flow and who will have access to those routers. At each router each packet can be intercepted, and related packets can be reassembled by unwanted parties to reproduce the original message.

While the packets of each message can travel through different routes, all of them have to pass through the same entry point to and the same exit point from the Internet. At these points (which are usually unique) all packets can be intercepted, and the original message can therefore be reassembled with relative ease. Therefore, in case of the Internet, the security risk is the greatest at the entry and exit points.

Similar interception risks exist in other transport and communication systems. Telephone messages can be easily intercepted by tapping into a line. Since typically the number of different owners of telephone circuits is relatively small compared with the number of Internet parts owners, the number of potential telephone interceptors is smaller than their Internet counterparts, and their ranks can be better controlled. It is difficult to assess the comparative risks of interception in various transport systems. We are not aware of any hard evidence to the effect that such risks are any higher than the security risks in other transport and communication systems.

At the same time, the Internet potentially offers greater opportunities for automated high-volume fraud. For example, the proliferation of credit card transactions on the Internet and the openness of the network to third parties create possibilities to intercept names, numbers, and expiration dates of a very large number (hundreds of thousands) of accounts. This information can be used to forge credit cards. These forgeries can be "automated" through computer programs that scan the Internet round the clock to perpetuate fraudulent procedures.

SECURITY REQUIREMENTS
FOR ELECTRONIC TRANSACTIONS

In general, there are three major security requirements in electronic communications:

- **Confidentiality** of information—information should not be accessible to parties who are not authorized by the sender of that information.
- **Integrity** of information—information should not be alterable or lend itself to tampering with on its way from the sender to the recipient.
- **Authentication** of sender—the identity of the sender of information should be verifiable in a reliable manner.

Modern cryptography (the science of encryption) provides means for simultaneously satisfying these requirements. The essence of cryptography is to encrypt (cipher or code) a message in a way that the resulting coded message can be decrypted (deciphered or decoded) only by holders of the appropriate "key." In general, the term "key" refers to the password and the procedure required to decipher the encrypted message. In electronic communications over the Internet the encryption and decryption procedures are commonly known, and the term key refers only to the secret *password*. The password is actually a number since electronic messages are just sequences of 0's and 1's.

Cryptography is a very old science. It was traditionally based on a one-key system. Both the encoder and the decoder used the same key to encrypt and to decrypt a message. As a result, the key had to be kept secret by all parties. This is why such systems are called *secret key cryptosystems.* Secret key cryptography is routinely used by the military and by the federal government. DES (Data Encryption Standard) is a widely used secret key cryptosystem. For example, DES is used for encrypting PIN numbers in ATMs. DES was endorsed as an official standard by the U.S. government in 1977.

A secret key cryptosystem cannot be used directly for electronic commerce because each merchant–customer pair will have to possess a distinct secret key. This means that each customer should have a separate key for each merchant he or she transacts with. By the same token, each merchant should have a distinct secret key for each of his or her customers. There is, therefore, no feasible solution for selecting and maintaining all these distinct secret keys.

Website Cryptosystems

Alternative cryptosystems, which made electronic commerce possible, were invented in 1976. These so-called *public key cryptosystems* are based on two keys. Each participant generates a pair of keys. One of them, the participant's *private key,* is kept secret from everybody else. The second one is the participant's *public key,* which is made publicly known. The underlying mathematics of encryption and decryption is such that if one key (either public or private) is used to encrypt the message, then the key of the other type is needed to decrypt the coded message. In other words, a message encrypted with the public key can be decrypted only using the private key. Consequently, knowledge of the public key cannot be used to decrypt a message encoded with this public key. Conversely, a message encrypted with the private key can be decrypted only using the public key. The most commonly used public key cryptosystem is RSA, invented in 1977 by Rivest, Shamir, and Adelman, and sold by RSA Data Security, Inc. (http://www.rsa.com).

To better understand the public key cryptosystems, consider the following information exchange. Alice wishes to send a confidential message to Bob. Alice uses Bob's public key to encrypt her message. Only Bob's private key can decrypt the message. Hence, as Bob decrypts the message using his private key, he can be certain of the confidentiality of the message. But Bob cannot authenticate the fact that Alice was the one who sent the message because anyone could have used his public key and pretend to be Alice.

To enable Bob to authenticate her identity as the sender of the message, Alice has to send Bob a message encrypted with her private key. Now everybody can decrypt this message because Alice's public key is known to everyone, and everyone, including Bob, can ascertain that Alice was the sender of the message. Hence, the authenticity of this message is established because only Alice knows her private key.

Finally, to assure Bob that her message is confidential *and* authentic, Alice has to send a message encrypted twice. Alice first encrypts her message with her private key and subsequently encodes the encrypted message with Bob's public key. This way, only Bob can decrypt the resulting message (assuring its confidentiality), which only Alice could have sent (assuring its authenticity).

In practice, the aforementioned theoretical procedure is not used directly because of the very poor computational performance of public key cryptosystems. The old secret key cryptosystems are about a hundred (!) times faster than public key cryptosystems. As a result, a practical hybrid procedure combining the two techniques has been developed to secure on-line information flows.

To assure confidentiality of the message, Alice (the sender) generates randomly a secret key and subsequently uses this random secret key to encode her message. She then uses Bob's public key to encrypt the random secret key and sends this encoded secret key together with the encoded message to Bob. At his end, Bob first uses his private key to decode the random secret key and then uses this secret key to decode the message. Confidentiality is assured because nobody except Bob knows Bob's private key, and the chances of randomly generating the same secret key are negligible. Here, a public key cryptosystem is used for encoding/decoding of only a very short random secret key. As a result, the time requirement is significantly reduced.

To assure integrity and authentication of her message to Bob, Alice adds a so-called "digital signature" to her message. This digital signature is designed to provide an irrefutable proof that the message was not altered, and was signed by Alice. Digital signatures are based on a procedure of "message digesting," which computes a short fixed-length number (called *digest*) for any message (of any length). Several different messages may have the same digest, but it is extremely difficult to produce any of them from the digest. Even the slightest change in the message generates major changes in the digest. Consequently, a message cannot be altered without significantly affecting the digest. Therefore, a digest can guarantee the integrity of a message if it is appropriately protected (otherwise, a fraudulent message can be fabricated together with its digest).

To complete the procedure, Alice encodes the digest of the message with her private key and then sends her message to Bob together with its encrypted digest. This encrypted digest is Alice's digital signature. When Bob receives Alice's message, he uses her public key to decrypt the digest. Subsequently, Bob runs the same message digest algorithm on Alice's message to obtain its digest independently and to check that this digest coincides with the digest that arrived with Alice's message. If the two digests coincide, Bob can be assured that the message was not altered (proving integrity) and has been authored by Alice (providing authentication).

Messages can be authenticated but not confidential, or confidential but not authenticated. To achieve *both* confidentiality and integrity with authentication, Alice should first create her digital signature for the message, then encrypt the resulting authenticated message with a random secret key, and ultimately encrypt the secret key with Bob's public key.

For illustration purposes, consider how these techniques are employed in securing communications over the Internet. When Alice surfs the Internet using a secure Web browser (e.g., Netscape or Internet Explorer) and wants to communicate with a secure Web site run by Bob using a secure Web server (e.g., Netscape Commerce Server), Alice's browser will first obtain Bob's server public key. The browser then generates a random secret key (session key), encodes it with the server's public key and sends it to the server. After the server decodes it using its private key, both the browser and the server know the secret session key and can communicate confidentially by encoding their messages with this secret key. The cryptographic algorithms used by Netscape[1] can be seen in its **Help** | **About Netscape** screen (see bottom of Figure 7-1). RSA is a public key cryptosystem, RC4 is a secret key cryptosystem, and MD2 and MD5 are message digest algorithms.

---

[1]Netscape Communications Corporation has not authorized, sponsored or endorsed, or approved this publication and is not responsible for its content. Netscape and the Netscape Communications corporate logos are trademarks and trade names of Netscape Communications Corporation. All other product names and/or logos are trademarks of their respective owners.

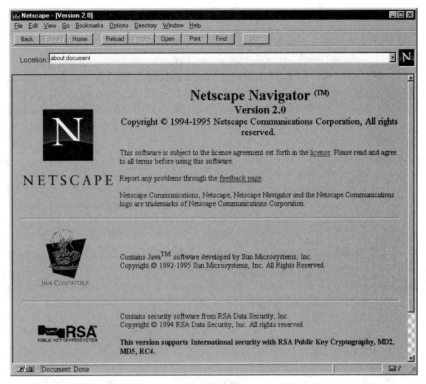

FIGURE 7-1 Netscape Information Screen (Copyright © 1996 Netscape Communications Corp. All rights reserved. This page may not be reprinted or copied without the express written permission of Netscape.)

Note that all the aforementioned procedures are publicly known. Only the secret keys and the private keys are unknown. Also, there are no mathematical proofs of the relative difficulties in deciphering these procedures. It is, however, universally believed that they are extremely difficult if not impossible to break. The longer the key the more difficult the process of breaking the code. Moreover, linear growth in the key size leads to exponential growth in the difficulty of breaking the code. As faster computers permit longer keys, advances in hardware make these cryptographic procedures more difficult to break.

How secure should on-line systems be? Faster computers can handle longer keys, thereby providing more security. From a cost-benefit viewpoint it is possible to oversecure a system. There is clearly an optimal level of security. The key should be long enough to make the cost of breaking the code exceed the benefits. It should not be much longer than that, if excessive costs associated with the cryptographic systems (e.g., hardware and software costs) are to be avoided.

There remains the problem of verifying the identity behind a public key. Who guards the guards? How can Bob be sure that "Alice's" public key really belongs to Alice rather than to an impostor who claims to be Alice. One solution is to have trusted authorities (called *certificate authorities*) whose public keys are publicly known and trustworthy. Any party can request (or buy) from a certificate authority a digital certificate, that is, this party's public key digitally signed by this certificate authority. If Bob receives a digitally signed message from Alice together with

Alice's digital certificate, Bob can then use the certificate authority's public key to extract Alice's public key from her certificate and be sure that it belongs to Alice.

VeriSign, Inc. (`http://www.verisign.com/`) is in the business of providing digital authentication services and products for electronic commerce and other forms of secure communications (see Figure 7-2). The company was founded in 1995 as a spin-off of RSA Data Security. Its investors and partners currently include Ameritech, Visa International, Netscape, Open Market, and IBM.

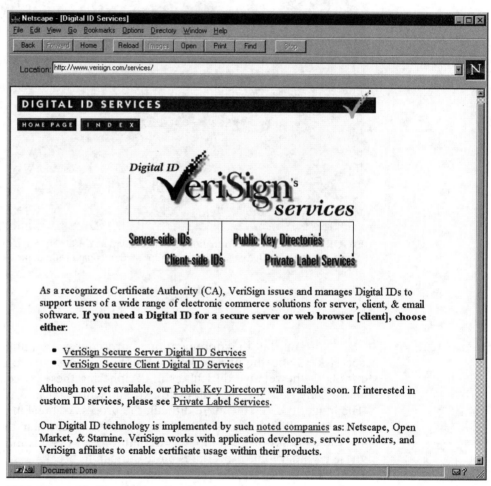

FIGURE 7-2 VeriSign Services (Reprinted with permission by VeriSign Inc.)

SECURE ELECTRONIC TRANSACTION (SET)
SPECIFICATIONS BY MASTERCARD AND VISA

**Website
Secure Electronic
Transaction (SET)**

With the growth in Internet commerce, issues of security of information flows on the net have come to the forefront of developments in Internet technology. A variety of products for securing the Internet information flows are currently available on the market. Interoperability and a degree of standardization of these security products are needed to facilitate a faster development and wider acceptance of Internet commerce. A major milestone along these lines was the February 1996 announcement by Visa and MasterCard of the common specifications of secure electronic transactions (SET) (see Figure 7-3).

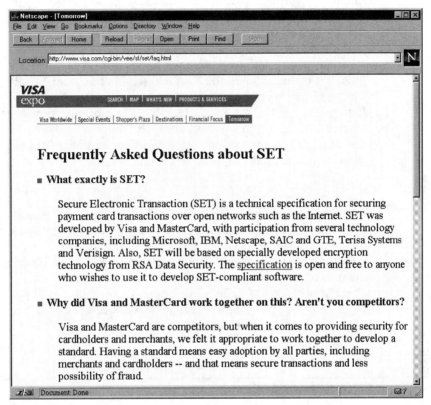

FIGURE 7-3 Visa SET FAQs (Reprinted with permission by Visa International. Copyright © 1996 Visa International.)

Both Visa and MasterCard make this specifications draft freely available on-line and solicit comments from interested parties. According to the draft:

"The Secure Electronic Transaction (SET) specification is divided into two separate documents: the SET business section and the SET technical specification.

"The SET business section provides an overview of the potential opportunities for bankcard associations to participate in the future growth of electronic commerce . . .

"The SET technical section contains the information and processing flows for SET protocol. It is intended as an introduction for anyone interested in the processing of bankcard transactions on electronic networks. It is also intended for vendors developing software that will inter-operate with other implementations of SET. The scope of the SET technical section is limited to the payment process and the security services necessary to support the payment segment of electronic shopping. To provide these services, SET, in addition to defining the electronic payment protocol, also defines the certificate registration and issuance process." See

http://www.visa.com/cgi-bin/vee/sf/set/intro.html

PUBLIC POLICY ON ENCRYPTION

**Website
Encryptions**

Encryption is an important and controversial policy issue. The International Traffic in Arms Regulation (ITAR) defines cryptographic devices (including software) as munitions. The U.S. government limits exports of cryptographic products, making it practically impossible to obtain an export license for a software product implementing strong encryption algorithms. In the past the U.S. government investigated people who made effective cryptographic products publicly available on the Internet.

These restrictions have been highly controversial. As a result, the U.S. Congress has commissioned the National Research Council (NRC) to prepare a report on the U.S. encryption policies. The report, released in May 1996, says that ". . . no law should bar the manufacture, sale, or use of any form of encryption within the United States, and that export controls should be relaxed but not eliminated. The development of encryption technologies should be driven largely by market forces than by government-imposed requirements." See

```
http://epic.org/crypto/reports/nrc_release.html
```

Public sentiment in favor of relaxing current U.S. policy on cryptography is growing. The NRC believes that its recommendations, if adopted, "would lead to enhanced protection and privacy for individuals and businesses in many areas, ranging from cellular and other wireless phone conversations to electronic transmission of sensitive business or financial documents."

Another noteworthy development in public policy on encryption occurs in the area of digital signatures. Digital signature laws have been passed in a number of states, with Utah and California taking the lead (see a detailed discussion in chapter 9).

SECURITY OF ON-LINE SITES

The best efforts to secure information flows on the Internet will come to naught if the end points are vulnerable. The end points are the computers engaged in communications over the Internet. These computers are vulnerable to break-ins by third parties. For example, an unauthorized person may find out the password of a legitimate user and get access to the information on the computer system. A more sophisticated break-in can occur when a computer cracker gets access to a computer system exploiting some weaknesses of the software running on it.

There have been numerous breaches of Internet sites' security. One of the most notorious incidents was the so-called *Internet worm* created by two Cornell University computer science students in November 1988. That worm managed to bring down a significant number of Internet hosts, including some Department of Defense systems. In response to the incident, the Advanced Research Projects Agency (ARPA) created the Computer Emergency Response Team (CERT).

The following quote from the CERT Web site provides a testimony about the current status of on-line site security: "From January through December 1995, the CERT Coordination Center received 32,084 email messages and 3,428 hotline calls. We handled 2,412 computer security incidents during this period. More than 12,000 sites were affected by these incidents, which involved 732 break-ins and nearly that many probes and pranks." See

```
http://www.cert.org/cert.report.95.html
```

Investor's Business Daily (June 24, 1996, A6) quotes the FBI's special agent in charge of the San Francisco division saying that in a recent survey of companies, "42% of those who responded said they'd experienced some unauthorized intrusion into their computer system in the last 12 months. Also, it found that 47% of those surveyed felt it could have been a foreign competitor or foreign government. We feel that's a very significant problem, one the FBI is particularly interested in."

The frequency of on-line site security breaches points to the need for countermeasures ranging from relatively simple password protection to very sophisticated "firewalls" separating corporate networks from the open Internet.

Every on-line site restricts the number of people who are allowed to structure and modify it. Otherwise, it would have no control over its activities. It follows that any on-line site needs a certain amount of security. The most basic way to protect an on-line site is to restrict remote login by requiring a login name and a password. However, this rudimentary protection can be easily compromised if a user fails to keep her password confidential. Outsiders may uncover passwords by trial and error, or steal them along their way over the Internet. The so-called *one-time passwords* can impede such intrusions.

A one-time password system includes some special software running on the Internet host and a special personal card (synchronized with the host computer) that generates a new password each time the user wants to log in. The computer recognizes the password, which is never used again and therefore becomes useless. The security of this system is compromised if the card is lost but not canceled.

More sophisticated protection of an on-line site can be accomplished by constant screening of the incoming Internet traffic. This screening can be done in several ways. The simplest way is to configure the router that connects the site to the Internet to do the so-called *packet filtering*. This filtering requires some analysis of the packets to screen out those packets that are considered unwanted. The criteria used for deciding which packets are unwanted are determined by the security policy of the site. The restrictiveness of the criteria is set by weighing the tradeoffs between security costs and benefits. Additional security is costly, inconvenient, and time-consuming.

Security policies are usually determined by management's attitudes toward risk. Such policies are commonly characterized by the *Four P's* of computer security, as being *paranoid, prudent, permissive,* or *promiscuous.* The paranoid policy disconnects the computer system from the network since any risk is considered too high. Obviously, in the absence of a connection, packet filtering is not needed. The prudent policy limits network access to a few applications considered safe (e.g., E-mail and WWW only). Filtering rules in a router can be set up to let through only packets carrying information for the allowed applications. The permissive policy allows all network applications, except for a few that are considered unsafe (e.g., telnet). Filtering rules in a router can be set up to let through all the packets except those carrying information for the prohibited applications. The promiscuous policy does not impose any restrictions on the network connection. Here again, no packet filtering is needed. Ultimately, however, what is prudent is decided by the cost/benefit circumstances of each particular case.

Packet filtering is an example of a firewall providing a rudimentary perimeter defense for an on-line site. A *bastion host* running application or proxy servers is a more formidable firewall. A bastion host is fundamentally a buffer computer designed to shield the internal network from potentially hostile Internet users. It runs only the absolutely essential programs that were designed to avoid any security holes. A bastion host runs trusted versions of Internet applications (say, E-mail and WWW) and acts as an intermediary between the internal network and the external Internet.

Internal computers connect with external ones through the bastion host. For example, rather than requesting a Web page directly from the external computer hosting it, an internal computer asks the bastion host to request that page on its behalf. The bastion host then requests that page and forwards it to the internal computer. As a result, outsiders interact with the bastion host only and therefore cannot inflict any damage on the internal computers. Moreover, outsiders may know little, if anything, about the configuration of internal computers.

Since the bastion host keeps track of all the active network connections, it can exercise a much more intricate control over the network activities. For example, it can detect an http packet that lacks any specific functional purpose for being let through into the internal network, although it has been identified by the packet screening router as "legitimate." Extensive log keeping of network activities is another important feature of firewalls. This allows system administrators to analyze suspicious probes and thereby continuously modify and improve their defense system.

Firewalls are like ramparts of a fortified citadel. They protect from an enemy charging from the outside but cannot protect the citadel from a "Trojan horse" that is successfully smuggled in. Firewalls can be effective in protecting internal computers from unauthorized access by outsiders. They are generally useless against insiders who may inflict damage intentionally or unintentionally. For example, no firewall can protect against a virus[2] attached to a legitimate E-mail message or stored on an infected floppy diskette brought in by an employee. In fact, many experts claim that the internal threat to corporate networks (internal risk exposure) is much higher than the external one.

Firewall technology, however, can be used to reduce internal risk exposure. In addition to building firewalls to defend the perimeter of an internal network, the network itself can be segmented into smaller compartments using firewalls. For example, the subnetwork of the personnel department may have to be separated by a firewall from operating departments to protect sensitive employee data. This segmentation of the internal network limits the damage an insider can do by preventing it from spreading beyond the affected segment.

CONCLUDING REMARKS

As companies increase their reliance on commercial transactions over the Internet, and public accounting firms increase the use of professional electronic communications with their clients, more messages on the Internet will have to be restricted and secured. Accountants will be required to know more about the technologies and professional implications of alternative Internet security systems. Indeed, accountants may also be required to participate in auditing Internet security arrangements designed to protect the integrity of financial information and transactions.

---

[2]For a discussion of how to protect your computer from viruses, see appendix B.

Problems

1. Describe the major security requirements of electronic communications.
2. Describe the differences between secret key cryptosystems and public key cryptosystems.
3. Explain why a secret key cryptosystem by itself cannot support electronic commerce.
4. Compare the risk of giving your credit number over the phone with the risk of sending it over the Internet in the nonencrypted E-mail message.
5. What is the Secure Electronic Transaction (SET) standard? Why is this standard needed?
6. What is the current U.S. export policy concerning encryption products? Discuss the pros and cons of this policy.
7. What is the difference between securing Internet information flows and securing Internet sites?
8. What is an Internet firewall, and how does it increase security of an on-line site?

C H A P T E R

Electronic Commerce

8

INTRODUCTION

Electronic commerce (EC) is a broad term encompassing electronically conducted business activities and transactions. Through the use of computer technology and standards, the flow of business information and the conduct of commercial activities can be remote, automatic, and electronic.

The WWW greatly facilitated the growth of electronic commerce over the Internet by bringing point-and-click usage and a simple publishing language (HTML) to the Internet, so that millions of users with only basic computer literacy could conduct business on the Internet easily and with low cost. In this chapter the present scope of electronic commerce and its major manifestation and practices are reviewed, future prospects and opportunities are contemplated, and implications for the accounting profession are discussed.

For Internet purposes it is useful to classify goods as *bitable* (soft goods) and *nonbitable*. The first can be delivered through the net (e.g., software, information, or money), while the second class requires physical delivery of goods (such as shoes or automobiles). Apart from the physical delivery of the goods, the entire sales process can be completed over the net in both categories.

It is also useful to classify goods as *commodity* or *noncommodity* goods. For Internet purposes the former are the goods that the consumer does not need to see, try, touch, smell, or taste in order to buy. The latter are less appropriate for electronic commerce as direct contact is necessary. With consumer experience, goods can evolve to commodity from noncommodity items. Bitable commodity items are the best prospects for electronic commerce.

Even commodity items have *bitable attributes*. Progressively, with the customer's experience the shopping decision may reduce a noncommodity item to a commodity item through experience and judicious understanding of some of its attributes. For example, after trying and purchasing a few times, a customer may realize that female Levis jeans are a good fit with a waist size of 28 and a length 30. The decision will then be based on price (a bitable attribute) and size (a bit-describable attribute).

Electronic commerce on the Internet can be currently viewed as consisting of the following two areas:

- Direct selling over the Internet.
- Using the Internet for activities that support and facilitate commerce (e.g., electronic marketing, transaction processing, and electronic finance).

Most opportunities in the second area will present themselves through advertising, subscription services, and transaction processing.

Website Subscription services

Subscription services are technologically related to the concept of micropayments, and while the security and standards of payments over the net are evolving, electronic commerce has started slowly. Subscription services will allow the user to buy access to valuable information for his/her activities (e.g., stock prices, analyst reports, test results, etc.).

Website Transaction services

Transaction services will progressively take care of the "back office" functions of many businesses, use the Internet as the virtual private network, and allow for substantial buying and selling over the Internet.

Website Advertising

Advertising on the Internet is in its embryonic stages. According to the *Los Angeles Times*[1] (June 10, 1996), out of $125-billion, U.S. advertising market on-line advertisement in 1995 was about $80 million. At the same time, the newspaper cites Jupiter Communications projections of on-line ads growing from about $340 million in 1996 to $5 billion in 2000. This rapid growth indicates a promising future for Web advertising. Some of largest U.S. advertisers seem to be convinced. In April 1996, Proctor and Gamble (with an annual advertising budget in excess of $3 billion) signed a deal with Yahoo (http://www.yahoo.com)—the most popular Internet directory.

Differentiating Business to Business from Person to Business

While most current discussion of electronic commerce revolves around consumer-oriented commerce, a large portion of EC will be of the business-to-business variety. This variety involves a mutation from EDI (electronic data interchange) concepts to a wider set of activities formalized initially through mutual agreements and progressively developing industry standards that will eventually lead to purely blind, automatic transactions, where no specific deals and agreements between the parties are necessary.

Possibilities with Electronic Commerce

- What if you were able to make changes to any technical drawing from a computer and then immediately share the modifications with all end users instantaneously through the usage of groupware associated with the Internet?

- Imagine bidding for and winning a contract without extensive procurement of RFPs, handling reams of paper, leaving telephone messages, and waiting indefinitely for answers.

- Consider using a computer to find, immediately, all the information needed to prepare a competitive bid.

- Suppose you were able to access data instantly, from old billing information to complex technical specifications—no more searching through stuffed filing cabinets only to find a faded, dirty, unusable original.

- Think of your management or auditors being able to trace instantaneously all the steps of a transaction by a client.

- Think of your security officers identifying fraud while someone is trying to break into a system.

- Now imagine customer involvement with the development or improvement of a product or service: Consider what it would be like if companies could come together to share tal-

---

[1]Behal, Bob, Menachen, Lauren & Nymberg, Hogan, "Advertising on the Internet," unpublished manuscript, 1996.

ents and unite resources to go after opportunities normally beyond the realm of any of the individual companies. Picture an environment where a company is not only electronically linked internally but also linked externally to any location in the world.

These are some selected activities being facilitated by the combination of computer and electronic commerce technologies. The trend in electronic commerce is to mold the vast network of small businesses, government agencies, large corporations, and independent contractors into a single-business community with the ability to communicate with one another seamlessly across any computer platform.

Integration means more than coming together externally, it also encompasses internal integration. In an internally integrated organization, incoming orders are received electronically, and the information goes not only to production but also to shipping, billing, and inventory systems automatically—without any human intervention. Internal integration also means that critical data are stored digitally in formats and on media that permit instantaneous retrieval and electronic transmission.

While technology is important to integration, human resources are indispensable. Electronic commerce principles require coworkers, customers, and even former competitors to work together to solve problems, improve services, create new products, and pursue new markets. One essential feature of electronic commerce is data continuity, which is the concept of having data created, modified, and saved in such a way that it can be used throughout the life cycle of a manufactured product, as well as through the value chain[2] of complementary products. The understanding of the value chain, and the increased connectivity of the value chain facilitated by internetworking, can provide substantive competitive advantage. Figure 8-1 displays a visualization of how the value chain can benefit from partners sharing Intranets (Extranets), the corporation with its own Intranet, and the buyers from access through the Internet.

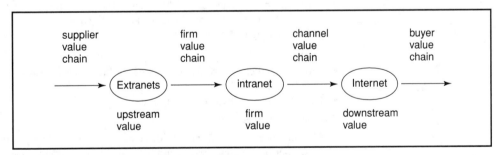

FIGURE 8-1 Internet-Enhanced Value Chain

Table 8-1 enhances the view of the role of the Internet in the value chain as a tool of infrastructure as well as a direct tool in the corporation's primary activities.

---

[2]Michael E. Porter and Victor E. Millar. "How Information Gives You Competitive Advantage," *Harvard Business Review,* July–August 1985. Figure 8-1 and Table 8-1 were adapted from this article.

TABLE 8-1   Internet/Intranet Role in Corporate Activities in the Value Chain

Primary Activities	Inbound Logistic	Operations	Outbound Logistics	Marketing & Sales	Service
Support activities					
Infrastructure	Planning models	Intranet	shared Intranets	Internet presence	Electronic customer care
Human Resources management	Automated personnel scheduling				
Technology development	Computer-aided design	Electronic market research			
Procurement	On-line procurement, automated warehouse	Flexible manufacturing	Automated order processing	Telemarketing, remote terminals for sales	Remote servicing of equipment

Source: Adapted from Porter and Miller, 1985, op. cit.

First we discuss how direct selling over the Internet is currently conducted. Subsequently, we review various business activities that support and facilitate commerce over the Internet.

The Shopping Process in Electronic Commerce

Website
The shopping process in electronic commerce

The consumer shopping process is usually composed of several distinct steps. These steps are outlined below. Business-to-business commerce, while in some respects is similar, presents a very different set of problems.

1. The search stage
   - Customer searches for sites of competing products
   - Customer surfs through the merchant's site to learn about product offerings and conditions such as price, delivery times, availability, etc.

2. The purchase stage
   - Customer places selected product in a virtual shopping cart
   - Customer pays for the products with a credit card, with electronic money (E-money), or by charging it to a charge account

3. The delivery stage
   - Customer takes electronic delivery of bitable goods or waits for vendor to deliver non-bitable goods
   - Customer tracks the order (if nonbitable)

4. Post purchase stage
   - Manufacturer (or vendor) provides customer with on-line product support
   - Customer corresponds with vendor (or manufacturer) by E-mail
   - Customer contests/discusses billing

In many cases, on-line communication between the customer and the vendor are still supplemented with conventional ones (telephone, FAX, regular mail, etc.). As an illustration of the stages and experiences, we will go through the search for a book in the Internet.

The Search Stage

The user will typically use a search engine to find the desired product or alternative sources of information. Increasingly, Web-based businesses also advertise in traditional publications. For example, Amazon Books advertises in the *New York Times*. A search on the Yahoo search engine (Figure 8-2) provided a set of bookstores from which Amazon is chosen. Figure 8-3 shows the Amazon homepage.

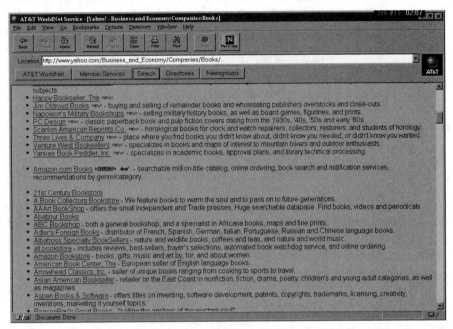

FIGURE 8-2 Yahoo Search for Bookstore (Text and copyright ©1996 by Yahoo!, Inc. All rights reserved. Yahoo! and the Yahoo! logo are trademarks of Yahoo!, Inc.)

FIGURE 8-3 Amazon Homepage (Amazon.com site as 2/97 reprinted with permission by Amazon.com)

This Web site advertises a very large catalog (claiming more than two million items). The acquisition process is facilitated by the virtual shopping cart. The customer can browse through the bookstore and use a powerful search engine (Figure 8-4) to locate the desired book. The Amazon site may provide selected information about the book (e.g., summary, notes about the authors, table of contents, sample chapters, reviews) to browse through. Chosen books are placed in the "shopping cart" for subsequent purchase.

The same type of service is found at the CDNow site (`http://www.cdnow.com`), where a buyer can search, view content, maybe sometimes listen to some sections of a CD, and place the chosen CDs in a shopping cart.

The search engine of the Amazon site (see Figure 8-4) allows customers to search for a book by its title, the name of its author(s), or by other criteria. These types of search engines are character oriented and very similar in nature, if not identical, to the large search mechanisms in the Internet such as Yahoo and Digital's Altavista. In Figure 8-5 we see that a search for the author 'Vasarhelyi' yielded four titles that can be readily ordered.

Desired items are placed in "shopping carts" or "shopping baskets" as illustrated in Figures 8-6 and 8-7 for Amazon and the Harvard Business School sites.

Vasarhelyi has twelve book titles in print, while the Amazon search engine found only four. However, a more complete search engine would have found additional titles under the topic of "Artificial Intelligence" (e.g., volume 1 of the series). Such problems illustrate the nonlinearity and heterogeneous nature of search indices.

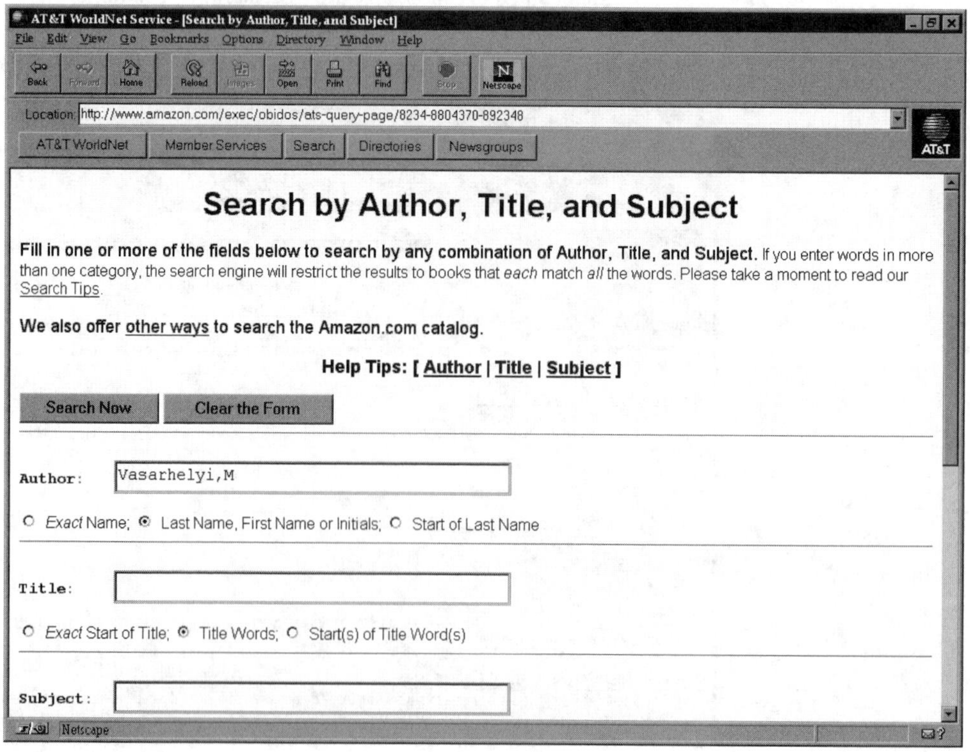

FIGURE 8-4 Search by Name in the Amazon Site (Amazon.com site as 2/97 reprinted with permission by Amazon.com)

The search results displayed in Figure 8-5 demonstrate how electronic catalogs can facilitate shopping experiences. The building of electronic catalog is becoming a major Internet industry. Later in this chapter we discuss the iCat company that specializes in the custom building of electronic catalogs. The work involved in the maintenance of the catalogs is substantial. In the future it will have to be performed in conjunction with mainframe-based legacy inventory systems.

After the first generation on Web utilization which focused on fixed topic page publication, a second generation of databased variable context publishing is emerging. These are typically based on a relational database and include a constantly updated content benefiting from updates due to changes in technical specifications, new product offerings and stock-outs.

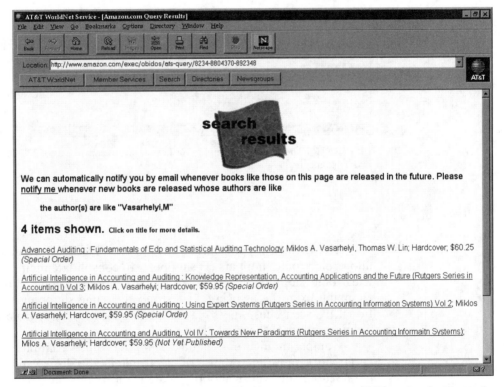

FIGURE 8-5 Search Results in the Amazon Site (Amazon.com site as of 2/97 reprinted with permission by Amazon.com)

The Purchase Stage

Once the search and decision processes are completed, the customer is transferred to a "secure area" where his or her browser will communicate with a secure server and transmit purchase information and credit card information. Shopping sites may give the shopper the option not to use a secure browser as some shoppers may not have updated secure browser software.

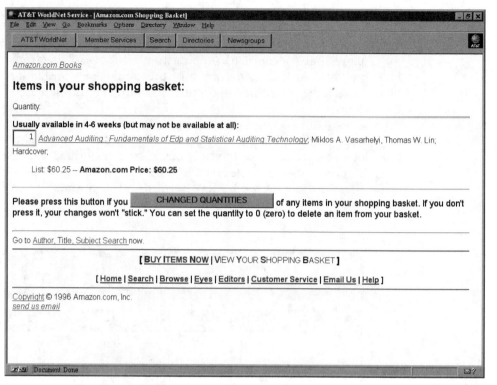

FIGURE 8-6 The Amazon Shopping Basket (Amazon.com site as of 2/97 reprinted with permission by Amazon.com)

The virtual shopping basket (as shown in Figures 8-6 and 8-7) is easy to use. It allows electronic shoppers (E-shoppers) to consolidate their purchases from a site. Electronic shopping malls that encompass more than one merchant may facilitate shopping from the associated sites into the same shopping cart. On the international EC scene, customers may be buying electronically from Paris, London, and Tokyo vendors at the same time.

Comparing Figures 8-6 and 8-7, we see some variations in forms of shopping carts, with a more mature use of electronic media displayed at the Harvard Business School site whose shopping cart is more elegant. The reader should notice three distinct areas on the page: the top area with hot buttons to other regions of the site, as well as an interesting "on-line consultant" feature; the middle of the page with the items in the shopping cart, each with a button "remove item;" and the bottom of the page with the icon that can transfer the shopper to the virtual checkout counter.

In addition to Web shopping at the HBS site, faculty members may participate in E-mailing lists of special interest. For example, such lists may inform instructors of new cases as they become available. The site can also discriminate among customers. For instance, it allows professors to purchase teaching materials that are not available to the general public. In fact, the site has an area accessible only to instructors. Faculty members must request access permission to this area in writing using college stationary (to confirm their qualifications).

Many sites ask customers if their credit card information can be kept on file. Currently, security experts advise against that, as the custody of credit card numbers is more risky than the electronic transaction itself. The transaction is then confirmed by E-mail to the customer. Some cyber-stores will also have an electronic care (E-care) module facilitating interaction between the customer and the store. This module usually allows the customer to check on the status of orders and perform other activities.

The shopping cart has a minimum order size. At the checkout counter, some items are repriced based on the category of the buyer. This dynamic nature of pricing and purchasing make cyber-shopping very different from regular shopping. While this is still not common in electronic commerce, there is no reason why a commerce site cannot link the electronic medium with some form of telephone connection (such as Internet phone) with the vendor. For example, during the visit the customer could press a button and talk to an expert on the item being considered (on-line consultant), have some form of low-band video interface with the store, or be connected to a chat line that specializes in technical discussion around the vendor's merchandise. In particular, this may be of great value for software, hardware, and technical item purchases as well as technical support.

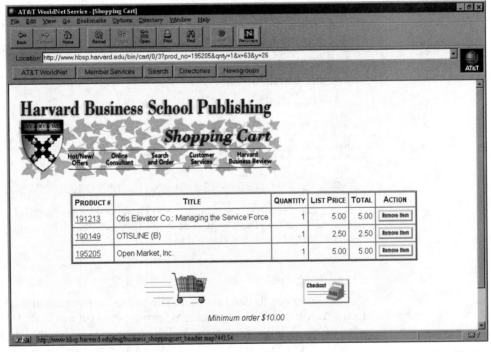

FIGURE 8-7 The HBSP Shopping Cart (Reprinted by permission of Harvard Business School Publishing. From the HBSP Worldwide Web site: http://www.hbsp.harvard.edu. Copyright © 1996 by the President and Fellows of Harvard College; all rights reserved.)

When the customer pays on-line using a credit card, the bookstore seeks authorization for the dollar amount of the purchase. Once the approval is obtained, the order is processed and confirmed. This transaction can take just a few seconds. How soon the customer will enjoy the book depends on the form of delivery.

Books are bitable, but at the current stage of technology a book transferred electronically is not as aesthetically pleasing and convenient as a book in traditional print form.

Figure 8-8 shows the HBS's checkout counter that gathers credit card data[3] and the method of shipment. The bottom of the screen, not shown in the figure, has a submit button. If the customer makes a mistake, say, by not filling in shipping instructions, he receives an error message asking to use the **BACK** key in the browser to fix the mistake in the form and resubmit it to the vendor.

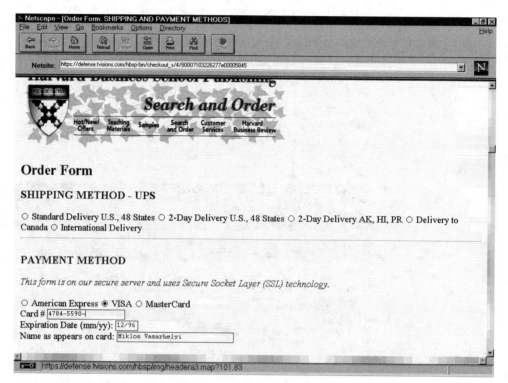

FIGURE 8-8 The HBSP Checkout Counter (Reprinted by permission of Harvard Business School Publishing. From the HBSP Worldwide Web site: http://www.hbsp.harvard.edu. Copyright © 1996 by the President and Fellows of Harvard College; all rights reserved.)

The Delivery Stage

Bitable goods can complete the full cycle over the net. Purchases of information and software are becoming commonplace on the Web. File transfer protocol is often used to deliver software and documents from a protected area. Alternatively, customers can consume information on-line while they are charged on a per connection time basis. The HBS site, as mentioned earlier, has a faculty-only area for the distribution of sample cases. The area is password protected and contains selected cases in the Adobe portable document format (PDF). The site directs faculty to download the Adobe Acrobat reader and gives guidance on its usage. The PDF files have a backdrop watermark stating "DO NOT COPY." While this is a

---

[3]The reader should compare the status lines of the Harvard Business School (HBS) screens. The broken key image of the shopping cart screen becomes a nonbroken key in the HBS checkout counter showing secure protocol interchange.

practical process and gives HBS some copyright protection, it does not take full advantage of the Web technology. As a result, users often have to download large files and read them on their PC just to find whether the case is appropriate.

To deliver nonbitable goods, electronic malls often have agreements with package carriers (e.g., Federal Express) for delivering items directly from wholesalers and manufacturers. After customers choose items from the mall's electronic catalog, often consolidating databases of many suppliers, whenever suppliers cannot or will not deliver the product, carriers are dispatched and the tracking information is copied to the mall's system.

Post Purchase and Communications (E-Care)

A crucial step in the electronic shopping process is E-care. While telephone support and visits to service counters have been traditionally the methods of customer service for nonvirtual businesses, E-care is a core service of e-commerce. The public is increasingly accepting cyber-commerce, but this process is full of hesitations, concerns, and technical pitfalls. All of the above stages of EC require some degree of E-care. The *search stage* often requires some clarifying explanations. The *purchase stage* often requires the verbal transmission of payment information. The *delivery stage* requires tracking and answering customer requests. Finally, the *post purchase stage* requires product support, responses to billing questions, and information about complementary products.

An emerging line of thinking in this area focuses on passing much of the burden of communications support to automated E-care. Customers will call in and talk to automated voice response systems (VRS), send E-mail, fill out forms on the Web, send faxes, receive FAQs through voice systems, read FAQs on the Web, and so forth. Table 8-2 displays some forms of customer inquiry and response that combine different technologies with traditional telephone service.

> It pays off to create a robust E-care mechanism even for traditional sales channels.

Many computer firms have realized that the same information support systems that their system engineers use to field customer questions may be opened to customers. This opening of information may create some legal problems and requires substantial adaptation as customers will not have the same type of training and experience as system engineers. On the other hand, it often facilitates significantly interaction with customers and decreases customer service costs. While the emphasis of this book is on the Internet, it should be noted that companies are finding that even for the traditional sales channels, it pays off to create a robust E-care mechanism. As an increasing number of customers have E-mail and Web access, automation of traditional response channels can save labor and at the same time provide a level of service not previously deliverable. Consider the following examples:

- airlines now offer automated VRS for flight departure and arrival information
- banks offer electronic VRS for balance, deposit, and check information
- package carriers offer access to their databases for package tracking
- brokers offer quote information on the web or VRS
- long-distance carriers offer resolution of some billing disputes by automated services

TABLE 8-2 Technologies for E-Care

Customer Communication	Tools	Response
Telephone	VRS	Voice
		Specialized voice routing
E-mail	Boilerplate answers	E-mail
Web	FAQs	E-mail
	Web diagnostic systems	Surf monitoring
Fax	Fax boilerplate answers	Fax
		Voice

The Amazon and HBS sites have E-mail response systems and send E-mail to confirm orders. However, the maturity of E-mail interface with vendors is variable, and if a customer communicates with the vendor by E-mail, responses may or may not be received. One of the authors sent an E-mail to an access provider, on-line malls, a discount broker, and two bookstores. Two of the communications were never even acknowledged, the brokerage house responded within twenty-four hours, the access provider responded in a week with an apology for the delay and promising to respond to the question rapidly (but never responded), and the two bookstores responded rapidly and precisely.

Offering technical support on the Internet has become a given for most hardware and software vendors. But what is actually offered through the site can range from a mere listing of E-mail addresses, to a keyword-searchable knowledge base, to the ability to initiate a formal support request on the Internet.

Dun & Bradstreet Software Inc. has gone a step further to the cutting edge of WWW-based support. Its SmartStream Assistant, based on agent technology that notifies the help desk when there is a problem, runs in the background when a user has any of D&B's SmartStream suite of client/server applications open.

When a problem occurs, SmartStream Assistant captures the user's configuration information and forwards it to the user's system administrator—who may be able to take care of the problem immediately—as well as to the D&B help desk. This approach eliminates the bounce-back effect of help desk people needing to call back and request configuration information in order to recreate the problem. With SmartStream Assistant, the help desk person has all the critical information to solve the problem—all without human intervention. Between 65 and 70 percent of D&B's support calls are now being taken electronically, either over the Internet or through a dial-up connection. Problem log information can be patched from SmartStream Assistant into a Microsoft Corp. Access database. From Access, event reports to track exactly what happened and when it happened can be generated.

EXPERIENCES IN DIRECT SELLING OVER THE INTERNET

Website
Bitable attributes

As discussed earlier, it is useful to classify goods as bitable (soft goods) and nonbitable. Bitable goods are the first main target of the Internet. Their customers are already used to much of the electronic medium and accept the advantages and limitations of the medium as part of life. While bitable goods get most of the press, the issue is also the bitability of attributes of a particular good. For example, perfume is not an easy item to sell over the Internet to a customer who has never tried it before. Its attribute "smell" is not bitable at all and cannot be represented by another attribute. On the other hand, once a perfume is bought and liked, it becomes a very good item to purchase over the Internet. Marketing research shows a high degree of consistency over time on perfume purchases (repeat buys), consistent quality, a very price-sensitive item with large margins, and highly transportable.

On the other hand, many nonbitable products may be candidates for first sales over the Internet if they can be well represented by pictures, technical descriptions, and detailed explanations. For example, computers are excellent items for an Internet purchase as extensive drawing, technical descriptions, and pictures can be made available on-line.

The following sections focus on the Web presence in selected industries including car sales, air travel, banks, and securities trading.

Car Shopping on the Internet

Website
Car shopping

Cars are neither a commodity nor a bitable good. Lately, however, car shopping through the Internet has been flourishing. It seems that Internet shoppers prefer to avoid the haggling and hassles often associated with purchasing a car from a dealer. Clearly, the whole purchasing cycle cannot be completed over the Internet. So far, nobody has succeeded in devising ways to test drive or physically deliver cars over the Internet. As a result, Internet shopping for cars is usually limited to the first few steps of the purchasing cycle.

Shoppers can find on the Internet abundant information about car models, including prices, various standard features, and available options. Most car manufacturers maintain Web sites with a lot of information about their models. Manufacturers' information, however, may be biased. The only available price quote is the manufacturer's suggested retail price (MSRP). Shoppers, of course, are much more interested in dealers' invoice prices. Consequently, many customers start their car shopping on the Internet by browsing Web sites of independent car information providers.

A number of well-established car information providers have invested significant efforts in creating well-designed Web sites. A good example is the Web site of Kelley Blue Book found at

`http://www.kbb.com`

This site provides comprehensive information about the standard features and pricing including the dealer's invoice price and MSRP for base models and all available options. This information is provided for every car model! Figure 8-9 shows the page of Kelly Blue Books with all of the 1997 models of Toyota Camry. There are a number of alternative sites on the Internet providing similar car information, for example, Edmund's Automobile Buyer's Guides (`http://www.edmunds.com`) and Autosite by Automotive Information Center (`http://www.autosite.com/`). The information provided by the sites varies in coverage and format. Autosite provides only limited information free of charge, but it is provided in a convenient matrix form (see Figure 8-10). All these information providers refer the customer to the same Web site that handles sales called Auto-By-Tel (see Figure 8-11). This site can be found at the following URL:

`http://www.autobytel.com/`

This site accepts purchase requests on-line. The prospective buyer has to fill out a form describing in sufficient detail the new car she or he plans to buy. It is necessary to provide a telephone number and an E-mail address. Auto-By-Tel forwards this information to a participating dealer in the locality of the buyer. The dealer then contacts the customer with a "low" price offer that reduces the hassle and haggling normally associated with a regular purchase of a car. The site encourages the customers to become informed buyers. It points them to auto information providers described above, suggesting that they find out the dealer invoice prices for the base model and all the options, current discounts, rebates, and various other dealer and buyer incentives. The dealers participating in this program are aware of the fact that they are dealing with educated buyers.

Subsequent phases of the car-buying process take place off-line. The buyer test drives the car and, if the deal is successfully closed, the car is delivered to the customer. The Internet-based phase of the process is, however, very useful. Most of the inconveniences associated with car buying are eliminated at this stage. A motivated customer may be able to collect a comparable amount of information about the car of her or his choice off-line. However, it is much more difficult for a sophisticated buyer to find off-line a dealer who will forgo conventional irritating selling tactics. Participation in this Internet-based car shopping process provides the dealers with an access to an additional market segment—the on-line car shoppers. The marketing expenses associated with this are relatively low. In addition, the off-line phase of the process tends to be much shorter, simpler, and less frustrating than the conventional one.

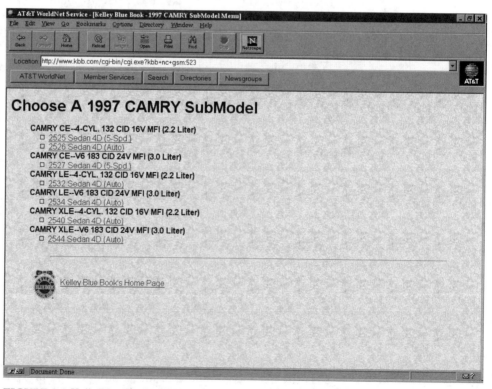

FIGURE 8-9 Kelly Blue Book's 1997 Models of Toyota Camry (Reprinted with permission by Kelley Blue Book)

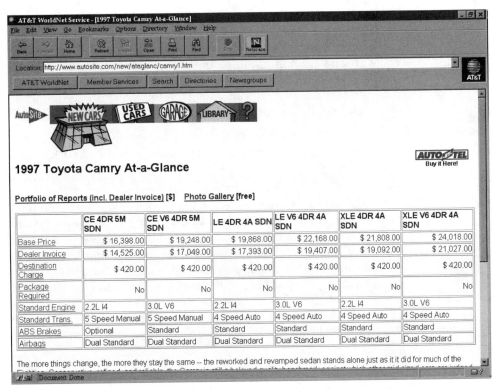

FIGURE 8-10 1997 Toyota Camry Listings (Reprinted with permission by the Automotive Information Center, a Thomson Corporation Company)

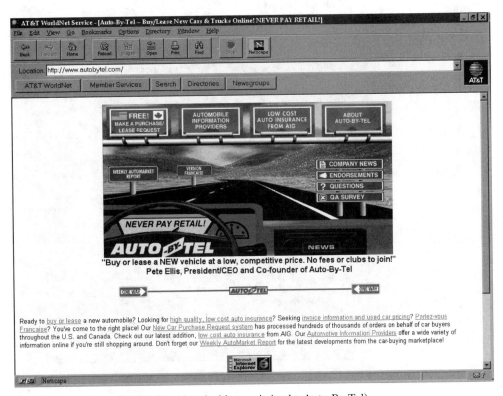

FIGURE 8-11 Auto-By-Tel (Reprinted with permission by Auto-By-Tel)

Among the successful examples of Internet-based businesses, car shopping is atypical in the sense that a larger part of the process takes place off-line. Airline ticket reservation over the Internet provides an example where all parts of the process are accomplished on-line, except that at this moment the printing and delivery of tickets is still done by the travel agent.

Airline Reservations

Website
Airline reservation

There are a number of Internet sites in this business. In the authors' opinion, one of the most convenient is the Internet Travel Network (ITN) located at

`http://www.itn.net`

This service is free, but it requires an on-line shopper to register. Registered shoppers have a direct on-line access to the reservation system that allows them to specify intricate travel plans including complicated itineraries, preferred airlines, and class of service. When a travel plan is submitted, the ITN searches the on-line air ticket reservation system and returns a number of choices (specified by the shopper) for each leg of the trip. The user can also obtain information about each type of aircraft and the airports.

A simple example of a round trip from Newark, New Jersey, to Chicago, Illinois, is shown in Figure 8-12. When this request was submitted, the INT returned a

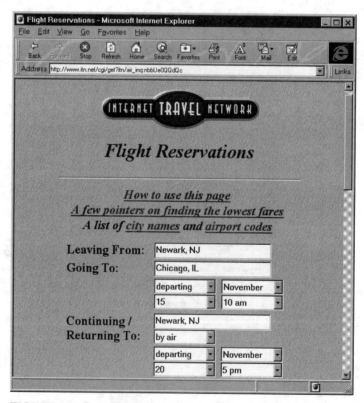

FIGURE 8-12 Travel Itinerary (Reprinted with permission by Internet Travel Network)

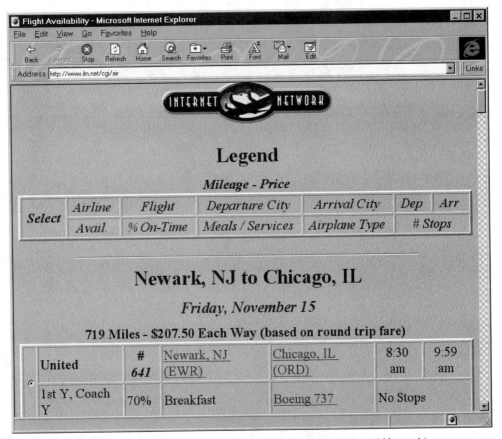

FIGURE 8-13 Flight Choices (Reprinted with permission by Internet Travel Network)

long list of flights sorted by price in ascending order. The beginning of this list is shown in Figure 8-13. The user should choose all the legs with the same airline to receive discounted round-trip fares. The selections are then priced together, and the final result is presented to the shopper (see Figure 8-14). This page allows the shopper to book the reservation and to choose a participating travel agency who will accept payment and issue the tickets.

Alternatively, the shopper can complete the purchase phase on-line through the Small World Travel agency that works together with the ITN. This requires filling in the credit card information as shown in Figure 8-15. Upon credit approval, the agency issues the tickets and mails them to the shopper using the address shown on the form.

In this example, the printing of tickets is done by the travel agency, and the delivery of tickets uses regular mail. It is conceivable that in the foreseeable future even these steps can be accomplished on-line with the delivery over the Internet of digitally signed tickets and the tickets printed by the shopper on a local printer.

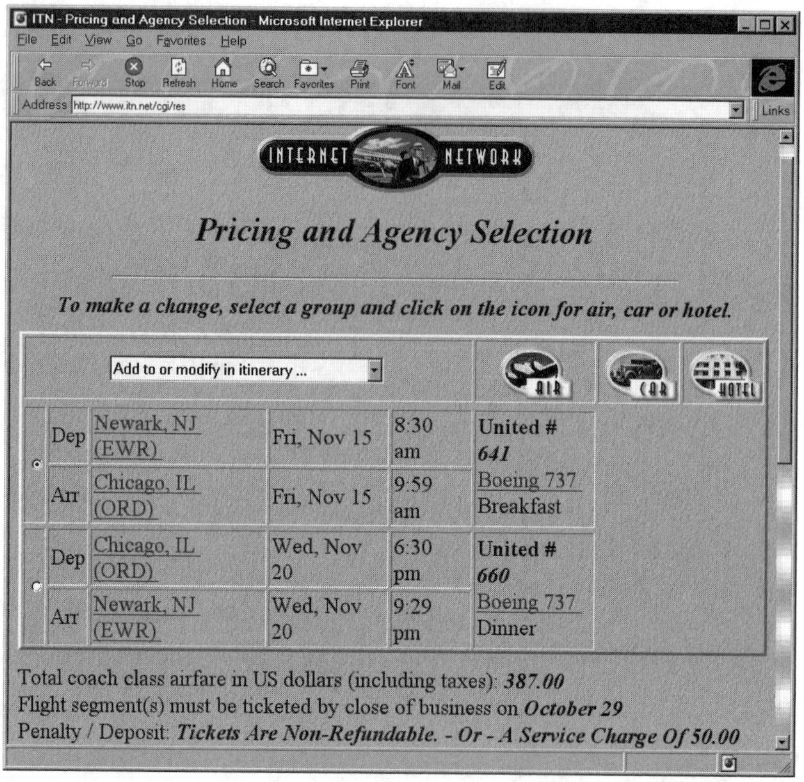

FIGURE 8-14 Final Selection (Reprinted with permission by Internet Travel Network)

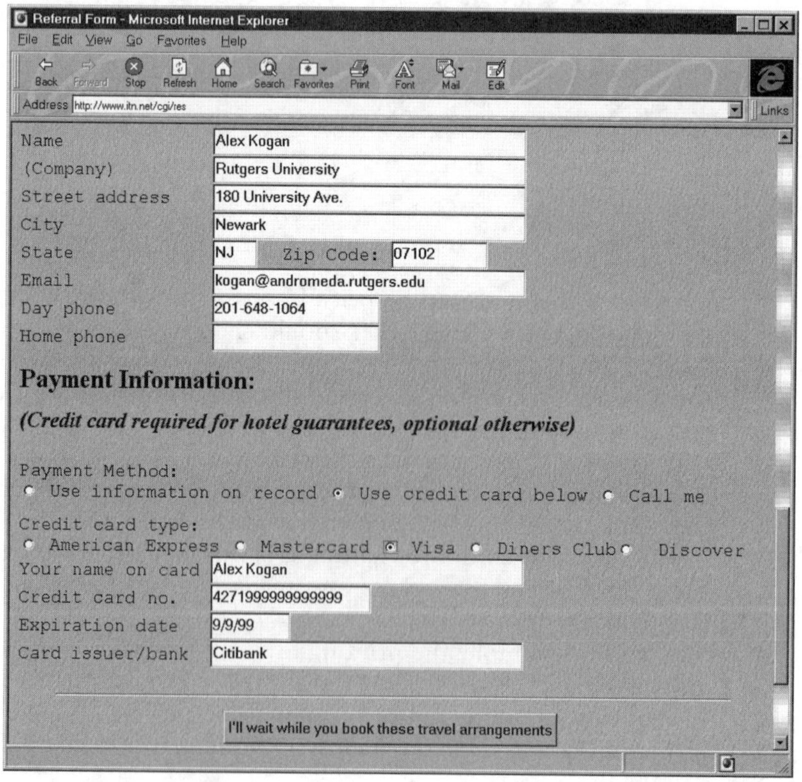

FIGURE 8-15 On-line Payment (Reprinted with permission by Internet Travel Network)

Banks[4]

Website
Electronic banks

A very significant part of business activities of banks and other financial institutions consists of information processing. Most banks' products are fully bitable except for the delivery of cash. The current intensive development of various concepts of electronic money will very soon allow banks to deliver over the Internet every element of their product mix. Virtual banks are sprouting all over the spectrum of services, with some entities having no storefronts to meet clients but doing so by going to the client's home physically or electronically. Retail banking has been revolutionized first by automatic teller machines and is being revolutionized now by home banking (also called PC banking).

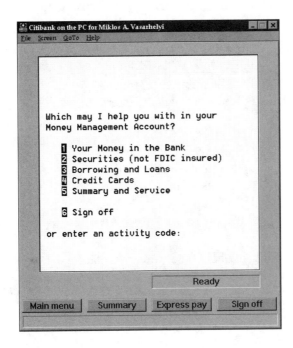

FIGURE 8-16 Citibank Access through Its Proprietary Network

Most major U.S. banks now provide their customers with the dial-up PC-based access to their accounts. For example, Citibank started its "Direct Access" service about ten years ago with a proprietary network and a dial-up access to the central computers of Citibank. In 1995, Citibank joined a network of banks who opted to provide consumers with on-line access through Prodigy (Figure 8-16)—the third largest commercial on-line service at that time. Citibank dropped its charges for PC banking and increased substantively its charges for telephone transactions and transaction services. Citibank apparently figures that eventually PC-based services will be much cheaper to provide.

On-line access to banking services over the Internet is being gradually embraced by various U.S. banks ranging from relatively small pioneers of the field like Security First Network Bank (http://www.sfnb.com) to the giants of the U.S. banking industry like Wells Fargo (http://www.wellsfargo.com, see Figure 8-17).

---

[4]A review of three bank offerings can be found in the October 1996 issue of *PC Computing*, pages 73–77 and can also be found at their web site http://www.pccomputing.com

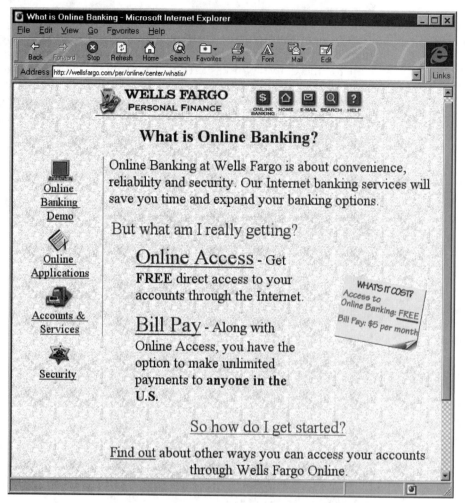

FIGURE 8-17 Wells Fargo On-line (Reprinted with Permission by Wells Fargo Bank)

Customers can open an account with Wells Fargo on-line over the Internet. Internet-based access is free. The bill-paying service over the Internet is also available for a low monthly fee ($5 in the fall of 1996). This service allows payments to anyone in the United States. It provides means for easily setting up recurring payments (mortgage, car loan, etc.). Payments can be scheduled in advance, and Wells Fargo will process the payment on the day it is scheduled. Payments are delivered either electronically (for those payees who accept electronic fund transfers) or by regular U.S. mail.

On-line access to Wells Fargo is based on secure Web servers. Customers sign on by entering their social security number and individual password. After signing on, customers have full access to their Wells Fargo accounts. The Demo account summary is shown in Figure 8-18. A single click takes a customer to the account history detailing all the transactions within the last forty-five days. The customer can see which checks have cleared the bank, what payments were made, and so forth (see Figure 8-19). Account history is available for credit accounts as well.

FIGURE 8-18 Wells Fargo Demo Account Summary (Reprinted with permission by Wells Fargo Bank)

On-line access provides very simple means for transferring money from one account to another. It is even more significant that customers can pay their bills on-line if their Web browsers are secure enough. Wells Fargo claims to be the first bank to require domestic grade security[5] for on-line bill payments. Customers can easily enter one-time payments or schedule recurring payments. Figure 8-20 shows that a customer can check and, if needed, change any of the pending payments.

According to Wells Fargo, the following service requests can be made online:

- Order more checks for your checking account
- Request copies of cleared checks
- Request copies of past statements for your account
- Request an address change on your accounts
- Set up an automatic savings plan
- Request direct deposit of your paycheck
- Order travelers checks
- Order cashier's checks/official checks
- Order foreign currency
- Inquire about a bill payment
- Ask questions about your account

[5]Domestic grade security uses 128-bit encryption keys, while international grade security is limited to 40-bit keys (see chapter 7).

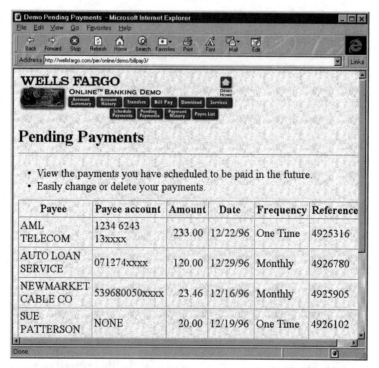

Balance Detail

CHECKING 0065-206xxx	Amount
Beginning balance as of 06/24/96	$785.59
Available balance	$785.59

Account History

Date	Description	Amount	
06/21/96	AML TELECOM	$61.11	
06/20/96	CHECK # 173	$86.60	
06/16/96	NEWMARKET CABLE CO	$23.46	
06/12/96	CHECK # 171	$25.00	
06/11/96	EXP ATM DEP/TRSF	$227.25	+
06/11/96	POINT OF SALE	$85.03	
06/08/96	STAMP PURCHASE	$6.40	
06/03/96	TRF-OTHR WF ACCT	$120.00	
06/03/96	ATM WITHDRAWAL	$40.00	
06/01/96	ON-LINE TRSFR	$200.00	+
05/28/96	AUTO LOAN SERVICE	$120.00	

FIGURE 8-19 Wells Fargo Account History (Reprinted with permission by Wells Fargo Bank)

WELLS FARGO
ONLINE™ BANKING DEMO

Account Summary | Account History | Transfers | Bill Pay | Download | Services
Schedule Payments | Pending Payments | Payment History | Payee List

Pending Payments

- View the payments you have scheduled to be paid in the future.
- Easily change or delete your payments.

Payee	Payee account	Amount	Date	Frequency	Reference
AML TELECOM	1234 6243 13xxxx	233.00	12/22/96	One Time	4925316
AUTO LOAN SERVICE	071274xxxx	120.00	12/29/96	Monthly	4926780
NEWMARKET CABLE CO	539680050xxxx	23.46	12/16/96	Monthly	4925905
SUE PATTERSON	NONE	20.00	12/19/96	One Time	4926102

FIGURE 8-20 Wells Fargo Pending Payments (Reprinted with permission by Wells Fargo Bank)

Security of financial transactions over the Internet is a major concern for all bank customers. Therefore, serious banking sites on the Internet tend to provide sufficiently detailed information to their customers about security arrangements. The Wells Fargo Web page devoted to security is shown in Figure 8-21.

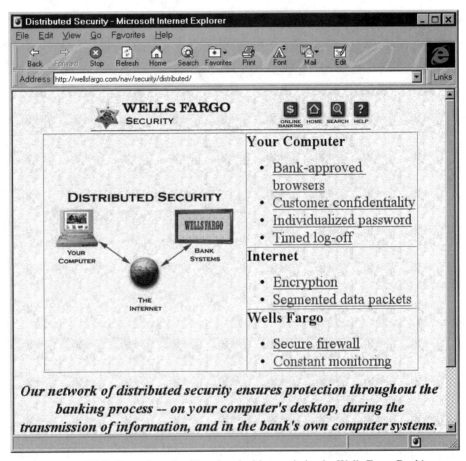

FIGURE 8-21 Wells Fargo Security (Reprinted with permission by Wells Fargo Bank)

Securities Trading

Website
Securities trading

Securities trading has become an important element of the EC landscape. Many brokers, including E-Schwab and National Discount Brokers, are arduously placing themselves in this line of business aiming at competing with traditional brokers and capitalizing on being discount brokers. They bank on their ability to interact automatically with the customers and the potential availability of on-line stock prices and portfolio updating. In order to use National Discount Brokers, users sign on to PAWWS (http://www.pawws.com) and choose NDB as their brokers.

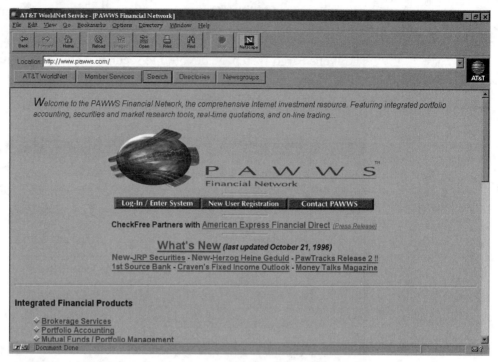

FIGURE 8-22 PAWWS Financial Network (Reprinted with permission by Check Free)

PAWWS (Figures 8-22 and 8-23) is a sort of electronic infrastructure for different E-brokers and the home for many financial services. Its homepage presents a security feature that requires registration by the user and a password to be designated by the user. Its main menu presents the features of reporting (portfolio status), transactions (connection to brokerage services), stock information (stock prices for a fee), market information, and utilities. An attractive news archive titillates the visitor with financial information tidbits. More-detailed financial information comes with a cost.

The user registers (opens an account) with one broker or several brokers and "links" these accounts to PAWWS (see Figure 8-24). Therefore, there will be at least two levels of password security (the broker's and the PAWWS's passwords). The setup is somewhat confusing even to relatively sophisticated users. Many of the financial and brokerage systems are progressively using electronic payment systems to provide and transfer resources between different institutions and customers.

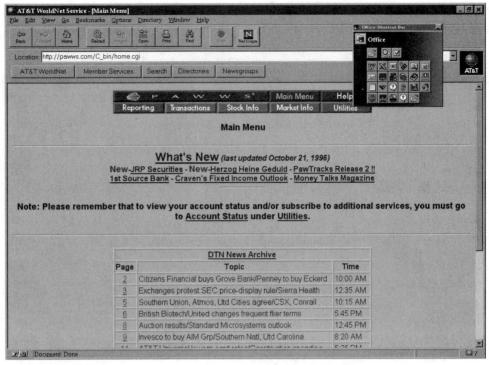

FIGURE 8-23 PAWWS Main Menu (Reprinted with permission by Check Free)

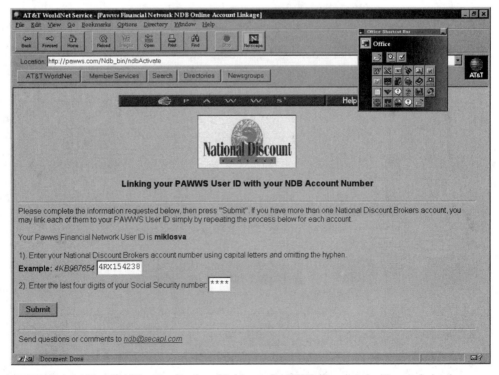

FIGURE 8-24 National Discount Brokers Linking to PAWWS (Reprinted with permission by Check Free)

ELECTRONIC PAYMENTS

Website
Electronic payments

Many of the electronic store fronts described above allow customers to pay for their purchases on-line using secure Web servers. In most cases such on-line payments are made by credit cards, with the final stage of credit card payment processing done by conventional means.

On-line Credit Card Payments

Since the credit card information is transferred using secure Web browsers and servers, the risk of being intercepted while in transit over the Internet is virtually eliminated (as described in chapter 7). In spite of the fact that in these cases transmitting credit card information over the Internet is not riskier than doing so by phone, both Visa and Mastercard advised their customers against sending their credit card information over the Internet.

In the scenario described in the previous paragraph, the main risk exposure is at the merchant's site, where employees who have access to this information are in a position to misuse it. Similar risks exist with all types of credit card payments (e.g., in person, over the telephone, by regular mail). The SET standard, jointly developed by Visa and Mastercard and described in chapter 7, provides a way of drastically reducing, if not eliminating altogether, such risks.

The SET specification is based heavily on the use of public key cryptography, digital signatures, and digital certificates. To participate in SET-based payments, each cardholder has to obtain a cardholder certificate from a card-issuing financial institution (called an **Issuer**). This cardholder certificate is a digital analog of a credit card with one important difference—it does not contain the account number and the expiration date. The cardholder certificate is digitally signed by the Issuer. This digital signature serves as a proof of the legitimacy of the credit card.

A vendor participating in SET has to obtain a merchant certificate from his or her financial institution (called an **Acquirer**). The merchant certificate is digitally signed by the Acquirer and proves that the merchant accepts the credit card in question.

Two very crucial parts of the credit card information—the account number and the expiration date—are not disclosed to the merchant, only to the Acquirer or to a designated third party. This eliminates any potential misuse of credit card information at the merchant's site, making SET-based transactions safer than regular credit card transactions. All other parties in SET transactions (Issuers, Acquirers, etc.) also need digital certificates since they need to digitally sign electronic documents. Digital signatures not only allow the authentication of documents but also insure their integrity, that is, that the documents have not been tampered with.

How do customers know that they are purchasing from a valid merchant? Before they purchase, the merchant needs to provide them their certificate. The merchant can do this in a variety of ways, such as by sending a copy to the cardholder by electronic mail or by publishing a copy on the Internet that anyone can easily inspect.

Seeing that the merchant has a valid digital certificate, the customer can now buy a book. As an example, the reader should go back and look over the book-purchasing process illustrated by the Amazon purchase.

Credit card transactions and the SET standard are very important for electronic commerce to succeed. There are, however, a number of distinctive features of credit card payments that may affect their suitability in certain types of electronic transactions. For example, credit card payments carry information about the payer. This may carry an advantage by providing a proof of payment and consumer protection. On the other hand, a payer might prefer to remain anonymous. Also, the transaction costs associated with credit card payments are relatively high (at the very least, in dozens of cents per transaction). This is less of a drawback if transactions involve dozens of dollars, but such costs become prohibitively expensive when a transaction involves only a couple of cents.

Electronic Cash and Checks

New Internet-based electronic payment systems are currently being developed. Ecash by DigiCash. NetCash and NetCheque© by USC-ISI, CyberCoin by Cyber-Cash, NetBill by CMU, and NetChex by NetI are among the best known. Although none of these fancy new schemes is anywhere close to the penetration of credit card payments, they may reach a much wider acceptance in the near future. While secure credit card payments are supported by SET, these and other Internet electronic payment systems aim at developing digital analogs of cash, personal checks, and traveler's checks.

The various concepts of electronic money mentioned above, as well as imaginable future schemes of electronic payments, can be categorized along several important dimensions. The first dimension is that of anonymity. Electronic payments can be either *identified* or *anonymous*. For example, as was mentioned above, all the credit card payments are identified. Electronic analogs of personal or traveler's checks are identified as well. Among the systems listed above, the identified types of electronic money are NetCheque©, NetBill, and NetChex (`http://www.netchex.com/`). CyberCoin may be classified as semi-identified, since the financial institution transferring electronic coins to a customer does know the identity of that customer, while a merchant receiving a CyberCoin payment does not know who the payer is. The homepage of CyberCoin is located at

`http://www.cybercash.com/cybercash/shoppers/coingenpage.html`

The concept of an electronic check is a relatively straightforward digital implementation of conventional checks on the basis of public key cryptography. **Electronic check** is a debit-payment instrument that includes the name of the payer, the name of the payee, the name of the payer's financial institution, the payer's account number, and the amount of the check. When an electronic check is submitted for payment, it is digitally signed by the payer. The payee also digitally signs an electronic check before depositing it.

A typical example of electronic checks is the NetCheque© system (see Figure 8-25) developed at the Information Sciences Institute of the University of Southern California. Its homepage is located at

`http://nii-server.isi.edu/info/NetCheque/`

The NetCheque© system allows the use of multiple accounting servers. It means that customers and merchants can use electronic checks for payment even when they have accounts with different financial institutions.

The NetBill electronic commerce project is developed at the Information Networking Institute of Carnegie Mellon University. The homepage of the project can be found at

`http://www.ini.cmu.edu/netbill/`

At the time of this writing (fall 1996), the project was in its Alpha trial, on the Carnegie Mellon campus. In this system, all the customers and merchants have to communicate with the central NetBill server.

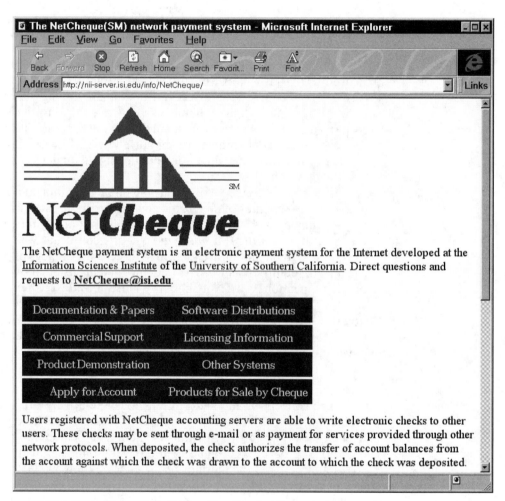

FIGURE 8-25 NetCheque© Homepage (Reprinted with permission by the University of Southern California)

The anonymous type of electronic money is electronic cash represented by DigiCash and NetCash. Ecash by DigiCash is strongly anonymous in the sense that even in the case when the issuing financial institution, the merchant, and all the other third parties taking part in transaction processing collude, there is no way for them to figure out the identity of the payer. In the case of NetCash the protection of anonymity is somewhat weaker. If the parties mentioned above collude, they can figure out the identity of the payer, although that would be a violation of the rules.

One of the oldest and the best-developed electronic cash systems is Ecash (see Figure 8-26) by Digicash whose homepage can be found at

http://www.digicash.com

Electronic currency comes in the form of electronic bank notes that can be disbursed (again, electronically) to a customer. These electronic bank notes are identified by a serial number and a denomination and are digitally signed by the issuing bank. Assuming that the bank's digital signature is recognized by the general public, electronic bank notes should be acceptable as a form of payment. To engage in a transaction using electronic bank notes, both the customer and the merchant should establish E-cash accounts with the issuing bank.

The electronic bank note scheme described above may be vulnerable to abuse if special counter measures are not taken. The most widely discussed problem of such a system is the problem of double spending. Since copying electronic information (i.e., files) does not present a serious challenge, any customer or merchant can create copies of electronic bank notes with relative ease and present the same notes for more than one payment. To prevent this from happening the issuing bank maintains an on-line database of spent bank notes, and it checks every note submitted for payment against the notes in the database before accepting it. This is the reason why even in the case when E-cash is exchanged, and the payee does not intend to deposit electronic notes immediately in the bank, the payee still has to submit all the electronic notes to the bank to check that those notes have not been spent.

Since the anonymity of electronic cash is its most fundamental property, an important feature of every E-cash scheme is how this anonymity is achieved. In all E-cash schemes the payee has absolutely no way of establishing the identity of the payer (if the payer does not disclose it voluntarily). The issuing financial institution may or may not be in a position to keep track of the identity of the recipient of electronic bank notes. If the serial number of the bank note is chosen by the issuer (the case of NetCash), it is possible for the issuer to record the identity of the recipient, although this is generally prohibited and considered to be unacceptable policy in all E-cash schemes. In this case the consumer confidence in anonymity relies on the trust in the issuing institution.

The protection of consumer anonymity is much stronger in the case of E-cash by DigiCash. The founder of DigiCash, Dr. David Chaum, developed a special cryptographic technique called **blind signatures** that allows issuers to digitally sign bank notes without knowing their serial numbers. In this approach the serial number of the bank note is randomly chosen by the consumer's software. The bank note is then encrypted in a special way and sent to the issuer who applies a blind digital signature to the encrypted bank note and returns it to the consumer. The consumer can now decrypt the original encryption without destroying the issuer's signature. This bank note will be accepted by the issuer since the issuer's signature can be verified. The use of blind signatures makes it technologically impossible for the issuer to keep track of the identity of bank note recipients.

To prevent *double spending,* the issuer maintains an on-line database of all the bank notes that have been spent and checks that the bank note submitted for payment is not in this database. Since the issuer never knows the serial numbers of bank notes in circulation, it is required to keep in the on-line database all those bank notes that have been spent, even those spent a very long time ago. The size of this on-line database will keep growing over time, making it increasingly longer and, possibly, more expensive to clear bank notes submitted for payment.

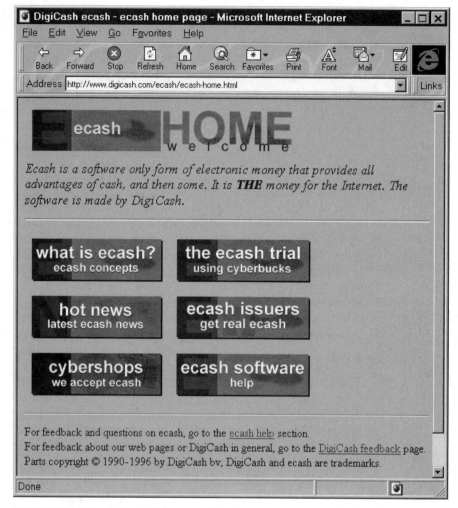

FIGURE 8-26 Ecash: Ecash Homepage (Reprinted with permission by CyberCash, Inc.)

After a successful trial by DigiCash that involved a fictitious currency called the Cyberbuck, E-cash is currently being used by several banks around the world. The first U.S. bank that started issuing E-cash denominated in U.S. dollars is Mark Twain Bank of St. Louis, Missouri (see Figure 8-27), found at

http://www.marktwain.com/

Mark Twain Bank started issuing E-cash in the fall of 1995. To transact in E-cash, customers have to open WorldCurrency Access accounts that are deposits of Mark Twain Bank. The bank succeeded in signing up dozens of merchants who now accept E-cash. There are a number of different fees that the bank charges for E-cash transactions. A transaction fee is between 2 and 3 percent of the transaction amount for merchants and 4 and 5 percent for customers when E-cash is converted to regular currency. The bank waives some of these and other fees for certain customers and merchants.

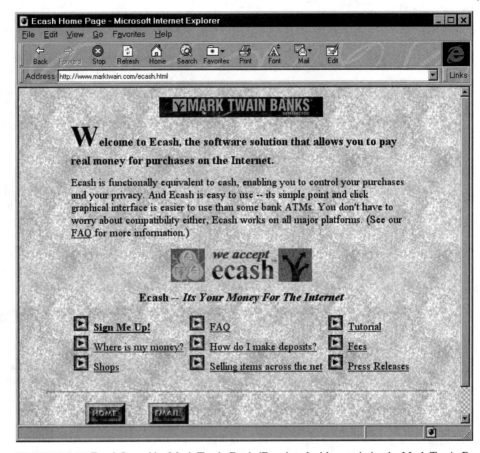

FIGURE 8-27 Ecash Issued by Mark Twain Bank (Reprinted with permission by Mark Twain Banks)

Smart Cards

Website
Electronic money

Electronic money is not limited to the Internet-based payment systems. A very important dimension of electronic payment schemes is whether the transaction can take place *off-line* or whether all the payment-processing parties have to be *on-line* (connected to the Internet or a private network). All the payment schemes mentioned above are on-line payment schemes. Although the ambition of Internet service providers is ubiquitous access all over the world, the reality is that for many years to come there will be a significant number of transactions for which the on-line requirement is too rigid. It may not be cost-efficient or even possible to satisfy. Additionally, since every transaction using on-line types of electronic money requires access to certain databases, there is a cost associated with such access. It is therefore difficult to invent a system that does not have per transaction fees. This may be a serious detriment to the wide acceptance of electronic cash.

A solution to off-line electronic payment transactions is provided by various kinds of the so-called **smart cards.** A **smart card** is a hardware device, typically a plastic card of regular credit card size that contains a chip—a microprocessor and memory elements that implement its functions. In addition to the card itself, a smart card payment system also includes a card-accepting terminal and a software system designed to handle smart card transactions.

One of the oldest and best-known E-cash smart cards is Mondex by NatWest and Midland banks in the United Kingdom (see Figure 8-28). The home site of the card is located at

http://www.mondex.com

One of the unique features of the Mondex card is that it is designed to be a multi-currency card and can operate in any currency. The value is stored on the card, and transactions involve a transfer of value from one card to another. The security of the Mondex card is based on the standard public key encryption technology described in chapter 7.

Each card has a unique sixteen-digit identity number stored on the chip. Mondex cards are protected by using personal identification numbers, and the owner can lock the card to prevent it from being used in the case of loss. If the card is not locked and lost, the value is lost as well, as it is the case with regular paper currency. If the card is locked, there is no incentive to steal it since it cannot be used by anyone except the owner. Therefore, even if a locked card is lost, it is more likely to be returned to the bank, identified, and the value returned to the customer.

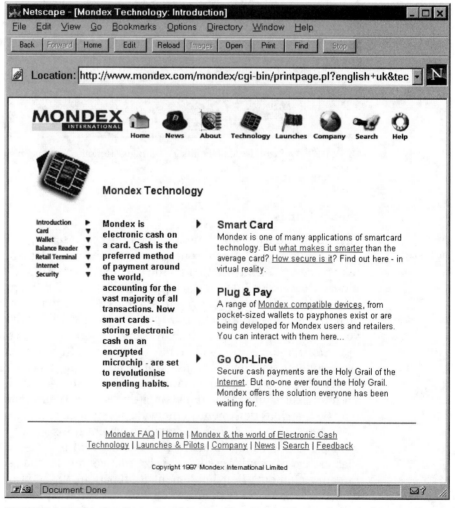

FIGURE 8-28 Mondex: Facts about Mondex (Reprinted with permission by Mondex International)

In addition to the card, a number of devices facilitate its use by consumers. The two most important ones are the balance reader and the electronic wallet. The balance reader is really just what the name suggests—a small electronic device to read the balance on the card. The balance can also be read using a more sophisticated device—the wallet. The main use of the wallet, however, is to keep a significant sum of electronic money and to transfer some of that money to the card as needed. This allows one to keep the wallet in a relatively safe place (home, office, hotel room, etc.) and to carry only the card with a very limited sum of money. The wallet can also be used to transfer money from one card to another.

The security of Mondex transactions is ensured by the card's chip. Each Mondex card involved in a transaction generates a unique digital signature that is recognized by the other card in the transaction. No centralized processing system is therefore needed for Mondex transactions. As a result, the value is directly transferred from one party to another, and there is no per transaction fee.

A sum of money can be transferred from a bank account to a Mondex card using specially equipped ATMs or the telephone. This transfer can also be accomplished over the Internet if a special Mondex card reader is attached to a PC. In this case Mondex cards can be used for paying over the Internet (if the payee also has a Mondex card and a reader attached to the computer).

NatWest started the development of Mondex in the early nineties. The first large-scale field test was undertaken in 1994 in one of NatWest's major computer centers in London. About six thousand NatWest employees were issued Mondex cards to be used in the centers' restaurants, coffee bars, shops, and ATMs. The trial was successfully completed, with over one million card-based purchases made by the end of 1994. The experimental launch of Mondex took place in July 1995 in the town of Swindon with population of almost 200,000 people, located about seventy miles from London. This experiment is expected to run for about two years and involve about forty thousand consumers and one thousand merchants. Upon the successful completion of this experiment, a wide roll-out of Mondex is expected all over the world.

INFRASTRUCTURE AND ACTIVITIES SUPPORTING ELECTRONIC COMMERCE

Basic Platform

To make EC possible, providers and consumers should share common Cyberspace through Internet access. While it is popular to imagine a ubiquitous Cyberspace, the development and growth of Cyberspace will be guided by basic economics, like all other social phenomena. Some products and types of transactions will initially be too onerous, cumbersome, or insecure to be practical on the Web/Net. On the other hand, when more economically justifiable transactions are established in the Cyberworld, the incremental cost of other activities will be much smaller, and they will become viable.

Netscape Merchant System

Netscape has developed its "Merchant System" with the basic architecture described in Figure 8-29. This architecture separates the main participants: the client and the merchant. It places the financial server outside the main stream of transactions. The staging server is designed for merchants to load, review, and update product displays, pricing, and special offers. Only the server administrator initiates the delivery of new product information into the production environment. The shopping basket resides locally on the client. Billing is processed in a single checkout payment form. The transaction server handles credit card authorization. Secure E-mail is used for order fulfillment. Merchants can determine what products are being viewed.

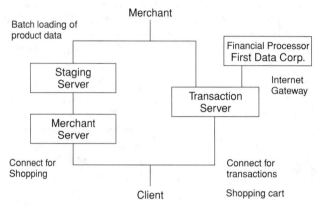

FIGURE 8-29 Netscape Merchant System

The Netscape Merchant System supports the Netscape Socket Layer (SSL) open-security technology and utilizes integrated Oracle RDBMS databases. It allows for audibility of all transactions and product browsing statistics.

VeriFone Internet Payment Product Suite

Website
VeriFone

The VeriFone Internet Payment Product Suite builds on the Netscape Merchant System to complete financial transactions. It can be used with the Netscape Merchant System or other systems that pass over payment services in one single transaction and expect some confirmation for fulfillment. Figure 8-30 describes the essence of the architecture.

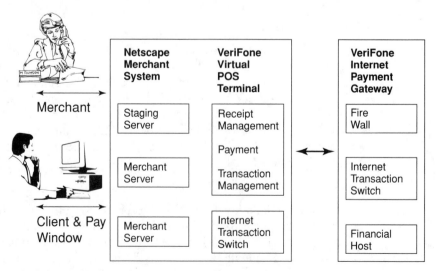

FIGURE 8-30 VeriFone Internet Payment Product Suite

The VeriFone Internet Payment Product Suite has many features that illustrate systems of the future. While we list many of these features, the discussion that ensues evolves around these features and their accounting-related matters, not representing any specificity to VeriFone.

PTAL Application Layer

- Multiple security protocols (SET included). Security is currently the major concern of Internet users, and no conclusive standards have emerged; consequently, multiple standards must be acceptable.

- Application program interfaces (APIs). For integration with merchant accounting, inventory management, and order entry, interfaces with operating processes must come directly from the Internet application. Auditors must understand the nature of these interfaces, the handoffs, backups, and so forth.

- APIs for other EC providers (Open Markets, etc.). While currently only a few protocols and commerce suite vendors exist, in the future there will be a large number of commerce providers, with different offering and common standards of hand-off.

Virtual Point-of-Sales (POS) Functionality

- Back-office support for reports, settlements, and reconciliations

  On-line transactions and open systems allow for continuous financial reporting with on-line real-time financial statements. The advent of open systems with multiple parties selling, buying, and servicing leads to the need for developing new types of more-informative financial statements. More information is particularly useful for narrow-margin vendors and virtual shops. The rapidly changing nature and availability of products on the Internet require virtual malls to understand margins and manage purchases and sales accordingly, to be able to survive in a very competitive environment (a recent survey counted more than three hundred virtual malls).

> The advent of open systems with multiple parties selling, buying, and servicing leads to the need of developing new types of more-informative financial statements.

- Authorization

  Many direct cues (such as appearance, alternate identification, location, etc.) are lost in electronic commerce. Consequently, authorizations assume much larger roles. Narrow margins allow for much less absorption of losses than the 200 or 300 percent markups sometimes found in high-fashion retail. Current authorization routes and rules as adopted by credit card companies will have to change with the Internet medium.

- Capture

  The Internet medium does not require clerical help to capture and record transactions. Actually, recording is inherent to the transaction itself, which does not happen unless recording procedures are in place. On the other hand, population controls and integrity controls become much more important as there is little or no supervision in the economic transaction process.

- Returns

  Returns authorizations and justification are less amenable to automation process than sales.

- Voids/Chargebacks/Disputes

  Again, these are less amenable to automation than sales and must have ratios and frequencies monitored on a real-time basis.

Payment Gateway

- Merchant account management tools

  On-line merchants function in a strange environment. They must have a set of tools that is equivalent to the one they use in their normal environment, often with similar metaphors such as cash register, inventory counts, and so forth.

- Conversion to host legacy formats

  While many vendors started as cyber-businesses, the large majority of future electronic merchants will work both over the Internet and in more traditional venues. Furthermore, their traditional venues will be much larger in volume and dollar sales. It will be cost-efficient for many processes, such as fulfillment, returns, and advertising, to function together. Consequently, EC data have to be integrated with the legacy systems downstream.

- Automatic merchant settlement uploads

  The usage of alternate suppliers, credit cards, authorization services, fulfillment by third parties, and other methods of EC lead to a larger percentage of "settlements" than traditional sales. Accounting and auditing for these is of much higher importance than before.

Pay Window on Client Browser

The client browser (on the customer's PC) assumes great importance in the process. A pay window will pop up at the completion of a customer visit. Later in this chapter we illustrate this process.

- Stores transaction records

  To prevent incomplete transactions, the client will store, at least temporarily, data on transactions. Some EC systems may rely on substantive information, particularly on history residing on the client browser. Eventually, the client device may be the only linkage between the cooperating systems that must be used to complete a transaction.

- Links to PC financial software

  Financial software such as Quicken and Money support a very intuitive checkbook metaphor. Furthermore, these are very popular among customers, and millions of users are familiar with their usage. Consequently, users require progressively more and more integrative linkages. For example, many of the electronic banking systems have Quicken as a download medium. If the data are set up properly, they can be easily placed in TurboTAx. Conversely, PC financial software vendors are becoming one of the mainstays of EC.

- Supports multiple payment methods

  E-cash, credit cards, and E-checks are going to be used most of the time as alternates rather than exclusive forms of payment.

- Password protection

  Passwords are often used at the PC level, at the access to a service level, and at the execution of a transaction level.

The intrinsic internationalism of EC, as well as its around the clock nature, brings opportunities and problems to the accounting profession. Sales of transnational nature, while not new to the accountant or the auditor, bring legal problems, to be discussed in chapter 9, to the forefront but also create a plethora of reporting and auditing issues. Among these we mention the following issues:

- physical process observation is of very limited value
- supervision is not existent in certain instances
- records may not sit on a particular location
- fiscal year end may not be a meaningful, natural reporting time
- inventory counts may not exist
- important information may be in secure servers of third parties
- technology is changing so rapidly that standards are not available

- major security breaches or multi-million-dollar crimes have not yet occurred or have not been publicized
- the public in general does not understand the process
- accountants do not have a clue to the main issues in cyber-accounting

OMI's Electronic Commerce Offering

Website
OMI

In addition to Netscape and VeriFon, OMI also offers a popular electronic commerce product. This offer is described in Figure 8-31, which details its transaction server. The four main components entail the client, the merchant, the transaction server, and the transaction financial processor. The OMI offering recognizes the multiple-mode, multiple-route nature of electronic commerce.

OMI Electronic Commerce

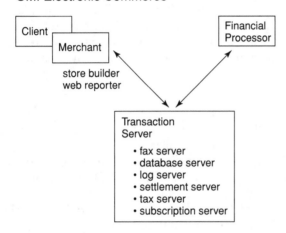

FIGURE 8-31 OMI Transaction Server

Based on the above extant systems, it is possible to generalize about some of the underpinnings of EC accounting and support. We define three main layers: the user/merchant layer, the transaction layer, and the information layer.

The User/Merchant Layer

Users will be clients in a client/server paradigm of Internet servers. Over the Internet, the number of servers is very large and out of the control of the organization. Merchants, also unlike the traditional mode of operation, do not control the means of commerce but are more likely to contract transaction infrastructures such as OMI and VeriFone.

The Transaction Layer

The basic transaction layer will manage the activation and execution of particular transactions of EC. While the basic platform provides mainly electronic publishing and display functions, most of the commerce steps fall into this category. For example, from the main steps in EC, only step 4 is performed by this layer.

The Information Layer

The information layer will help in the management of EC and will include among other things marketing information, accounting information, and site management information. The accounting layer, an often neglected part of the information layer, will become an important part of the process. In this layer, after the purchase is effected, a series of related transactions and records are to be effected and updated.

The transaction is

- recorded
- posted as a receivable
- flown through a general ledger
- positioned as a record for customer service
- matched with a payment
- connected to inventory for fulfillment

Many other recording, analysis, and reporting steps from the traditional accounting cycle may follow.

While the above steps are of traditional nature, EC is creating an environment where on-line posting and reporting are not only desirable but also feasible and ultimately necessary. A customer that purchases on-line will have little patience with waiting for a month for the status of the account. Merchants will also prefer to bill immediately, for cash-flow benefits as well as to refresh the customer's memory on an ephemeral electronic transaction, often performed on impulse.

EDI

Electronic data interchange[6] is the intercompany computer to computer communication of standard business transactions in a standard format that permits the receiver to perform the intended transaction.

EDI can be equated to "business-to-business" electronic commerce, of a particular and proprietary nature. Traditional EDI arrangements entail private EDI agreements among two or several companies that clearly establish protocols and file contents to be sent from one business entity to the other. Figure 8-32 illustrates two parallel flows: one utilizing EDI and the other focusing on paper flow. Later in this chapter, the same analogy will be made in relationship to electronic payments.

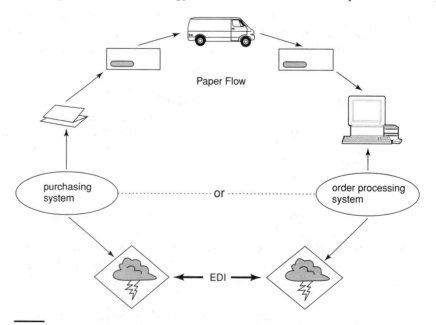

Paper Flow

purchasing system · · · · · · · · · or · · · · · · · · · order processing system

← EDI →

FIGURE 8-32
Paper Flow or EDI?

[6]Sokol, P.K., *From EDI to Electronic Commerce: A Business Initiative,* McGraw Hill, New York, 1995.

INTERNET TOOLS AND ELECTRONIC COMMERCE

Basic Tools

Through the usage of the interconnectivity possibilities provided by the Internet, manual business transactions are facilitated and progressively automated. In this chapter we revisit the basic Internet layers and services now with the view of business usage.

E-Mail

The advent of computer interconnections allowed for the development of synchronous and asynchronous messaging between computer sites whereby two parties communicate electronically passing typed messages between themselves (see Figure 8-33). In synchronous communications (e.g., TALK), the two parties are at their sites and type messages across a communications link. With the evolution of interconnectivity a set of common addressing conventions evolved that could be recognized by a wide set of networks and environments. This allowed for asynchronous communications where a party delivers a message to the network and the network delivers it to the other party's site and places it into a container (mail bin) accessible at any time by the other party. Also, at that stage, methods of routing evolved to give reliability to this connectivity.

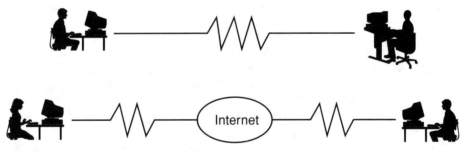

FIGURE 8-33 Synchronous and Asynchronous Communications

This party-to-party connectivity opens the way to tremendous commercial applications, incipient still at this stage, but of great potential for business. The three most noteworthy characteristics that make this of great potential are low cost per message, rapid delivery, and connectivity to corporate mailing lists. On the other hand, there are obstacles for this medium, in particular, the lack of habit by individuals in accessing mails, the lack of ubiquity of the medium, and still the unreliability of its delivery.

Low Cost per Message   While there is somewhat a large setup to get E-mail installed in a corporation, the actual incremental cost of the message is infinitesimal, in the tenths of a cent, when used intensively. With the advent of on-line services, such as America Online, even the setup became simple, whereby basic service can be purchased for $19.95 and each message has no incremental cost. Or, even a less-expensive approach entails a fixed fee, unlimited usage now being provided by Internet Access Providers.

Rapid Delivery   The speed of E-mail delivery is dependent on the route the messages take and on the characteristics of the mailers of the sending and receiving organizations. Typically, a mailer will query its mailbox at fixed intervals for waiting mail. Large organizations have mailboxes continuously on-line, but still there are delays on the way.

Individuals will typically have a mail server on a machine that is permanently on-line on the Internet and will download their mail to their PC when querying for mail. Some users will have scripts that periodically query for mail and bring it down to PCs. For example, when a user is an America Online client, the AOL mail server receives and sends all his or her mail. Periodically, say every six hours, the user's PC calls in to AOL and checks for mail. If mail is there, it is downloaded to the PC for reading. The opposite may also be set up (but is not usually the case) that when the mail server is queried, any mail to be sent is handed over to the mailer.

Connectivity to Corporate Mailing Lists   Traditional corporate mailing lists are databases that will often customize customer letters by linking a standard letter (message) to a variable addressee. Many word-processing packages exist with "mail merge" functions to facilitate this process. While the physical manipulation of paper is cumbersome and expensive, the actual management of the mailing database (list) is probably the more expensive and difficult part of the process. The use of E-mail and LISTSERV (Figure 8-34) technology decreases the physical manipulation of messages (estimates say that a $1.00 cost per piece of mail in a large bulk mailing may be reduced to $.15 or less) as well as allow for some automation of mailing list updates. Mailing list updates are onerous processes that often suffer from lack of systemacity, whereby organizations update their address lists on a haphazard manner.

Problems with E-mail   While it is pretty clear that E-mail and electronic mailing lists are going to have a major role in EC, there are still major problems to be faced. At the current time, we face the fact that many individuals do not have E-mail addresses or lack of habit of accessing their mail. It is highly misleading to find a business acquaintance that provides a business card with an E-mail address but that in reality does not regularly check his or her mail. As the medium is still not ubiquitous, only parts of mailing lists can be delivered, and some are not read by the addressee. While this is a problem, it is also similar to the fact that many customers do not open what they perceive to be "junk-mail." The decrease in costs of mailing through E-mail will eventually make electronic junk mail a major problem. Consequently, we already find, in the software market, "electronic agents" that screen E-mail and classify it into folders.

A third major problem is the lack of compatibility of mailers leading to unreliable delivery. While some mailers can provide confirmation of delivery, or even confirmation that the addressed party has read the mail, this is a very tenuous process that seldom is reliable.

The nature, also, of E-mail is changing. Traditionally, most E-mail was ASCII restricted to traditional characters, while now most mailers support the attachment of special files as *.DOC file (for word documents),*.XLS file (Excel documents), and so forth. Many of the mailers are "MIME" compliant, allowing for a much wider set of attachment and easy readability after decompression, encryption, etc. The process is still very heterogeneous, with often reading files presenting major difficulties to most users.

Another point to be made is the progressive advent of voice mail still a separate medium from E-mail. Users must use computers to pick up and send E-mail and telephones for voice mail. The rapid progress of voice recognition, or more, voice synthesis, will bring into being (with already some limited offers in the market) **universal mailboxes** mixing these two forms of communication. Users may read their E-mail and at the same time hear voice attachments, or conversely, call into their E-mail system. Furthermore, there is no reason why document sharing, faxes, and white boards cannot be part of this universal mailbox approach.

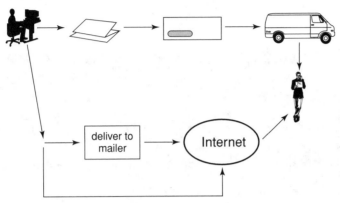

FIGURE 8-34 Mailing Lists Manual and Listserv

E-mail and Public Relations[7]   The rise of electronic mail as a legitimate and accepted form of corporate public relations has created opportunities for news sharing that are unprecedented. One of the most common PR uses of E-mail is for the distribution of press releases.

An E-mail press release has some subtle but crucial differences from its traditional paper counterpart. Knowing what some of these differences are and adjusting for the electronic medium can mean a much better response to your releases by the folks you are hoping will cover your company news. A badly formed and formatted E-mail press release can often mean the recipient hits the "delete" key before even attempting to read it—the very opposite of your intended goal. Too often, companies simply take the exact release they originally created for paper distribution, cut and paste it into an E-mail message, and let it fly. For example, in electronic form you must include an E-mail address and a URL in a prominent location. Targeted organizations, which receive messages through cybermedium, expect to answer the same way.

FTP

The file transfer protocol is widely used as a portion of the commercial transaction, whereby a large number of bytes must be delivered over the Internet. In electronic commerce, for bitable goods, it is often the delivery portion of the transaction. While the World Wide Web now exceeds "ftp" in traffic over the Internet, still ftp is the workhorse of software delivery and of the delivery of large electronic files. For example, if you want to buy software from a software provider, you will normally surf their WWW site obtaining information, will choose the software to be purchased, will go through a secure layer to pay for the items, and then will

---

[7]Eric R. Ward, "PR and Awareness Building in the Age of Email." June, 1996 (netpost@netpost.com).

download the software through an ftp layer that may be embedded into a Web browser. Furthermore, the new marketing axioms of the Internet prescribe software to be *given away* on a trial basis. Consequently, directories can be found of large quantities of software just for the picking. Figure 8-35 and Figure 8-36 are screen shots from the Ziff-Davis' PC Computing site that allow for the download of 1001 software titles somewhat for free. Some of these software are shareware, others a free update, others a free Beta, others a limited time demo.

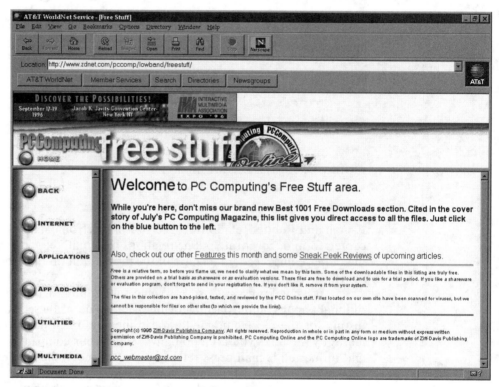

FIGURE 8-35 Free Downloads

Figure 8-36 lists the nature and capabilities of the "free stuff" area. The materials are organized by topics, such as Internet, Applications, App Add-Ons, Utilities, Multimedia, etc.

The user will enter the area by clicking on the items of their choice and will, in most instances, be routed to the provider's software pick-up area. The downloading is performed, in most cases, by the ftp process embedded into the browser.

The reader will, however, find that some of the software is not free, some of it is a simplified version for demos and sometimes has been moved or is not available any more. On the other hand, it also happens that that there are many free jewels of software available that fulfill some of the real needs of the user.

Of great importance, is to devirus imported software to avoid risks, especially in the less-known sites.

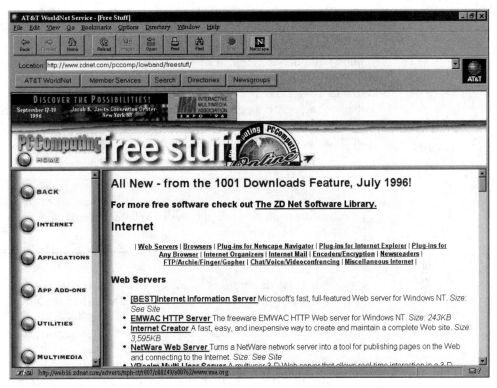

FIGURE 8-36 Free Stuff—PC Computing's 1001 Downloads of Internet Stuff

World Wide Web

The World Wide Web brought respectability to the Internet as a consumer medium. Prior to the WWW, Internet usage was mainly restricted to computer-literate individuals and technical professionals including computer scientists and engineers. While many business people were progressing toward word processing and analytical use of computers with spreadsheets, the use was restricted and specialized. The WWW brought point-and-click usage to the Internet and a simple publishing language (HTML), whereby millions of semi-computer-literate businesses could afford to publish on the net. This wide range availability also made the net a prime candidate for commerce and allowed that the substantial investments in infrastructure necessary for the deployment of a ubiquitous communications medium start to be deployed. While packet switching is a very efficient method of information transport, the cumulative demand placed initially by E-mail and ftp and now by the WWW commands major investments in infrastructure. Internet brownouts, and major backbone downtime, are symptomatic of this state-of-affairs and, while shocking to many users, simply illustrate a new stage of industry in its infancy. While today's AT&T long-distance networks expect nearly 100 percent uptime, the U.S. telephone system was hardly all that reliable in its infancy, say, in the 30s. It is not, therefore, unreasonable to expect that the digital superhighway will initially be sputtering and fraught with discontinuities. Again, the telephone analogy will indicate that the superhighway will require hundreds of billions of dollars of infrastructure investment to bring telephone-like reliability and universal access in the United States to the Internet. Recent technologies such as wireless transmission,

ATM switching, satellite relay, and very high speed ATM-based backbones will allow different solutions for the Infra-net-structure than current basic telephony. The U.S. government, earlier this century, allowed monopolistic status for telephony, aiming to reach universal access and homogenous service throughout the United States. Once these objectives were reached and the industry had grown to maturity, AT&T was forced to (1984) divest of its local operating companies, leading again to competition in the telephone markets, and more recently to competition in the local access markets prompted even by new more-distributive technologies.

> The superhighway will require hundreds of billions of dollars of infrastructure investment to bring telephone-like reliability and universal access in the United States to the Internet.

The great dilemma is whether history will repeat itself by consolidating the many players in the Internet markets and whether the government will intervene to allow for the massive necessary investments for a real information superhighway. While monopolization and tight government controls are unlikely in the current political and technical climates, the nature and volume of investments will bring substantial consolidation on the number of players in the markets, through acquisitions, growth, and strategic alliances. These events will be fueled by the advent and commercialization of the World Wide Web.

WWW Forms as Methods of Collecting Information   Web forms using CGI/Perl scripts are the main form of information gathering on the Web today. While the technology is rather simple, the tooling still is not around to make it a task easily accessible to everyone. Technical people are needed to design questionnaires, implement them on Web pages, collect data into common files, and, probably the most difficult task, interface them with databases and legacy mainframe systems.

ACCOUNTING FOR ELECTRONIC COMMERCE

While there is little in electronic commerce that is intrinsically different, for accounting purposes, many opportunities and issues emerge for accountants.

- The business is on-line, so why should its accounting not also be on-line.
- The opportunity of accounting reporting serving for marketing and logistic management is real and opportunistic.
- Drill-down (drill-up) reports can make an accounting system also an executive information system.
- The exposures for on-line transactions are larger and faster than those of traditional medium.
- Bitable items bring in inventory and sale measurement items that inventory counts cannot resolve.
- The nature of supervision changes considerably.
- Auditing techniques will have to be developed and adapted to the medium.

The whole set of EDP and systems auditing issues reaches much wider significance as not only the client's accounting / financial systems are computerized, but also most of its sales and procurement are on-line and integrated with the first.

Information Systems Auditing

Information systems controls can be divided in three major areas: information processing facility controls, development controls, and application controls. Electronic commerce adds emphasis to concerns with the network reliability, security of access, privacy of communications, and abilities to measure accesses to the site.

Counting Hits

Website Counting hits

The Internet is a challenging medium for market research in general, and for the purpose of assessing the audience in particular. While regular magazines cannot easily measure their readership and circulation numbers, it is possible to trace who visited the site, which pages they visited, and some estimation of how long they stayed in each place. If a questionnaire is added to the site, visitors may be requested to provide some basic demographic information before they get what they are looking for or before they can exit the site. Most servers have software in place to track Web visitations. Log files exist that allow for extensive analysis of site traffic, timing, popularity, and so forth.

The Web is a method of proactive contact with the clientele. While advertising in magazines or TV only gives a vague idea of how many people are observing a message, hit counts give a direct objective measure of the number of users that perused or received partially a file (a message of the business).

As a Web page may be composed of many files, a hit does not mean the reading of a full page, but the download of a component part of the page. Consequently, if a homepage has one HTML main page and five different gif's, then its download would lead to six hits.

Advertisers tend to use the number of impressions, the number of times a banner was downloaded as an objective measure, and more often than not base charges on their number.

While these are objective measures, companies are more interested in finding out questions such as (1) who received our message; (2) from the people that received our message, how many acted upon it following a link or obtaining more information; and (3) how many ultimately bought the product.

These questions lead to the need of a different form of accounting—the accounting for access to a Web site and ensuing actions. Several firms are now dedicated to selling software, providing access attestation services, and/or contracting to increase page traffic.

Measuring Paths of Usage

Unlike traditional sales media, the Web allows for the analysis of the routes that led a customer to visit a site. While post purchase questionnaires, such as in warranty cards, are widely used, they only give a glimpse to the reasons that led a customer to buy a specific product.

Web surfing logs provide a view of the entire route followed by a client in the search of the product or clear evidence of impulse buying. Furthermore, long-term analysis of surfing routes can be among the best indicators of users' preferences and ability to buy. On the other hand, issues of privacy are major in the examination of this information. Users do not feel too kindly on snoopers of their surf routes, and many civil liberty organization have specifically condemned the practice. Laws and ethics are still being developed to deal with the issue.

Usage of Database and Query for Satisfying Some Accounting Functions

While systems such as OMI's Electronic Platform have already incorporated database technology into their proprietary offerings, database access and compatibility is still the Achilles heel of Internet-based commerce. Technology for remote query and storage with interface to HTML pages and CGI scripts is still evolving, and no clear database interface standards have emerged except for a loose set of SQL-like practices that vary from vendor to vendor and from site to site. Unlike the traditional environment, where a plurality of database products and standards is acceptable and may be desirable, a public medium like the Internet requires some communality of standards. Intelligent agents will be much more desirable tools, if they can be designed to access databases in a plurality of locations and remain resident until enacted.

Many Internet-based functions can benefit from a distributed environment and replication of similar functions in tens of different hosts that would cooperate within a loose hierarchy. For example, a corporation with many departments or areas can run transactions in local hosts, drop these transactions into local electronic journals, then post them into the local general ledger. Derivative functions and reports are run either locally or in an aggregate form depending on the nature of reports designed, needs of clients, legal requirements, and so forth. Corporate records and reports aggregate on a systematic or *ad hoc* basis many of these functions. For this vision to come to pass, database coherence and commonality of standards are necessary.

Internet Demographics

Obtaining market research and demographic information about Internet users can be difficult. However, instead of contracting with a research firm to survey users, companies can browse the limited demographic information now available on the Web. Here we list some of those sites (educational institutions conducting voluntary surveys with willing Internet users or commercial firms offering survey results).

Georgia Tech's GVU Center (available on the Web at `http://www.cc.gatech.edu/gvu/user_surveys`) recently completed its third Web-user survey. They found that the mean age of Web users is thirty-five, 80 percent are male, and the top five uses of the Web are browsing, entertainment, work, educational research, and business research.

VALS survey effort takes a different approach, with interesting results. This survey claims to explore "the psychology of people's choices and behavior on the Web." The results indicate that 64 percent of Web users are male, and 36 percent are female. For more information, point your browser at `http://future.sri.com/`.

MIDS Internet Demographic Survey, at `http://www.mids.org/mids/ids2/.index.html`. The site includes a survey summary and information on how to measure Internet usage. Survey-Net (`http://www.survey.net/`) provides a demographic breakdown according to buying habits, religion, and other topics.

The Hermes Project, a research project on the commercial uses of the Web, offers information on how to track usage at Web sites, as well as providing results of its survey of consumers on the Internet. Connect to `http://www.umich.edu/~sgupta/hermes/` and take a tour of this site.

One interesting research project for the Internet, conducted by CommerceNet (`http://december.commerce.net`) and Nielsen Media Research, involves more than on-line surveys—people are contacted by phone and asked to provide detailed information about how and if they use the Internet. When you connect to the site—at `/cgi-bin/surveys/082195.surveypl?f=commercenet.`—check out the sample on-line questionnaire. It is very well done and may inspire you to create your own user survey to implement on your company's site. Some more recent data indicates that women are now close to 35 percent of the US Internet user population.

INTERNET IMPACT UPON DIFFERENT INDUSTRIES

These days few organizations are making money over the Internet. However, most large corporations already see the inevitability of its usage in many aspects of business. Bill Gates of Microsoft states that in ten years it will be as inconceivable to do business without the Internet as today doing business without a telephone. Industries are spending substantial resources developing strategies to face the electronic avalanche. It is clear that some industries will cease to exist in their current form and that other well-placed businesses will be the winners. Clearly, industries with bitable products will be most affected and possibly revolutionized. We shall discuss briefly some effects on six industries: (1) computers and software, (2) banks, (3) education, (4) publishing, (5) retail sales, and (6) information.

Computers and Software

Worldwide over 9 million computers are estimated to be on the Internet at the end of 1995. Furthermore, the number of computers placed in private networks, bridged or connected by a Gateway to the net, is difficult to estimate. If we consider that the average life of computers tends to be three years and the net has doubled each of the last thirteen years, it is reasonable to estimate that in terms of servers and hosts 3 million new computers in 1997 is not an overstatement. Just these numbers added to software costs lead the computer industry to more than 10 billion dollars in revenues associated with the Internet.

Software was the first product transmitted over the net. Methods of software marketing are being dramatically changed by free download offers and electronic distribution. While mainstay software, except for the Internet-related products, is still being distributed in boxes, progressively more and more of the technical support is placed on free receptacles on the Net.

It is reasonable to expect that a substantial parcel of this industry will trade over the net prior to other industries. While most industries are limited in EC as major segments of their clienteles are not computer literate, the computer industry benefits from high computer literacy among its customers, and this will accelerate the electronic future of the industry.

Banks

Banks, and other sectors of the financial industry, are mainly information providers. Their product is fully bitable except for the delivery of cash. With the progressive development of E-cash, every element of the product mix can be delivered over the net. Virtual banks are sprouting all over the spectrum of services with some entities having no storefront to meet clients but doing so by going to the client's home physically or electronically. Retail banking is being revolutionized first by automatic teller machines and now by home banking or what is called PC banking. Citibank dropped its charges for PC banking and increased significantly telephone transactions and transaction services. The largest U.S. bank concludes that eventually PC-based services will be much cheaper to provide.

While security and database standards are not consolidated, there is some concern for security in direct Internet access. Some banks, however, like Banc One of Ohio, are already providing full services on the Internet. It is reasonable to expect that the retail financial institutions will become primarily virtual entities over the years, with some degrees of specialization by clientele and geography. It is also reasonable to expect that cross-national retail banking with U.S. and Japanese banks will become a major force.

Publishing

All publishing houses see the Internet and electronic media with fascination and apprehension. They understand that their world, as they know it, is ready to disappear or completely change. They also understand that new copyright rules are needed, but they do not know what will emerge. Earlier in this book we discussed some basics of electronic publishing. Those basics will catapult the major revolution in publishing. Among many noteworthy effects, we find

- great investments in CD-ROM in the publishing industry
- trend toward electronic full text in libraries
- full-text editions of classics, with expired copyrights, available for free in the WWW
- custom news by many newspapers and magazines
- superiority of search mechanisms and indexing in magnetic medium
- availability of mega-libraries of content in many places
- some publishers getting involved in providing electronic content competing with TV and movie producers
- increasing role of multimedia in some forms of traditional print such as encyclopedias
- the progressive availability of broadband access (principally cable modems) to the home
- fuzziness of the separation of industries from traditional publishing
- large number of WWW sites by publishers
- custom tailoring of textbooks and book lists

Education

The educational field has been one of slow change. While the seventies already predicted the replacement of instruction by CAI (computer-assisted instruction), we are now witnessing university telecommunication networks, remote education, and across the United States (and the world) and progressively the effects of the revolution in publishing discussed above.

Education will continue to be labor intensive but with the progressive control of the problem of pornographic content on the Internet, primary and secondary schools will go full fledge into Internet-based education. It is clear that public authorities in the United States are aware of the needs and are starting to invest large amounts in the necessary infrastructure.

Remote learning, computer-based learning, and electronic libraries are tremendous opportunities for educators and at the same time prime avenues for electronic commerce, in fields that traditionally have been somewhat out of the commerce stream.

Retail Sales

Earlier in this chapter we illustrated electronic malls and commerce presence on the Internet. Bitable goods first, and then commodity-like products that one does not need to touch, smell, or try to buy, are of great promise for commerce. The basic axiom that one has to go somewhere to buy something is starting to change. With the improved quality of individual distribution logistics (post office, Federal Express, etc.), the axiom will change quantitatively, and the consumer will progressively have the store come to him in most purchases. Such a change will mean substantive economic displacement, and configurations of department stores and major retailers will have to adapt accordingly. We are probably going back to the point where catalog (now electronic) shopping will become a more substantial segment of the economy.

Information

We have identified "subscription services" to be one of the three mainstays of current electronic commerce. With the progressive development and acceptance of micropayments, a key link of information commerce will be in place. The Internet is a natural medium to sell information. Advertising, as discussed in this chapter, is a natural venue of transmitting information.

As an example, today one can subscribe to financial newsletters that were previously only in the hands of institutional investors, find any 800 number, look at a directory of more than 60 million households, find free information from the U.S. government, buy access to an updated Encyclopedia Brittanica, contract for dating services, explore places to travel, restaurants to eat, vines to drink, and thousands of other information services.

THE COTTAGE INDUSTRIES OF ELECTRONIC COMMERCE

EC spawns major changes in the way we do things. While some are interpreting it as only a new channel of commerce, a more insightful examination will show a paradigmatic change in means of commerce. Certain venues of commerce, when performed electronically, are so much more efficient that it will be inconceivable to continue doing business as usual and remain competitive. For example, in high-volume business-to-business commerce, Internet-based EDI will be the norm, not the exception. Consequently, many new forms of business are emerging. Some of these forms will eventually replace traditional modi operandi.

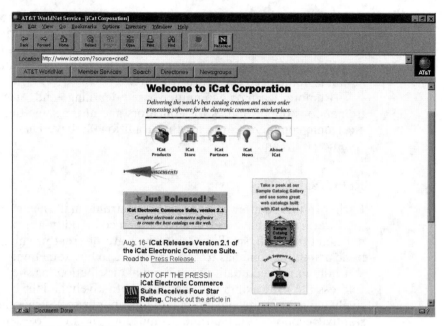

FIGURE 8-37 The iCat Homepage

A case in point are emerging cottage industries related to the Internet. These industries include Internet access providers, equipment sellers, publishers, browser developers, and so on. Consider, for example, specialized companies that design and implement electronic catalogs [see Figure 8-37 and one of their Products (Dean & DeLuca) in Figure 8-38].

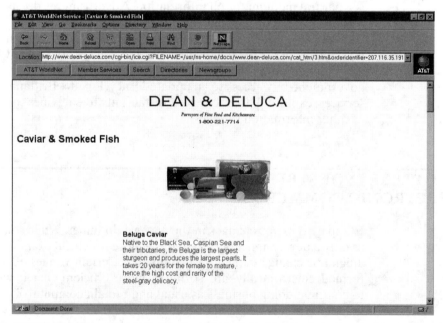

FIGURE 8-38 The Electronic Catalog of Dean & DeLuca Designed by the iCat Corporation (Reprinted with permission by iCat Corporation and Dean & Deluca)

Direct Selling and Infrastructure: The Case of Shopping Malls

A recent survey found more than three hundred Electronic Shopping Malls serving a wide variety of geographic, product, and generic domains. Often, these Shopping Malls consist of nothing more than an electronic storefront connected with a series of Databases of their suppliers. They benefit from low real estate costs (no stores and low-cost locations), no inventories, and the ability to shop around constantly for the lowest price. Consequently, many E-mail sellers claim to offer discounts of 10 to 50 percent.

These virtual providers may expand the traditional channels with little incremental cost, may provide round-the-clock service with little extra overhead, may utilize cheaper pools of labor (such as use employees from India to staff telephones off-hours), may keep very large lists of products, and may also consider the entire world as their market. With the progressive internationalization of markets and increased sensitivity and flexibility of export/import regulations, international mail order is becoming a reality.

In Figure 8-40 we describe the architecture of a virtual provider. Traditional media are enhanced by the Internet. The provider has links with the databases of suppliers and wholesalers. Once a sale is affected, and all the steps described above are completed, delivery is carried out either by the provider or by a contracted carrier.

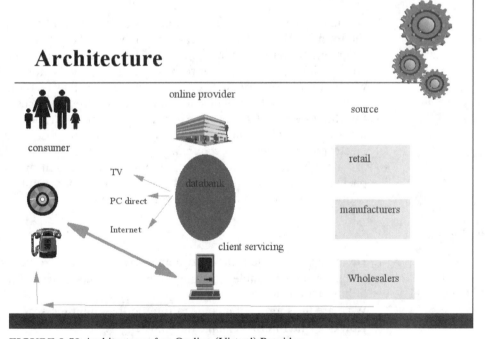

FIGURE 8-39 Architecture of an On-line (Virtual) Provider

The consumer visits the virtual provider through the phone, interactive TV, PC direct, Internet, and so forth. She or he may supplement the information received directly by using a PC-based database or a regularly distributed CD/ROM. The Virtual provider has its own database, a rich set of client-servicing features, and its own databank linked to retailers, manufacturers, wholesalers, and so forth. When the customer requests a product, databases are queried, best offers found, choices made, and, if a purchase ensues, delivery is scheduled. If the provider has its own delivery methods, they are activated. Otherwise, the virtual provider initiates some form of package delivery service.

CUC's Shopper Advantage Mall is an example of a series of electronic-shopping malls that are evolving in the Web. It can use a "shop-by-room" metaphor whereby the user roams through rooms or a "shop-by-department" metaphor, more like a two-dimensional department store.

Even for experienced computer users many domains of the Internet or electronic commerce are strange and difficult to use. When buying through the Internet, one may worry that the images shown are not representative, that one's credit card number can be stolen, that someone's message may be intercepted, and that one may betray the competence in the usage of computer tools. To reduce this danger, the technology has to become friendlier, less expensive, more intuitive, and simple to use.

With experience, standardization, and technical progress, these fears are progressively decreasing, and commerce over the Internet is increasing. The years of 1994 and 1995 were the years of the growth of the Internet. The next five years are the years of the popularization of Internet commerce. Electronic commerce in addition to supporting traditional commerce is giving birth to dynamic and exciting new industries and activities.

CONCLUSIONS

A remarkable evolution in technologies, standards, and practices is taking place on the Internet. While the next years are the years of electronic commerce, we are just beginning to define the information structure needed to run electronic commerce. Accounting will play a major role in facilitating this evolution. Accounting services will become a form of electronic commerce as well as its tool.

Accounting firms will sell *financial accounting* services over the Internet and for the Internet. Corporations and management accountants will increasingly focus on managing commerce, on understanding its cost structures, and on selling electronic *management accounting* services. Some forms of electronic *tax services* are already emerging, for example, on-line tax consulting, tax packages, and tax package interfaces with financial packages. The opportunities for accountants are many and will be explored in the years to come.

Problems

1. Describe classifications that may help to explain the electronic commerce phenomena.
2. Discuss what is a bitable attribute and how it can be analyzed for better understanding of Internet Phenomena.
3. What are the sources of income of Internet-based businesses?
4. How does the Internet change the value chain?
5. How can you divide the electronic shopping process?
6. What is the shopping cart metaphor?
7. Compare E-commerce for banks as opposed to some form of electronic shopping mart.
8. Why is E-care such an important part of the E-commerce process. Did anything change from the traditional processes?
9. What are the major security considerations in E-commerce?
10. What are the major marketing considerations that make E-commerce different from traditional commerce? You must think about the processes and make a comparative analysis.

CHAPTER

Some Legal Aspects of the Internet

9

INTRODUCTION

In this chapter we discuss some of the key legal issues likely to affect Internet users in forthcoming years. The purpose of this discussion is to provide a selective review of some outstanding legal issues arising from the rapid development of the Internet. The reader should bear in mind that this review is neither exhaustive nor legally authoritative. The authors of this book are not legal experts. Users who are in need of professional assessments of the legal propriety or consequences of any specific action taken on the Internet should consult legal experts and primary legal sources.

Developments in Cyberspace technology and practice pose many new, often unanticipated, legal problems of which users should be aware. For the time being, in many instances, it is the non-Cyberspace legal framework that provides the general guidelines to what can and cannot be done in Cyberspace. This legal framework is being gradually adapted to adjudicate some of the unique problems concerning Cyberspace. At this time, we can only allude to some of the more acute legal problems emerging on the Internet. In many areas one encounters as many unresolved issues as definitive answers.

INTERNET FREE SPEECH AND FREE EXPRESSION

Website
Free speech

The 1996 Communications Decency Act (CDA) outlaws the on-line distribution of "indecent" material. Immediately after its passage, hundreds of Web sites colored themselves *black* (see Figure 9-1), reflecting concerns over infringements on Internet freedom. The reader can see extracts of the act in appendix C.

Numerous organizations challenged the constitutionality of the new law in court. In a unanimous decision, a panel of three federal judges in Philadelphia ruled that the CDA unconstitutionally restricts freedom of speech by violating the free speech protections of the First Amendment, as well as the due process rights of the Fifth Amendment.

After President Clinton's signing of the telecommunications bill, hundreds of Web sites turned their pages black.

SOME SITES FOCUSING ON FREEDOM / CENSORSHIP AND RELATED ISSUES

The Center for Democracy & Technology
http://www.cdt.org/speech.html
Voter's Telecommunications Watch
vtw@wtw.org
Society for Electronic Access
http://www.sea.org/

On Feb. 15, a Federal judge temporarily blocked enforcement of the 1996 Communications Decency act by ruling the term *indecent* unconstitutionally vague but upheld the section that makes it a felony to use a computer network to display, in a way accessible to minors, materials that depicts or describes "in terms patently offensive as measured by contemporary community standards, sexual or..."

FIGURE 9-1 The Center for Democracy and Technology

The court held that content-based regulation of the Internet, however benign in its purpose, "could burn the global village to roast the pig." The exceedingly broad and vague definitions of "indecency," the judges unanimously concluded, significantly curtail legitimate speech.

The United States appealed the verdict by invoking analogies between the Internet and broadcast media. Courts have tolerated stricter control of broadcast content on the grounds that the "scarcity" of air frequencies turns radio and TV audiences into "captive" consumers.

STATEMENT BY THE PRESIDENT[1]

The Justice Department is reviewing today's three judge panel court decision on the Communications Decency Act. The opinion just came down today, and the statute says we have twenty days to make an appeal.

I remain convinced, as I was when I signed the bill, that our Constitution allows us to help parents by enforcing this Act to prevent children from being exposed to objectionable material transmitted though computer networks. I will continue to do everything I can in my Administration to give families every available tool to protect their children from these materials. For example, we vigorously support the development and widespread availability of products that allow both parents and schools to block objectionable materials from reaching computers that children use. We also support the industry's accelerating efforts to rate Internet sites so that they are compatible with these blocking techniques.

[1]Copyright 1995 PR Newswire Association, Inc., March 28, 1995, Tuesday.

Whether these "scarcity" considerations hold for the Internet is debatable. There are no known physical limits to the expansion of Internet services. The only relevant constraints to Internet capacity seem to be economic. Treating Internet users as "captive" audience is therefore a questionable proposition.

Recently, the U.S. Supreme Court agreed to hear the case. Many legal experts are of the opinion the criteria set in the CDA to determine what is indecent on the Internet are much too broad to withstand constitutional challenges.

In future cases concerning Cyberspace, the courts may have to decide whether the Internet constitutes an entirely new medium with so many unique features as to make most analogies with legal precedents in other media spurious. The Internet encompasses a transitional telecommunications network and a transnational corpus of content, residing in millions of computers, in different countries, geographic regions, and legal jurisdictions. It is therefore arguable that an entire new set of concepts, rules, agreements, understandings, and practices are emerging and will affect not only many legal aspects of computer uses but the information society as a whole.

INTELLECTUAL PROPERTY AND COPYRIGHTS

Website
Intellectual property

This section provides a brief review of selected key aspects of the U.S. copyrights and Intellectual Property law and their applicability to on-line publications and the exchange and dissemination of information over the Internet. Copyright infringement is a major concern because of the large number of files available on the Internet. For example, numerous software programs are accessible on-line. Some are free, some are not. Some are copyrighted, some are not. Some of them are distributed on a trial basis for a limited amount of time with no software protection upon the expiration of the trial.

At the time this book goes to print, the existing copyrights law of the land generally applies to Cyberspace. It is therefore important to start with a brief review of the major provisions of the U.S. Intellectual Property and copyright Law. In February 1993, President Clinton formed the Information Infrastructure Task Force (IF) to articulate and implement the vision of the Clinton Administration for the National Information Infrastructure (NII). Within the IF, a working group on Intellectual Property Rights was established to examine the intellectual property implications of the NII and make recommendations on any appropriate changes to U.S. intellectual property law policy. The subsequent discussion is largely based on the September 1995 report of this working group.

Copyright Law

The U.S. law of copyright is grounded in the U.S. Constitution that empowers Congress to "promote the Progress of Science and useful Arts by securing for limited Times to Authors and Inventors the exclusive Right to their respective Writings and Discoveries" (U.S. Constitution, Article I, section 8, clause 8).

When it enacted the Copyright Act of 1909, Congress has interpreted this constitutional clause to mean that the constitution does not confer any natural rights on authored works. Rather, copyrights are granted to promote public welfare by encouraging and providing economic incentives for free expression of creativity and invention. At the same time, to assure the ultimate uninhibited dissemination of new and original ideas, the duration of this protection is limited.

> the constitution does not confer any natural rights on authored works . . . copyrights are granted to promote public welfare . . .

As for the scope of copyright protection, U.S. law extends such protection to any "original work of authorship fixed in any tangible medium of expression, now known or later developed, from which they can be perceived, reproduced, or otherwise communicated, either directly or with the aid of a machine or device" (17 U.S.C. section 102(a) 1988 & supplement V 1993).

Based on the interpretation of this fairly broad provision, the courts have formulated three basic requirements for copyright protection—*originality, creativity,* and *fixation.* In the context of copyright law, an original work is simply a work of independent creation (i.e., not copied from another). It need not be innovative to be original. To qualify as creative, a work must show only a low level of creativity. As for fixation, a work is considered fixed when its embodiment is sufficiently permanent or stable to allow its communication or reproduction for a nontransitory period.

Website Copyrights

It is very important to bear in mind that the current law is flexible enough to cover any method of fixation presently known or likely to be developed at a later time. A work may be fixed in any stable form (e.g., words, numbers, notes, sounds, pictures). Note that works in digital form (generally encoded in a sequence of zeroes and ones) are legally covered. Likewise, floppy disks, compact discs, optical disks, and other digital storage devices are encompassed by the definition. Interactive works have also been regarded as sufficiently fixed to qualify for copyright protection.

An electronic transmission, in and of itself, would not fix a work (e.g., a transmission projected briefly on the screen). However, electronic transmissions from one computer to another, such as E-mail, have been generally found to qualify as fixed, even if they only resided on each computer in operating memory (RAM).

Presently, both published and unpublished works are protected by federal copyright law. However, the status of the work, as either published or unpublished, is legally significant. Among other things, for unpublished works, deposit requirements for registration with the copyright office differ, and the scope of the fair-use defense may be narrower. Generally, a copyrighted work is protected for the length of the author's life plus another 50 years.

A key concept in copyright protection is that *ideas* are *not* protected, only their *expression* is. It is, for example, legal to use ideas, concepts, methods, or procedures presented in an article, as long as the expressions used by the original author are not copied. Also, copyright does not prevent users from copying from a prior author's work items that are not original (e.g., facts and materials in the public domain).

Fair Use

The Fair Use Provision of the Copyright Act specifies certain limitations to the exclusive rights of copyright holders to their works. These limitations are related to the "fair use" of a copyrighted work, which permit, subject to specified legal provisions, restricted forms of quotations from and reproduction of such works. Four criteria are specified in the law for the determination of fair use: (1) purpose and character of use, (2) nature of copyrighted work, (3) relative amount of work used, and (4) effect on the economic value of the work.

Criterion (1) for fair use takes into account the following considerations: (a) commercial nature or nonprofit educational purposes of the work, (b) specific purposes of the work, and (c) degree of transformation of the work. In general, the burden of demonstrating fair use is eased if it can be shown that (1) the use is for nonprofit educational purposes; (2) the use is for the specific purposes of criticism, comment, news reporting, teaching, scholarship, or research; and (3) the use has significantly transformed the work rather than merely copied the original.

Criterion (2) evaluates the original work in terms of the degree of protection it deserves in the first place. In general, the more original and important the contribution of the original work, the more protection it is likely to get. Criterion (3) examines the quantity and substance of quotations from or reproduction of the original work relative to its totality. There is no predetermined numerical threshold for the use to be qualified as fair, but lower relative quantity and substance of use ease the defense of its fairness. Criterion (4) assesses the economic effects of use on the actual or potential market for the original work. The lesser the estimated adverse economic impact of the use on the original work, the easier the demonstration of its fairness.

The reader may have observed by now that the criteria for the determination of fair use are subjective. As a result, a priori assessments as to whether certain uses of original material can be effectively demonstrated as fair may often be difficult. At the same time, the stakes can be high. Adverse fair use rulings may damage reputations and result in harsh financial penalties for infringements on copyrights. Caution and prudence are therefore called for when original works are used, and some obvious behavioral guidelines apply. It is reasonable to start with a careful examination if the material to be used is of the type protected by copyright. If it is, it should be assumed that this work is indeed protected. For protected works, the purpose, manner and the extent of use, as well as its economic impact on the original work should be thoroughly assessed. Whenever possible, it is advisable to seek competent legal counsel to determine whether the contemplated use can be successfully defended as fair in a court of law. In case of doubt, it may be prudent to act conservatively and seek explicit written permissions from copyright holders.

On-line Transactions and Licensing of On-line Works

Copyright ownership may be *transferred* to one or more persons. The exclusive rights of a copyright owner may be also *licensed* on exclusive or nonexclusive bases. Rights in copyrighted works may be negotiated on-line or off-line. Licensing arrangements vary. For example, some may be negotiated as two-party agreements, others as voluntary collective licensing. But what about new Internet uses that were not contemplated at the time of licensing? Should, for example, a public display on a Bulletin Board System (BBS) automatically fall within a scope of a license agreement negotiated before the advent of BBS? In general, do new technologies produce new uses for works that may require renegotiation of existing contracts to accommodate these uses? With the continuous proliferation of new Cyberspace technologies, such legal problems are bound to become more acute. They will have to be resolved by the courts.

On-line contracting and licensing raise potentially important and often unresolved legal issues about the validity and enforceability of such transactions. Some of these issues are discussed below in the context of electronic commerce. On-line licenses for use of works may pose special legal problems. These transactions are generally not considered "sales" but rather licenses to use or access the works. Therefore, the legal validity of these on-line contracts may be open to question.

Copyrights Responsibility of On-line Internet Services

What is the responsibility of on-line Internet services vis-à-vis copyright violations by their subscribers? This is an important legal issue as can be evidenced by the following cases.

Frank Music sued CompuServe (an on-line Internet service) because subscribers placed many pieces of their music on the system. In 1991 a federal court in New York declared CompuServe to be more like a library than a newspaper, therefore denying responsibility over content. However, another court held a BBS operator directly liable for the display of unauthorized *Playboy* copies on the service.

In general, copyright law imposes different standards of liability for *direct, contributory,* or *vicarious* liability. Direct infringes are held to a standard of strict liability that is determined without regard to the intent of the infringing party. However, U.S. courts have the discretion to consider innocent intent by infringing parties as a mitigating factor in determining damages. As a result, those found to be contributory rather than direct infringing parties are generally held to a lesser degree than the direct standard of liability.

Internet on-line service providers have been arguing that they should be exempt from liability for the conduct of their subscribers mainly on the ground that the mere quantity of material on the on-line provider's system is often so large as to make content control either impossible or prohibitively costly. Furthermore, even if control was feasible, on-line providers argue that they usually do not possess the information or knowledge to determine which materials represent copyright infringements. As a result, exposure to liability for infringement could allegedly drive many service providers out of business, thereby endangering the free flow of information on the Internet.

Others argue that on-line service providers should not be given a preferential legal status, as compared with book sellers, record stores, newsstands, and computer software retailers who arguably cannot analyze all the items they sell for possible copyright infringements. If the latter distributors are held strictly liable for infringing works and copies they deal with, why should on-line service providers be exempt?

Patents

An increasing number of patentable innovations will be developed, stored, transmitted, published, and made available on the Internet. As a result, an effective legal system providing orderly and consistent patent regulation and protection is an essential ingredient in the development and growth of the Internet as a primary information and communication system.

The reader should bear in mind that legal patent protection is different from legal copyright protection. Copyright protection applies automatically at the moment of fixation. As for patent protection, an inventor must specifically request such protection by filing a patent application that establishes the patentability of her/his invention. In general, an invention must be *new, useful,* and *nonobvious* to be patentable. There are no limitations as to the field of technology. However, certain important restrictions have been imposed through legal interpretations by the courts. For example, one cannot preempt use of laws of nature or mathematical truths. As a result, applications of mathematical principles to solve a mathematical problem are not patentable.

Electronic publications on the Internet may pose some special problems for patent protection. The time an invention was made, its public accessibility, its technical accuracy, and its informativeness are important factors in determining patentability. In contrast to printed documents, electronically disseminated information may contain little or no tangible evidence regarding the date the information was first publicly disclosed or regarding the content of the document as disclosed on that date. Also, the degree of distribution of or public accessibility to certain electronic documents may be either unmeasured or unmeasurable. Information is communicated over the Internet in various degrees of formality and completeness. Numerous items are disseminated in a much more preliminary and tentative form than in most traditionally printed material. The technical quality and accuracy of electronically disseminated documents is generally subject to greater variability. Yet, from a legal point of view, the content of documentation required to assess the novelty of an invention, as compared to prior state of the art, must be informative and technically accurate. All this can greatly complicate on-line determinations of patentability and patent infringements.

Trademarks

Many companies throughout the world have symbols and logos that they have protected by registering them as trademarks™. Companies register such symbols and logos in order to prevent other companies from using them to "pass off" their product or service as a product or service of the original company. As a result, many firms are apprehensive about individuals using trademarked logos on the Internet unless their explicit permission is given and the logo is stated to be a trademark of the holder.

In general, the role of trademarks is to identify a distinct source of products and services. First and continuous use of trademarks give users exclusive rights to the mark and prohibits unauthorized third parties from using them. Registration at either federal or state level is not necessary to maintain those rights in the United States. International protection of registered marks is regulated by international agreements (Stockholm 1967 and Geneva 1977) to which the United States is a party.

In accordance with legal precedent, electronic transmissions of data are considered as services. Trademarks can therefore be established and infringed upon electronically. These principles notwithstanding, numerous trademark conflicts in Cyberspace arise. Some of the conflicts center around the legal relationship between trademarks and the registration and use of site domain names on the Internet. For example, a former employee of the MTV cable network established a Web site—"mtv.com"—offering a daily report about the rock music industry. MTV owners sued for trademark infringement and unfair competition.

International Protection of Copyrights

Website
International copyrights

The reader must realize that international copyrights do not exist as such. Instead, a system of international conventions sets norms for the protection of intellectual rights to be implemented within the framework of national laws. The transnational nature of the Internet complicates international protection of copyrights. Consider a user in France who accesses a database in the United States and downloads a copy to a computer in Sweden. It is far from clear whose copyright law would apply to such a transaction. Copyright laws are territorial. The standards of protection currently embodied in international conventions leave room for national legislative determinations. As a result, copyright infringements in one country may not constitute infringements in another.

Many of those conflicts are regulated in part by several major international treaties. The Berne Convention for the Protection of Literary and Artistic Works of September 9, 1886, is the principal international copyright convention. This convention, revised many times, was finalized in Paris on July 24, 1971. It was ratified by Congress and put into effect in the United States on March 1, 1989. The Berne Convention includes detailed provisions for copyrights protection that are generally considered to constitute an adequate set of protective standards. These standards, however, may be insufficient to deal with the digital dissemination of copyrighted works.

The World Intellectual Property Organization (WIPO), consisting of 155 members including the United States, is responsible for the administration of the international intellectual property treaties. In addition to the traditional WIPO forum, the World Trade Organization (WTO) Agreement on Trade-Related Aspects of Intellectual Property (TRIPs Agreement) sets important standards for the protection of copyrights and related rights. Concluded during the recent Uruguay round negotiations with the United States as a signatory, this agreement also contains provisions to insure that the parties to the TRIPs fully implement obligations under it. Among its numerous provisions, the TRIPs agreement requires member countries to provide exclusive rights for authors and to prohibit commercial rental to the public of originals or copies of copyrighted works. The agreement also provides minimum standards for the term of protection for copyrighted works (the life of the author plus fifty years for most works) and confirms that all types of computer programs are "literary works" under the Berne Convention, thereby requiring each WTO country to protect them.

All major international intellectual property treaties embody the principle of *national treatment*. National treatment gives a foreigner in any signatory nation the same intellectual property rights and benefits that a citizen of that nation is entitled to. It is important to realize, however, that national treatment does not require one country to grant a foreign citizen rights reciprocal to the rights that this foreign citizen enjoys in his own country. Some argue that intellectual property rights should be granted by a country only to the citizens of those countries that agree to reciprocate by granting equivalent rights to its citizens. If adopted, such reciprocity will create a more demanding international legal environment that will force countries either to conform to a widely accepted legal system of intellectual property rights or be left out.

The United States and other countries that follow the Anglo-American or common-law legal tradition differ in certain important aspects of copyright protection from the civil-law tradition that originated in continental Europe. Under the civil-law system, the rights of authors to have their original works protected is strictly moral. Therefore the ability of authors to transfer or waive such rights is considerably more limited than under U.S. law. This, for example, may impede on-line licensing. Furthermore, under the civil-law system, only works that are original, in that they reflect the personality of the author, are entitled to author rights protections (similar to the U.S. level of protection). Productions that do not meet this originality requirement (e.g., producers of phonograms, performers, and broadcasters) are protected under a lesser system of "neighboring rights." By contrast, the U.S. law grants most such productions the full protection accorded to authors' rights.

The principal treaty for the protection of neighboring rights is the Rome Convention, adopted in 1961. This Convention is considered by many to include standards inadequate to deal with problems arising from current technological advances in Cyberspace. Its major and critical flaw is that it allows members to invoke reservations and exceptions that enable countries to avoid their obligations for the protection of important neighboring rights. The United States is not a party to the Rome Convention. The TRIPs Agreement, however, also allows members to impose the exceptions to national treatment permitted by the Rome Convention.

To attain stronger and more reliable levels of legal protection for intellectual property rights over a global Internet system, the differences between continental author rights and neighboring rights systems and the Anglo-American copyright systems have to be narrowed and bridged. Ways will have to be found to establish standards that could be implemented through either legal system.

On December 20, 1996, an agreement by WIPO countries has been reached in Geneva to broaden and extend international copyright law. This sweeping agreement, designed to address protection of works, related primarily to the development of digital technology and the growth of the Internet, covers two treaties: The WIPO Copyright Treaty protecting the rights of authors in their literary and artistic works, and the WIPO Performances and Phonograms Treaty protecting the rights of performers and producers of phonograms. The WIPO Copyright Treaty provides for the copyright protection of *computer programs* and *original databases,* and it also provides for the rights of rental (consistent with the TRIPs agreement). The WIPO Performances and Phonograms Treaty extends protections of the rights of performers to the distribution of their works and to rental rights. Both treaties have to be ratified by the U.S. Senate and other legislatures around the world before they go into effect in the respective countries.

The WIPO Copyright Treaty is based on provisions of the Berne Convention for the protection of literary and artistic works. The protection of this treaty applies to computer programs regardless of the mode or form of their expression (Article 4), as well as to "compilations of data or other material in any form, which by reason of the selection or the arrangement of their contents constitute intellectual creations" (Article 5). Article 6 of the WIPO Copyright Treaty gives authors of literary and artistic works "the exclusive right of authorizing the making available to the public of the original and copies of their works through sale or transfer of ownership." Article 6 also gives authors of computer programs, cinematographic works, and works embodied in phonograms "the exclusive right of authorizing commercial rental to the public of the originals or copies of their works."

Importantly, Article 10 of the WIPO Copyright Treaty permits countries who are parties to the treaty to provide in their national legislation for "limitations of or exception to the rights granted to authors of literary and artistic works under this Treaty in special cases that do not conflict with a normal exploitation of the work, and do not unreasonably prejudice the legitimate interests of the author." This provision would be consistent with "fair use" notions under U.S. law that allow individuals, under certain circumstances and for certain purposes, to make limited quotes from or limited copies of protected works.

The WIPO Copyright Treaty requires signatory countries to "provide adequate legal protection and effective legal remedies against the circumvention of effective technological measures that are used by authors in connection with the exercise of their rights under this Treaty or the Berne Convention and that restricts acts, in respect of their works, which are not authorized by the authors concerned or permitted by law" (Article 10).

According to the WIPO Performances and Phonograms Treaty, the definition of "performers" is broad. It includes "actors, singers, dancers, and other persons who act, sing, deliver, declaim, play in, interpret, or otherwise perform literary or artistic works or expressions of folklore" (Article 2). "Phonograms" are defined as any embodiment of sounds that can be perceived, reproduced, or communicated through a device. "Producers of phonograms" are defined as those who take the initiative and have the responsibility for phonograms. The Treaty affirms the exclusive rights of performers and producers of phonograms to authorize the broadcasting, communication to the public, making available to the public, distribution, reproduction, and rental of their works.

Broadly speaking, the WIPO Copyright Treaty and the WIPO Performances and Phonograms Treaty, if ratified by a sufficient number of states, are likely to strengthen international legal protection over the Internet of authors, performers, and producers against piracy or unauthorized use of their works. At the same time, the 1996 Geneva Agreement stopped short of extending copyrights to transitory copies that are made automatically by computers as they download materials from the Internet. The latter extension of copyright was supported by the U.S. trademark and patent office and by movie makers and record makers. It has been opposed by a coalition of academic, scientific, and consumer organizations out of concern that such copyright provisions may limit free access to data and inhibit the growth of the Internet.

LEGAL ISSUES AND ELECTRONIC COMMERCE

Electronic commerce is growing in popularity. Electronic purchasing of goods and services over the Internet facilitates ordering, shipment, and tracking. Customers can benefit from on-line access to a variety of services including financial and investment services, reservation, video demonstrations, and interactive purchasing. Payments may be made either through conventional methods or through on-line fund transfers between a consumer's bank and an on-line provider.

The law dealing with electronic commerce has not been fully developed. Important legal issues concerning the validity and enforceability of on-line contracting and licensing remain unresolved. According to common law, a contract is formed by mutual, voluntary assent by the contracting parties and by their "meeting of the minds" to be bound by a set of negotiated terms. Legal questions arise as to whether, and to what extent, these requirements are fully met in electronic transactions.

For example, it is not entirely clear whether under existing contract law an electronic offer of message or acceptance or the simple use of the "accept" or "return" key in response to a provider's offer or consumer's request constitutes a legally binding assent. Furthermore, in case of so-called "electronic agreements" to on-line contracts containing non-negotiable terms (e.g., "shrink wrap" licenses used by software publishers), it is doubtful whether such agreements were preceded by sufficient "meeting of the minds" among the parties to qualify as legally binding contracts. Another issue concerns writing and signature requirements. In case of paperless Internet transactions, legal question may arise at to whether messages are "written" and what constitutes an adequate "signature." Recently, several states, have been developing and/or enacting more detailed and specific laws with respect to electronic signatures.

Advertising on the Internet allows greater tailoring and customizing of the advertising message. Electronic magazines are increasingly able to adjust their messages in real-time based on information requests made by visitors. The personal nature and interactive opportunities of Internet advertising are likely to amplify legal issues related to manipulation, truth in advertising, implicit contracts, and invasion of privacy.

DIGITAL SIGNATURES

Digital signatures are functionally the electronic counterparts to handwritten signatures. They are a necessary part of electronic transactions in the same way handwritten signatures are an essential part of nonelectronic transactions. Legislation governing electronic signatures is required primarily to prevent misuse and forgery of such signatures, and to legalize reliable mechanisms for the certification and authentication of digital signatures.

The reader should bear in mind that there is little resemblance between handwritten and digital signatures. The visible portion of a digital signature generally includes the signer's name along with a digital signature certificate, serial number code, and the name of the certification authority. The digital signature certificate is a computer record that identifies the signer. Out of a pair of two keys, the public key and the private key, it contains only the public key and is digitally signed by a certification authority. The private key is encrypted when it is stored in the signer's computer and is used by the signer only during the signing process to "create" the digital signature (see the discussion in chapter 7). It is the responsibility of the signer to preserve the confidentiality of her/his private key.

In the process of signing, the signer enters his/her digital signature authorization code and uses special software (e.g., CivicLink), which, through the use of the authorization code, decrypts, for the duration of the signature, the signer's private key. Signers use their public keys to identify themselves to certification authorities. The public key "reads" the digital signature created by the private key to verify the authenticity of the digitally signed documents. Public keys are made available by signers to the parties they wish to have their signed documents authenticated by.

The state of Utah was one of the world pioneers in developing a legal system and adopting a comprehensive electronic signatures statute, known as the Digital Signature Act, or the "1995 Utah Act" (passed on February 27, 1995, and took effect on May 1, 1995). This act is in the process of being amended to make it more consistent with the guidelines of the American Bar Association's Section of Science and Technology.

The legal framework established by the Utah law provides for state-licensed certification authorities, on-line repositories (databases), and public key encryption software to facilitate the application of legally binding procedures for the digital signing of electronic documents. To that end, the Utah law confers on digital signatures a legal status similar to that of valid handwritten signatures and regulates their use in contract and evidence law.

Among some of its more important provisions, the Utah law establishes licensed certification authorities, although individuals who choose not to be subject to requirements of the act are allowed to use nonlicensed certification authorities. Under the Utah system, electronic commerce customers may face considerable liability for fraudulent use of their signatures, unless they are able to demonstrate that they have taken reasonable precautions to prevent misuses of their private keys. This contrasts with the limited liability ($50 in most cases) incurred by victims of fraud involving transactions covered by the Electronic Funds Transfer Act (e.g., credit card transactions).

The Utah law bestows on on-line databases of public encryption keys the status of "recognized repositories." An administrative agency is authorized to choose "appropriate" public key encryption algorithms. Each party involved in a digitally signed transaction with another party is required to verify the signature of the pertinent party through the use of a recognized repository. The act does not provide options for anonymous digital signature certificates. Published (i.e., publicly accessible) certificates are generally required to contain names of subscribers, their affiliations, and a dollar figure, termed "recommended reliance limit," which may be interpreted as indicative of financial condition or standing.

Following Utah, other states, including Arizona, California, Florida, Illinois, Georgia, Hawaii, Oregon, Virginia, and Washington, have passed, or are in the process of enacting, digital signature laws. These laws, which are essential for the smooth development of electronic commerce, often differ from state to state. For example, the Utah law is detailed and comprehensive, while the California statute (passed in October 1995) is brief and delegates regulatory powers to the state administration. Other states generally follow either the Utah approach (e.g., Washington, passed in March 1996) or the California approach (e.g., Florida, effective in May 1996). It is likely that efforts will be undertaken in the future to increase the degree of uniformity in digital signature laws among states and nations.

JURISDICTIONAL ISSUES[2]

In view of its global transnational structure, the Internet is a world community whose members interact across traditional jurisdictional boundaries. This gives rise to legal issues of jurisdiction, some of which will be discussed below.

Pornography and Jurisdiction

Consider the case of Robert and Carleen Thomas who were indicted and found guilty of obscenity for running a pornographic BBS (Bulletin Board Service) in San Francisco that required payment and written application stating that the client was a nonminor. A postal inspector in Memphis, Tennessee, obtained an account, downloaded materials, and then filed criminal complaint in Memphis. The Thomases were found guilty and sentenced to two years in prison. The case is pending on appeal.

This case illustrates the difficulties of applying "local" standards of obscenity in cyber media. What is a community standard? Should the court use *Tennessee, California,* or *Cyberspace* standards? The more serious question is on what jurisdictional grounds were the BBS operators brought into a Tennessee court in the first place?

A major legal test as to whether Tennessee has jurisdiction can be stated as follows: Could Robert and Carleen Thomas have reasonably anticipated being brought into court in Tennessee as a result of running their pornographic BBS in San Francisco? So far, a lower court answered in the affirmative. It remains to be seen whether higher courts will agree. Given the nature of the Internet, this is a very difficult question even for legal experts to answer definitively.

In 1996, the German state of Bavaria sued Compuserve and threatened to revoke its license to offer its services to state subscribers if it did not block access of its Bavarian subscribers to certain types of pornographic material. Eventually, Compuserve backed down, although Compuserve's attorneys argued that their company's services were analogous to those of Federal Express who merely transports mail and could not be held responsible for its content. The position of the State of Bavaria was that Compuserve provided services within its territory and was therefore bound by its laws that outlawed transmission and sale of child pornography.

---

[2]This section relies in part on legal research on jurisdiction performed by Shawn Edwards, which is posted on the Web at http://207.43.80.3:80/shawn/read.html.

Jurisdiction Abroad

The global reach of the Internet poses interesting jurisdictional questions. Suppose that Robert and Carleen Thomas were operating their BBS from Sweden rather than California. Could the Tennessee court assert its jurisdiction as it did in the case of California?

U.S. law does not preclude extraterritorial applications of penal provisions. In principle, the U.S. courts can exercise jurisdictions abroad provided that the *intention* of the legislator to give the law extraterritorial reach is demonstrated. Subject to such intent, extraterritorial assertion of jurisdiction must also satisfy additional requirements. U.S. courts have determined that these requirements have been met whenever it can be shown that acts committed by alleged offenders abroad were intended to produce detrimental effects within their jurisdiction.

Libel and Jurisdiction in "Cyberspace"

Some important jurisdictional issues are associated with Internet libel suits. Consider the case of Shirley Jones who brought suit in California against the writer and editor of a libelous article published in the *National Enquirer*. The author of the article and the editor of the *National Inquirer* were both Florida residents. The *National Inquirer* is incorporated in Florida. Its largest circulation is in California. The article was written, edited, and approved in Florida. One of the main disputes in this case was jurisdictional. Did California courts have appropriate jurisdiction?

The U.S. Supreme Court affirmed California's jurisdiction in this case. Chief Justice Rehnquist maintained that the article impugned the professionalism of Jones whose television career was centered in California. The article was drawn from California sources, and the brunt of the harm, in terms both of respondent's emotional distress and the injury to her professional reputation, was suffered in California. Thus, California was the focal point of both the story and the harm suffered. Jurisdiction over petitioners is therefore proper in California based on the *effects* of their Florida conduct in California. The Court reasoned that under the circumstances the petitioners should have reasonably anticipated that they could be brought before a California Court to answer for the truth of the statements made in their article. As a result, according to the Supreme Court, jurisdiction in California was proper because the intentional conduct of the defendants in Florida was calculated to affect the plaintiffs in California.

In another case, a court held that the operators of a Web site delivering E-mail or articles to Newsgroups may not be held accountable as distributors of libelous material if it "neither knew nor had reason to know of the allegedly defamatory statements."[3] The court likened the service provider to a public library, bookstore, and newsstand and refused to offer less protection to on-line services than the traditional forms of information publication. The court reasoned that to do otherwise would impose an "impermissible burden on the First Amendment."

> The court likened the service provider to a public library, bookstore, and newsstand

---

[3]65. *Cubby, Inc. v. Compuserve, Inc.* 776 F.Supp. 135, at 141 (1991).

Consistent with this logic, unmoderated Newsgroups would not be presumed to have knowledge or reason to know of defamatory statements. However, moderated groups would be expected to know or have reason to know of defamatory material because moderators review each article before it is posted to the group. This position is consistent with the "intentional conduct" requirement.

Gambling and Jurisdiction

Internet gambling-related sites range from casino guides similar to the one illustrated in Figure 9-2, Casino Guide, to many casinos offshore, in Europe, and other countries. With the exception of the provisions in the Wire Communications Act and the Indian Gaming Regulatory Act, gambling in the United States is controlled by state laws. Unresolved issues of *legal enforcement* arise from interstate gambling and off-shore gambling made possible by Internet gambling sites.

Most states in the Union outlaw any form of gambling. Consider, for example, the legal status of residents of a state that does not allow gambling who place bets over the Internet in casinos located within jurisdictions that legalized gambling. This type of gambling over the Internet is not addressed *directly* by any law. However, it is arguable that the Federal Wire Communications Act outlaws Internet gambling by prohibiting the foreign and interstate transmission of bets or wagers through the use of wire communications. To place bets over the Internet, users must go through telephone lines, which are wire communications, thus rendering Internet gambling illegal.

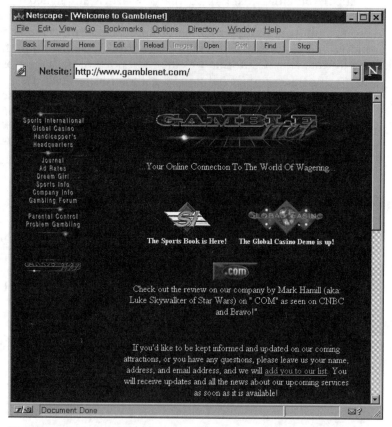

FIGURE 9-2 Casino Guide (Reprinted with permission of Intersphere Communications)

The illegality of Internet gambling, if established, poses questions as to appropriate enforcement. Is it practical for government to press charges against and collect penalties from casual Internet bettors? Can casinos and gambling companies providing Internet gambling services be effectively prosecuted if they reside outside state or federal jurisdictions? Is it reasonable to hold Internet service providers or telephone companies accountable for illegal transmission of bets? These legal enforcement issues remain largely unresolved.

COMPUTER CRIME[4]

Website
Computer crime

Crime on the Internet is a serious and growing problem. The concern is not so much over the fact criminals use the Internet but over the possibility that police might not be able to catch up with many of them. Techniques for encryption—scrambling messages so that only the intended recipient can read them—are now so advanced that they can be virtually untrackable, even with the biggest computers. Encrypted messages make Internet wiretapping nearly impossible. This is why the American government has banned the export of strong encryption technology, and law-enforcement agencies want to set up a system that allows them to decode messages sent within the country.

Statistics regarding computer crime over the Internet are at best sparse, ad hoc, and controversial. However, surveys appear to indicate a relatively high incidence of break-ins into commercial and institutional computer systems, as well as computer crime/misuse by individuals against their employers.

For example, a survey cosponsored by the FBI and a private group of computer security professionals found increasing rates of computer systems break-ins. However, only 8 percent of the sampled institutions responded to the survey. More than 40 percent of the responding corporate, university, and government sites reported at least one unauthorized use of their computers within the last twelve months. More than half the organizations surveyed reported that some "attacks" came from inside the organization itself; more than a third said they had been attacked via the Internet, a disconcerting statistic for businesses that want to conduct commerce in Cyberspace. About 75 percent of the executives who responded to the survey said they feared attacks from independent hackers and "information brokers." Nearly 60 percent said they consider their domestic competitors just as likely to try to break into their computers.

Attacks ranged from changing some information on the compromised computers to attempts to steal passwords or prevent legitimate users from gaining access to the systems. Some of the more serious incidents of computer crime have been committed by disgruntled employees against their employers.

Computer security experts have noted that individual personal computers, especially at home, are far less likely to be attacked than larger systems used by corporations and government agencies. The information most personal computers contain is not nearly as valuable as that of corporate databases, and the challenge in overcoming defenses is small.

Law enforcement officials are also worried that institutional victims of Cybercrimes rarely report the incidents to police. The FBI study states that only

---

[4]Based on the story at the *San Jose Mercury News,* May 6, 1996, which can be found at `http://cgi.`
`sjmercury.com/business/chips/fbi506.htm`

16.9 percent of suspected computer crimes were reported. The main reason for the low reporting rate is the reluctance to publicize computer system vulnerabilities.

Inadvertent Violations

On the Internet, many common "normal" activities may inadvertently break the law. The simple act of reading a document on-line often entails copying it in a user's hard disk. Internet providers often keep copies of popular Web sites on their local servers so their subscribers do not jam their long-distance lines. Then, there are innumerable violations without a commercial motive: copying an interesting electronic article and E-mailing it to a friend or putting it on a company LAN.

In some instances Cyberspace exhibits little, if any, respect for trademark law. For example, an arm of the Internet Society issues "domain" names to companies on request. But it does not usually check to see if the person requesting it owns the trademark or if somebody else does. Indeed, when a journalist took mcdonalds.com as a prank, the company had to threaten to sue him to get it back. Also, different companies may own the same name in different countries. As the writs fly, groups such as the International Trademark Association are desperately trying to find some solution.

CONCLUDING REMARKS

The fast technological developments in Cyberspace pose new legal problems and challenges. National and international legal systems are responding slowly. For the longer run, it is reasonable to expect the evolution of a body of law specifically modified for and attuned to the special needs of Cyberspace. The 1996 Geneva Agreement makes a promising start in this direction. In the meantime, users should operate under the prudent assumptions that in the absence of specific laws, existing general laws, subject to appropriate interpretation, fully apply to the Internet, and that exemptions or special considerations by legislators or courts will be rare. Likewise, law enforcement will tend to respond to Cybercrime in a manner similar to its treatment of other crimes. Investigative techniques and counter measures will have to be continuously updated to catch up with technological developments.

Problems

1. Describe the main legal problems that the emergence of cyberspace has been posing to society.
2. What are the issues of jurisdiction and the Internet?
3. Prepare a table talking about a set of legal problems and compare traditional with non-traditional (Internet) media.
4. Copyrights are an important element of protection of intellectual rights. What new issues have emerged in relation to the Web?
5. Has gambling changed in legal status with the emergence of electronic casinos?
6. Has freedom of speech been respected with the recent legal decisions described in the chapter?
7. What are the tradeoffs in protection of minors against pornography and freedom of speech?
8. In your opinion, will a new order of law emerge in the Internet?

CHAPTER

The Future of Accounting and Electronic Commerce on the Internet

10

INTRODUCTION

The first wave of the Internet focused on personal use and expression. The emphasis has been on Internet access and personal publishing. The second emerging wave is centered on ways to create and establish commerce on the Internet. In the initial phase of this second wave, as commerce platforms are being developed and offered, market players search for products and offerings that make economic sense. Currently, many of the Fortune 500 companies have presence on the Web and are planning substantive activity. Relatively few seem to know how to make money on the Web. Accountants, not known to be on the forefront of technology, are bound eventually to evaluate the medium and experiment with forms of commerce.

> No one really seems to know how to make money on the Web.

Website Cyber-services by accountants

As specific offerings like on-line tax consulting and remote auditing proliferate, demand for the electronic version of traditional services, such as accounting/bookkeeping services on the net, will follow. While many Cyber-services are not intrinsically different in the electronic commerce arena, their nuances, methods, and marketing will change considerably. The challenge for the profession is to offer a balance of services that are sound, that eventually will be profitable, and that satisfy the needs of electronic commerce and of society at large.

In this chapter some of the likely effects of the growth of the Internet on the accounting profession are briefly reviewed. As was previously discussed, the explosive growth of the Internet is bound to have a profound impact on the accounting profession. A growing Internet provides wider, less costly, and often almost instantaneous access to increasing amounts of on-line economic and financial information, and very fast means of transfer and retrieval of such information. This growing body of financial information has to be collected, classified, presented, analyzed, and audited by accountants. Much of this information will be available on-line, worldwide, and will be continuously changing. It follows that to be relevant and up-to-date and keep up with the requirements of electronic commerce, accounting information associated with electronic transactions will have to be accessible on-line in a continuously updated form.

A More Central Role for Accountants

Accountants will operate in an increasingly networked world, with most organizations and business enterprises connected to the net and having Web sites. Most professional accountants will access the Internet through their respective organizations, as well as privately by using home access through on-line providers. This means that as professionals charged with the primary task of collecting and organizing financial information to support business decisions, accountants will have to cope with immediate access to an ever-growing array of accounting data. Accounting systems will have to be adapted to interact with and incorporate increasing and faster flows of business intelligence about customers, competitors, and new products and technologies.

Website
Intranets

Within their organizations, most accountants also will be hooked to Intranets ("internal organizational webs"). Intranets use Internet technology and protocols but are typically insulated by protective "fire walls" from the external web and are usually accessible by only selected organization members and outsiders. Sooner rather than later, the Intranets will become the "organizational accounting homes" that will house most of the vast management accounting systems. It follows that accountants will be called upon to play a leading role in deciding where, and to whom, will on-line Intranet information items about costs, revenues, production, budgets, standards, variances, and quality flow.

Most business enterprises will set a hierarchy of Intranet sectors with a controlled and selective access on a need-to-know basis. The degree of access to, and protection of, any Intranet sector will depend on the sensitivity of the information it handles. At the same time, it would be rather difficult to imagine many Intranet sectors that could function effectively with no access to accountants. At the very least, certain organizational accountants will have to supply some information to most Intranet sectors and help to interpret that information.

Business enterprises would have to, and in many cases would probably want to, grant their major constituencies qualified access to and interface with their Intranets. These constituencies include investors (owners and creditors), customers, suppliers, employees, and governments. All such interfaces will need significant accounting contributions to their information design, content, analysis, control, and audit. Furthermore, accountants are well placed to play a major role in the design, creation, and management of the information links established between a subset of Intranet sectors and the Internet. These links will facilitate not only flows of information between business enterprises and their constituencies but also systematic and controlled flows of business intelligence. While the Intranet/Internet dichotomy is often discussed, the world will not be that simple. Corporations will open parts of the internal networks to suppliers and other parties that add value to or depend on their processes. For example, in just-in-time manufacturing arrangements, suppliers will examine inventory levels, orders, and production plans on the client's Intranet as part of their internal processes. Often, these "share processes" will become the main process for the client and the supplier.

The Business Environment

Continuously Interactive Customers and Suppliers

Internet technology will give buyers greater opportunities for frequent on-line interaction with sellers. Customers will require from companies more and better information over the Internet. Competitive pressures will require companies to provide much more information to the customers. This will include a greater array of high-quality post-purchase customer services. Company accountants will have to provide more information for these enhanced services, account for them, audit them, and possibly manage much more detailed individual customer records.

Companies and their suppliers will broaden and deepen the Internet-Intranet interfaces. Many long-term suppliers will have continuous on-line access to specification, production schedules, and sales forecasts of the companies to whom they supply materials, products, and services. Accountants of the supplying and supplied companies will have to participate in linking databases and information systems of the respective entities, and jointly designing, operating, and controlling those interfaces.

Business Intelligence

Most business intelligence activities in the open area of the Internet will constitute legal and legitimate gathering and interpretation of the enormous volume of unrestricted and unprotected business information being accessible on the Internet worldwide. In a global intensely competitive environment, deft collection and interpretation of business intelligence will play a very important role in enhancing competitive advantage. Management accountants will have to determine to whom in the decision-making chain should various items of business intelligence flow and how they should be merged with existing management accounting systems. Additionally, many business intelligence items have to be classified to be available for strategic planning, standard setting, and benchmarking. It is important to realize that with the spectacular growth of information available on the Internet, which is only expected to intensify, collection and analysis of business intelligence will become a continuous task for most large- and medium-sized companies. Permanent business intelligence units will be created, and management accountants will be important participants in these operations.

Technological Change

Accountants will be called upon to develop services designated to take advantage of the opportunities offered by worldwide connectivity and Internet technology. A few technological projections may give us a better picture of the future environment accountants are likely to operate in.

- *Computer systems will be on-line and virtually connected.* Organizations up and down the value chain will share processes and information.
- *Distributed intelligence systems will be prevalent.* Such systems distribute the loci of decisions. In the future, with many localized processes making decisions, there will be substantial decentralization of intelligence. For example, logistic truck routing will be made while en route considering information available at the time over the network.
- *Computer sites will harbor intelligent agents.*[1] Intelligent agents are software systems capable of exercising judgment in making choices. Among them we can find purchase agents,

Website
Intelligent agents

---

[1]M. A. Vasahelyi and V. J. Sareen, "Towards Intelligent Agents in Accounting: Background and Potential," Rutgers University Faculty of Management, presented at the AI/ES in Accounting Symposium, University of Huelva, Spain, September 1996.

bill-paying agents, and information-gathering agents. Eventually, agent-type technology will account for a substantial percentage of data entered into corporate systems and for a large part of transactions being processed in corporate systems. As intelligent agents require a receptor environment that is cooperative with third parties allowing interactivity and sometimes remote execution, they also are the potential conduit for fraud or viruses.

**Website
Future of computing**

- Computer systems will be *deskbound, distributed,* and *ubiquitous,* with many computer environments built into appliances. Even today, many appliances contain computer chips. However, these chips are not yet interconnected and subordinate to centralized environment controls. With chip-device integration and interplay, many support functions (e.g., menu planning, temperature control, energy management, and information routing) will be performed automatically without human intervention.

- Financial systems will be *distributed* and more often than not packaged. Individual development of applications, while more adaptive and easier to absorb, is expensive and error prone.

- Applications will be integrated along functional lines. While, today, applications tend to be local, value-chain-related computer systems will span entire production cycles and across organizations. Consequently, corporations will readily recognize common applications and re-engineer them for common use.

**Website
Continuous process
auditing**

- Monitoring systems will focus on exception reporting and will place heavy emphasis on funds transfer systems. The advent of an all-encompassing network, linking internal and public systems (Intranets and the Internets), will improve the identification and analysis of significant audit variances. For example, the CPAS (Continuous Process Audit System) effort at AT&T Bell Laboratories focused upon "audit by exception," as opposed to auditing actual reporting. In this case, corporate standards and forecasts are monitored and exceptions are brought to the attention of the auditor. The same observations are applicable to management accountants who focus on significant budget variances.

**Website
Viruses and hackers**

- Viruses and hackers will continue to permeate the environment. So far, viruses have been primarily inflicted, directed by a small number of hackers, as proofs of technical proficiency. A bigger risk is posed by the advent of a class of computer criminals geared at hacking for profit. For example, Trojan-horse software would have a sleeper characteristic that would give Intranet access to unauthorized users. Alternately, packaged software is aimed to have different organizations acquire and use the same type of software and to pass its development and maintenance to a single third party, benefiting from economies of scale. The nightmarish scenario of a software of wide distribution (say Windows 97) having built-in time bomb, or Trojan horses cannot be discounted. Many of the popular and widely distributed software systems have many millions of lines of code, and there is no practical way of assuring their complete correctness and integrity.

> . . . often . . . software has many millions of lines of code and there is no practical way of assuring its complete correctness and integrity

- Unauthorized invasions will be among the top security concerns. The opening of corporate systems to the Internet and file sharing along the value chain creates major weaknesses in the structure of corporate information systems. Exposures are exploding due to the natural desire to open systems to the clienteles, to decrease costs, and increase service.

These technological trends create a set of needs, exposures, and opportunities for measurement sciences and management. They also open up great opportunities for the accounting profession. New reporting methods, new auditing procedures, new attestation services, and additional analytical systems and technology call for changes in accounting support systems.

ON-LINE ACCOUNTING KNOWLEDGE PLATFORMS AND EXPERT SYSTEMS

The Internet is bound to serve as an ideal medium for the proliferation of on-line accounting knowledge platforms. These knowledge platforms will contain papers, lectures, conference proceedings, documents, standards, guidelines, and pronouncements. We will also witness the emergence of publicly available expert systems in such areas as auditing and tax, journals, books, cases, professional discussion groups, and expert systems in all of the important subdisciplines of accounting. As a result, a vast body of accounting knowledge with elaborate search engines will be available on-line for the use of accounting practitioners, scholars, educators, and students.

> we will witness the emergence of publicly available expert systems in such areas as auditing and tax

Website
Experts systems

On-line accounting knowledge platforms are also likely to contain expert systems in major areas of accounting practice. Given today's experiments in expert systems in the accounting and finance areas,[2] we will witness the emergence of publicly available expert systems in such areas as auditing and tax. They are likely to be effective in addressing relatively standard and routine problems, while the more sophisticated expert systems are likely to be restricted to paying customers.

Intranets as Vehicles of Accounting Information Dissemination

Website
Intranets

Intranets are increasingly prevalent in the United States and proliferate around the world. The advent of the common tcp/ip protocol with the availability of a large number of tools that are either free or inexpensive and work on many platforms, over regular networks (LANs and WANs), made the Internet tremendously popular with the consumer. These same features opened the possibility for interfacing business activities such as group support, networking, and shared data over the entire corporate range. The promise of this approach, initially introduced by proprietary packages such as Lotus Notes, made companies more responsive to interface opportunities. The open architecture of the Internet enhanced these opportunities.

The growth of Intranet-Intranet interface is forcing Lotus Notes to adapt, on-line services to adopt the HTML protocol, and relational database companies to accelerate their work on real distributed (over the Internet) storage and query.

HOW THE INTERNET WILL AFFECT ACCOUNTING

As discussed in chapter 8, accounting roles and needs will depend on developments in the Internet and the evolution of electronic commerce. Accountants will have to follow technology and record business activity in an on-line real-time mode.

---

[2]See M. A. Vasarhelyi, "Artificial Intelligence and Expert Systems in Accounting and Finance," vols. I, II, III, & IV, Markus Wiener Publishing, 1993-1997, for examples of this emerging technology.

Enhanced and Changed Disclosures

For example, the facility of electronic publishing and the ubiquitous nature of their display will tempt organizations to move from traditional reports to Web-published reports, first looking exactly like their paper counterparts. When IBM first placed its financial report on-line, it had pretty much the look of its printed counterpart. When the 1995 report was placed on the Web site, as shown in Figure 10-1, it already had some Internet medium enhancements—in this case, a Java script that allows the user to chart some trends in IBM sales of hardware and software. In the same site the visitor can download a Lotus file with much of the data of the statements avoiding tedious data punching. The reader should also notice the "adjusted, unaudited" notice in the header.

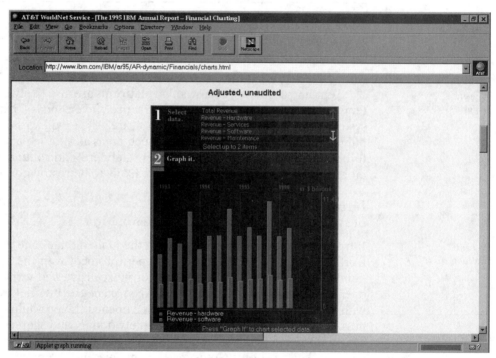

FIGURE 10-1 IBM's (http://www.ibm.com) Chart Builder (Reprinted with permission by IBM)

While interesting, these enhancements are just the tip of the iceberg. Firms, catering to special audiences, will increase their public disclosure (always concerned with the shadow of public liability) of data, maybe allowing drill downs to divisional or product data [e.g., drill downs to SFAS 14 (segment reporting) data].

Broader and Deeper Financial Disclosure

Internet interface opportunities among business enterprises and their owners and creditors are likely to broaden and change the nature of financial disclosure. Investors will be keenly aware of the fact that the firms they invest in have vast quantities of continuously updated information on-line. Likewise, the cost of disclosing this information will decrease dramatically. This awareness will increase pressure on the part of investors not only for more-detailed and timely disclosures but also for setting permanent on-line links to certain Intranet sectors. As a result, the growth of the Internet is likely to increase *the scope and frequency* of financial disclosure and to make certain accounting information publicly available continuously and instantaneously.

Scope of reporting will entail different *presentation methodologies* as well as *additional information content.* For example, with the IBM chart builder, interactive report presentation allows for the *presentation* of the data currently available in many forms, some of which best satisfy the individual information needs of the investor. It is also conceivable that organizations would offer supporting layers of information breaking down information from its balance sheet disclosed level to details (drilling down) that support their claims. Figure 10-2 illustrates this mode of reporting. The levels of detail naturally kept in corporate databases, and summarized along many dimensions for management purposes, can be made available to the world for little incremental cost. What will be at issue is the desirability of doing so.

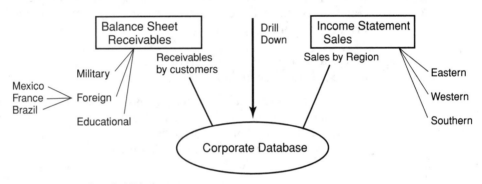

FIGURE 10-2 Leveled Disclosure

Many accounts (e.g., cash, receivables, inventory) are kept updated in real-time and used for the management of many essential functions. For example, cash balances in many banks are kept updated on an on-line real-time basis to allow overnight cash applications. Often these cash balances are updated with reliance on their bank's overnight clearing systems, illustrating reliance on shared data from cooperating systems. On-line applications allow for reporting at increased frequencies.

Website Innovation in disclosure

With the cost of disclosure significantly reduced by the use of Internet technology, the most important remaining barrier to expanded disclosure will be the danger of compromising the confidentiality of strategically sensitive information. This may put the disclosing firms at a competitive disadvantage, thereby potentially hurting the very investors who clamor for these disclosures.

These considerations are likely to result in individual large creditors and investors bargaining for wider and more-frequent private disclosure deals that will give them selective and restricted access to certain Intranet sectors of companies. The legal ramifications of selective disclosure to related parties are many and precedents have not been fully established. Ensuing developments will require accountants to design and manage specialized and dedicated information links between selected constituents and Intranet sectors for restricted types of financial disclosures.

From a public interest viewpoint, restricted private disclosure agreements over the Internet may give some large investors considerable advantages over smaller investors. Regulators will have to rule on the extent to which such differentiated disclosure patterns should be legally permissible. More complex SEC rules and FASB guidelines may result, confronting professional accountants with considerably more complex disclosure compliance and auditing tasks.

Tax Accounting

The federal government and local government are important constituencies of business. Internet technology is likely to increase the reliance of tax authorities on on-line interactive tax audits. The cost of specific audits will decrease, thereby permitting to audit more businesses more frequently and more intensely. Increasingly sophisticated on-line expert systems in tax accounting are likely to proliferate. Taxpayers and tax accountants may have to be more careful, meticulous, and alert. Likewise, on-line interactive audit technology will enable governments to audit more comprehensively and frequently business compliance with a host of laws and regulations that will create a more challenging environment for business and government accountants alike.

On-line Presentation of Strategic and Technical Information

Strategic and technical information associated with the financial statements of companies will aim at presenting future prospects of companies in the best possible way; IBM, for example, has a "future of computing" section with a description of their view of the business, as in Figure 10-3.

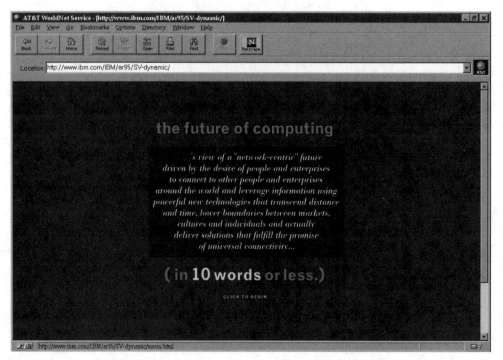

FIGURE 10-3 IBM's Future of Computing (Reprinted with permission by IBM)

Analysis and Comparative View

Information about companies on the Internet is now easy to find. Most of the largest have financial statements and/or 10K statements available on-line. Exposure to the world increases pressures to explain and discuss financial information. Thus, barriers to analysis and information are rapidly decreasing. Companies are striving for standardization and simplification. Accountants with specialization in Web disclosure are emerging, linking accounting skills to public relations and communications training.

Remote Computing Services

Remote tax consulting services, remote bookkeeping, remote financial statement preparation, remote auditing, and continuous auditing processes are progressively emerging as realistic services that may even make a profit. The scope and nature of these services, initially mainly a mutation of traditional services, are rapidly evolving.

Goodbye to Ledgers and T-Accounts, Hello to Databased Accounting

Ledgers, T-accounts, and paper-based journals are an anachronism. Computer-based packages are now integrated databases using distributed relational database systems to create views of the performance and management of a corporation. Relational database products (such as Oracle and Ingres) are progressively the base for a larger and larger percentage of financial applications, often segmented by organizational unit. For example, each division has its own financial set of systems located on a large workstation running Oracle, and one corporate system consolidating results. New accounting rules and new government rules relative to document format and retention will appear and redefine the field taking in consideration the new technological and cost realities. The advent of the Internet greatly facilitates the interface among computerized systems that are geographically and organizationally distributed.

Interactive Distance Auditing

Private accountants for companies and investors will have to design, administer, control, and audit much more complex information networks born out of a variety of Internet-Intranet fusion patterns among businesses and their constituencies. Public accountants will have to modify their audit and certification procedures to allow for more information being disclosed with greater speed and frequency.

The Internet will allow for greater reliance on interactive distance auditing. With exceptions for physical inspection of assets and inventory assessment and counting, Internet technology will make physical proximity and personal presence in auditing much less important. On-line access to materials, and remote transfer and retrieval of documents, will be enhanced by audio and video capabilities. This will make distance auditing via the Internet fully interactive. Costs of specific audit tasks will be significantly reduced. At the same time the variety, scope, and frequency of on-line distance auditing will grow. A large portion of on-line auditing will become continuous.

Continuous on-line distance auditing over the Internet is bound to increase opportunities for more timely detection of serious lapses in financial reporting and financial performance. Commensurably, obligations and legal liability of auditors will undergo substantial changes. Auditors will have to be much more alert and timely in their reporting, recommendations, and certification.

Other Attestation Services (of Virtual Nature)

The need for measurement of Internet activity, such as number of hits per site, number of impressions of an ad, number of purchases directly through the Internet, or purchases facilitated by the Internet, is generating attestation service needs. These areas are prime candidates for CPA involvement, and there is an acute need for the AICPA to provide professional approval and basic regulations for these activities. The Elliott Committee of the AICPA has been examining these issues and is expected to issue a report by the end of 1996.

Among the questions that a new environment may raise are

- What is the responsibility of auditors in relation to expanded information reporting and on-line disclosures?
- Is on-line auditing more like supervision than traditional auditing? Are auditors overstepping their boundary?
- Should auditors attest to software reliability, integrity, and being free of viruses?
- What type of professional services, if any, can accountants provide on-line?
- Can public accounting firms run electronic commerce finance servers and remain independent?

ELECTRONIC COMMERCE

How It Affects Different Industries

Chapter 8 indicated several industries that will undergo radical changes. Consequently, accounting roles will change inducing substantial revisions in risk priorities during an audit. We expect the publishing, information, and computer businesses to be radically different due to Cyber-commerce. Accounting will eventually evolve as a special segment of the information industry. On a slower vein we expect education and retail to evolve toward new venues of activity complementing current means and presenting substantial opportunities for profit. Capital-intensive industries will use the Internet for customer service, catalogs, and means of advertising but will not rapidly change in nature and approach.

Accounting Services

The expected growth in electronic commerce on the Internet (reviewed in chapter 8) will present accountants with new challenges. New accounting and auditing systems will be set up to meet the needs of electronic commerce. For example, new methods will be required to account for the effectiveness of advertising. Accountants will be called upon to design, monitor, and certify these methods. On-line selling of products and services will require on-line accounting entries, postings, reporting, and retrieval. Electronic signatures are bound to change required documentation for transactions and contracts.

Accounting rules and procedures for electronic transactions are likely to undergo significant transformations, partly due to changes in legal requirements (reviewed in chapter 9). For example, timing of revenue and expense recognition, as well as the recognition of assets and liabilities, may change if on-line contracts will be judged legally valid and binding at the moment an "enter" key is struck, or if the validity of such contracts becomes contingent on the types of electronic signatures and authentication procedures. Accounting for some intangible assets, such as on-line intellectual property, may be particularly affected by future legal developments (see discussions in chapter 9).

The Internet is likely to revolutionize financial service industries. On-line financial investment services could be broadened to include on-line issue of equity and debt. Securities trading could be largely performed on-line rather than on floors of stock exchanges. The use of digital cash and virtual banking will transform accounting for cash and cash transactions. All these developments will require modified and enhanced accounting services.

Defining the Cyber-consumer

The Internet is still mainly a personal phenomenon. The Nielsen/CommerceNet survey identifies more than 30 million users of the Internet, using more than 4 million computers in the United States and Canada. At this stage, more than 70 percent of the Internet is in these two countries with tremendous growth expected for Europe in the next five years. The Scandinavian countries, which have a comparable density of PCs per capita, are prime candidates of great usage as they also have high educational levels, high and well-distributed per-capita income, and great penetration of cable TV. Nordic weather is also conducive to indoor activities.

Currently, the Internet user is mainly male (65 percent), upper income (per family income of $60K), and well educated. With the progressive dissemination of computers, the advent of utility computer of low cost, and the progressive integration of personal computers as appliances, the demographics are going to parallel the general population with some degree of income thresholding.

Furthermore, many information services within the accounting domain will emerge. Family financial management will increasingly use tools as electronic payments, electronic shopping, on-line financial services, personal financial management packages, and tax preparation packages. The Internet is still mainly a personal phenomenon. As such, it generates demand for personal on-line accounting services. A sizable fraction of the 30 million Internet users will use this tool in their management of familiar finances. This segment of society is highly educated, high income, and still male dominated.

Costs and Benefits of Internet Commerce: An Illustration

Once technology is integrated into a process, there will be substantive trade-off between incremental utilization of labor and initial capital for entering on-line activities. The Internet requires substantive front-end investment for initial electronic commerce when an organization aims to set up its own processes.

Professional accounting associations will increasingly rely on the Internet to disseminate professional information and to sell their services to members and the public at large. For example, the Financial Accounting Standards Board can sell its statements and exposure drafts over the Internet, thereby accelerating the dissemination process.

As another example, consider the opportunities open to the American Accounting Association to use the World Wide Web to disseminate information and market its services. Let us assume that the American Accounting Association[3] decides to automate some of its processes to use Internet services. This example is

---

[3]The American Accounting Association is a professional society mainly of accounting professors, and currently about 10 percent of its members are practicing accounting professionals. This example is fictitious, designed to illustrate the issues of developing an electronic pressure.

hypothetical and is not based on any actual data or AAA practices. The AAA is a ten-thousand-member professional association, with 75 percent of its members in the United States and Canada. It publishes five major journals, several newsletters, and has a budget of about 2 million U.S. dollars. Publications account for 40 percent of its income. It has seven full-time employees who facilitate its publications, coordinate national and regional meetings, and maintain a wide set of member services.

With a small permanent staff, the organization relies on a very large number of voluntary hours contributed by its members. Its direction of its sections is voluntary, and officers are elected to mainly one-year terms. The journals and newsletters have their content contributed, and the Association is in charge of their production. The journals have small circulation and are very technical in nature. The newsletters focus mainly on the sections and are published mostly on a quarterly basis.

The headquarters of the Association has a small IBM 4000 that runs a proprietary association management software, three networked Macs, and some PCs. Much of the revenue of the organization is derived from the national meeting. Much of the time of its employees is dedicated to contacts with its members. International members often complain of insulation and difficulty in obtaining services from the AAA.

The AAA could benefit from a wide set of Internet services including E-mail communications with its many members and committees, distribution of newsletters by E-mail, listserv services to distribute information among many members, electronic publication of its journals, Web presence for information processes, and Web-based membership services including address updates, billing, account status services, sign-up for membership, sign-up services for membership in sections and regions, sign-up for meetings, and other miscellaneous communications with members.

For these purposes the AAA could consider having the following: computers for each (most) of its employees, a common server, a LAN, a Web site, and reasonable access to the Internet. Table 10-1 displays a preliminary budget for the setup of its operations with electronic commerce in mind. The cost estimate involves total cost of hardware being installed, while incremental costs make the assumption of utilizing existing facilities already in place.

TABLE 10-1 AAA Cost Estimates

	Cost	Incremental Cost	Yearly Operating Cost
Personal computers	$21,000	$10,500	$7,000
Local server	$5,000	$5,000	
LAN	$5,000	$5,000	
Router	$4,000	$4,000	
Miscellaneous equipment	$2,000	$2,000	
Software	$10,000	$6,500	$3,500
Internet access			$18,000
Technical support			$30,000
Incremental content prep.			$18,000
Personnel training	$5,000	$5,000	
One-shot facilities	$3,000	$3,000	
Total	$55,000	$41,000	$76,500

While these costs seem very high, they illustrate some of the front-end cost considerations that entail automation of computer processes toward electronic commerce. On the benefit side, as in many automation projects, some labor savings may be projected, but history tends to deny major labor savings in projects that do not contain processes that are completely re-engineered, with many jobs eliminated. In this case, of the AAA, substantial gains in quality of service, expanded services, domestic presence, and international presence are expected.

Several Dilemmas Will Face the AAA

- If the journals and publications become electronic, what will be the effect upon total revenues from publications?
- While members are accustomed to paying annual dues incorporating subscriptions, Internet consumers have been reluctant to pay hefty amounts for electronic journals, or for Internet-based services.
- What level of technical competence will be needed at the AAA headquarters?
- What will be the role of professional associations in an electronic world?

In the next section we describe a series of potential projects aimed at raising additional revenues and to facilitate the association's electronic evolution. It can be seen as a hypothetical plan of implementation for the AAA.

New Sources of Income

A. The Article Library Project The AAA owns a large number of articles from old issues of its journals, magazines, and newsletters. This project will sell old articles from academic journals. Each article, more than a year old, will be sold for $2.00 for any requesting AAA member or $5.00 for AAA nonmembers. This process will have limited security, with articles being downloaded under a password arrangement and automatic electronic billing to the requester.

The selling process may unfold in the following sequence:

1. User signs on an open area.
2. User fills a form with personal data and an E-mail address.
3. E-mail is sent to user with a temporary password (one day) to access a restricted (but not locked) area.
4. User searches for key words (this process could be prior to 2).
5. A particular article is found.
6. The article(s) is (are) downloaded by the user (ASCII or pdf).
7. E-mail is sent to the user as a bill, alternatively a credit card procedure can be followed, or E-mail for members and credit card requests for nonmembers.

This procedure may expose the AAA to the following risks:

- Nonpayment by certain requesters.
- Electronic duplication of the articles by third parties (copyright notice in each page). While articles in traditional paper form also have the risk of unauthorized duplication, electronic medium makes this substantially easier.
- Loss of some revenue from past issues.

B. The Common Advertising Project The AAA obtains advertising revenues through advertisements in its magazine. This project entails selling additional advertising through its Web pages. Incorporating banners (files printed during the download process) and deeper details (page linked to touch-sensitive banners) including forms to request information, automatic ordering, and extensive product information upon request.

The selling process is as follows:

- The AAA, in addition to its normal ads, sells Internet imprints at, say, $.03 an impression for a banner, and $.06 for ten screens of additional information, and 2 percent of the value of an order.
- The user gets a banner of a particular product while visiting the AAA site and may route down the clickable banner.
- The user may also just get a banner or an imprint.
- Alternatively, the user has to register prior to entering the AAA site along the lines of project A, and at that time he or she will provide substantive personal data. Or, if the user is an AAA member, this information may be found in the member files.
- The user gets a banner of special interest to his/her profile for which the AAA can charge higher advertising fees. For example, if the member has young children, some children's services (e.g. diaper service) are advertised, or for MAC user, MAC software and Mac-based tax services are advertised.
- E-mail is sent to the user as a bill, alternatively a credit card procedure can be followed, or E-mail for members and credit card requests for nonmembers.

Possible exposures are as follows:

- potential non-payment by certain requesters
- some perception of overcommercialization of the AAA
- servicing costs for these items
- risk from a new medium of customer servicing
- the need to create a process to respond to E-mail requests

C. The Membership Services Project   The AAA has a large number of members who call in for miscellaneous services that encompass changes in address, membership status, service orders, communications to the AAA, etc. This project entails the collection of those membership communications and passing them over to the AAA for updating. A certain degree of automatic answering for queries is called for. This includes capabilities of directing queries to existing AAA information, taking of orders for publications, and, where systems permit, automatic updating of AAA databases is also enclosed.

The benefits from this project are from the savings in the processing of these communications. On the other hand, some loss of personal contact will occur.

The process for this project is as follows:

- The member signs up in a restricted area with his or her membership number and some unique personal information that is current in the AAA records. Additional data for the AAA databases is also collected as E-mail address, Internet-related interests, etc. (here the AAA may be able to sell some services of third parties like the subscription of an Internet magazine).
- The member navigates to the area where the service can be provided and enters her information.
- E-mail is sent to the member confirming the transaction requested, and a special password is mailed to the member for using the member area.
- The information collected is sent to the AAA for processing (assuming that the current association management software does not take automatic updating).

- Summary reports are prepared on a daily basis for the AAA as a control for manual updating.

The exposures are as follows:

- unauthorized users may sneak-in by mistake
- as processes are automated, there will be less human scrutiny and observation
- increased transaction processing costs
- lack of person-to-person contact with the membership, but increased international and around-the-clock responsiveness to the membership; international members will have immediate access to information at no incremental cost

D. The Journal Project   The AAA has journals it publishes for its membership. This project envisions the journals to be posted electronically at a discount (the discount is afforded by savings from printing and mailing). It also proposes a restricted subscriber area in the Web where some additional information can be found, such as data from the articles, other electronic goodies, and material excluded from the publication. This area may contain articles rejected due to space reasons or updated information that the authors may wish to convey to the readers. The area could be permeated with ads and related product offerings.

The selling process is as follows:

- The member signs up in a restricted area with his or her membership number and some unique personal information that is current in the AAA records. Additional data for the AAA databases is also collected as E-mail address.
- Arrangements analogous to those in the preceding project are made for electronic journal subscription.
- E-mail (listserv) is sent to the user with current journal issue, and an area in the Web is populated with the issue and some complementary materials. The user may opt not to get E-mail but to be able to pick up the issue for a period of twelve months (when the issue falls into project A).
- The information collected is sent to the AAA for processing (assuming that the current association management software does not take automatic updating).
- Summary reports are prepared on a daily basis for the AAA as a control for manual updating.

The possible risk exposures are as follows:

- unauthorized users may sneak in by mistake.
- some erosion of the paper-based subscription may occur; on the other hand, this process may also stimulate paper-based subscriptions.
- additional electronic publishing costs.

E. The Newsletter Project   The AAA has newsletters it publishes for its membership at no extra fee. This project proposes the newsletters to be posted electronically, article by article, and at discount corresponding to the incremental printing cost being given to its adopters. It also proposes a restricted subscriber area in the Web where some additional information can be found, such as data from the newsletters, bibliographies, less-important matters, and be posted on a regular basis. Each committee member would have an area to post newsletter items of their choice.

The selling process is as follows:

- the member signs up in a restricted area with her membership number and some unique personal information that is current in the AAA records. Additional data for the AAA databases is also collected as e-mail address.

- arrangements analogous to project A are made for electronic journal subscription

- E-mail (listserv) is sent to all newsletter recipients choosing the electronic form when the newsletter is issued. Prior to that date items of the newsletter that become available are posted in the area

- summary reports are prepared on a daily basis for the AAA as a control for manual updating

The AAA may be exposed to the following risks:

- unauthorized users may sneak-in by mistake

- some erosion of the paper-based subscription may occur; on the other hand, this process may also stimulate paper-based subscriptions

- some publishing costs

In conclusion, there are many paths to introduce an organization to the Internet, corporate policies, politics, economics, and a vision of the future modulate this path.

Security of On-line Accounting Systems

Website Security

The vast explosion of business information on the Internet and Intranet systems, the nature of Internet technologies, and the sheer number of users multiplies the opportunities for security breaches and fraud. This puts additional burdens on company accountants to guard against, detect, control, and counter business espionage and financial fraud. Certainly, the role of forensic accountants will grow. They will have to become increasingly familiar with security technology over the Internet, including Web site security and transactions security. Accountants in general will have to play an important role in designing information systems and information flows that meet security requirements. Additionally, detection and prevention of fraud and espionage will require a mix of accounting and technologic knowledge. Forensic accounting will also become increasingly preoccupied with counter intelligence.

OTHER RELEVANT ASPECTS OF THE FUTURE ENVIRONMENT

Intelligent Agents

The explosive growth in external business information potentially available to business enterprises is likely to tax and even overwhelm the capabilities of businesses to screen, absorb, and assimilate such information. Intelligent agents in the form of software packets capable of "roaming" throughout the Internet to locate and identify relevant and important business intelligence items will be increasingly demanded, developed, and deployed. These agents will be *intelligent* in the sense that they will contain heuristics (i.e., logical procedures based on broad principles and guidelines) enabling them to *exercise judgment* and *learn* as they continuously screen and classify information. Furthermore, intelligent agents will develop increasingly sophisticated capabilities to decide which information items are material significant for which type of decisions, who are the decision makers who should receive them, in what form, and how they should be interfaced with the internal management accounting information systems.

On-line Accounting Education

Website
Online courses

Some forms of on-line accounting education are likely to have a promising future. Basic accounting courses covering the accounting cycle, as well as materials covering GAAP (Generally Accepted Accounting Principles) and their applications, are well suited for on-line courses. The same is true of standard applications of information systems to auditing and the basic mechanics of preparations of tax returns. Reviews for professional accounting certifications (e.g., CPA and CMA examinations) also can be handled effectively on-line. In particular, continuing accounting education seminars, programs, updates, and discussions may become attractive to accounting practitioners who would like to meet their continuing professional education (CPE) requirements without the need to personally attend professional meetings.

Accounting for Usage-Sensitive Pricing of Internet Services

To avoid increasing congestion, the Internet service providers will have to, sooner and later, charge users for their services on a *usage-sensitive* basis. Usage-sensitive pricing will ration use by the value of services to users, as reflected by their willingness to pay. It will make possible differential pricing by quality, speed, and priority of service, and diminish trivial use of the Internet. As a result, Internet usage will become more efficient and the incidence of blackouts and brownouts will diminish.

The accounting system required for the institution of usage-sensitive pricing of Internet services is currently not in place. Nor is it clear, given the present technology, whether it is either technically or economically feasible to operate such an accounting system. The major problem is that the Internet traffic measurement system is not fine enough to gauge degrees of usage by individual users of various Internet networks through which information packets flow. Problems of instrumentation and design will have to be resolved before effective usage measurement and costing systems are developed.

The Future of the Internet and Communications

Telephony in the form of public networks is a twentieth century phenomenon. At its early stages the industry encompassed thousands of small independent telephone companies. As a new technology, telephony not only created a new industry with many new jobs, but also changed the ways of doing business. This business phenomenon was also a mechanism of social change affecting the fabric of society and the personal habits of individuals. The need for cost-efficient universal interconnection was used to justify the "natural monopoly" held by AT&T until 1984. In this process the government facilitated and subsidized the requirement of universal access, and the system created a very reliable ubiquitous network.

In the late sixties a new network interconnecting computers came into being. It grew gradually into becoming a global telecommunication infrastructure which presently allows millions of people and hundreds of thousands of business entities to communicate and share information. Internet has found a lot of devoted users whose way of life was in many cases changed by this new communications medium. Its decentralized structure leads many observers to believe that the Internet is intrinsically open and democratic. There is still some concern about whether the Internet will scale up to support the ever increasing numbers of new users. Major commercial enterprises are now making major investments in developing the Internet technology, while many more companies are investing in developing their presence on the Internet. The biggest telecommunications companies like AT&T, MCI, Sprint, British Telecom, French and German Telecoms, as well as some of the regional Baby Bells, and smaller networking companies such as BBN, UUNET and PSI are rapidly increasing their bandwidth and working on the security and reliability issues with the ultimate goal of creating and selling the so-called "virtual private networks" which are based on the Internet technology, but at the same time robust, reliable and secure enough to support mission-critical corporate communication. To facilitate interconnection, the founders of the Internet introduced open standards, and as a result, the Internet technology has become a de facto inter-networking standard. The existence of an open standard makes the formation of technology based monopolies on the Internet difficult, if not impossible.

It is impossible to overestimate Internet's growth potential. Despite explosive growth, only a tiny percentage of the businesses all over the world are presently connected to the Internet. The U.S. is the unquestionable leader on the Internet, but even in this country less than 30% of the population have access to the Internet. At the same time, the Internet seems increasingly congested, with frequent "brown outs" during peak traffic hours. On the other hand, the analogy to telephone systems in the 30s, where thousands of independent not interconnected phone systems existed, makes this seem natural, and quite acceptable.

> Corporations can reduce the Internet lag by buying more and faster servers, bigger links to the Internet, and carefully planning the growth of their usage.

Much of the congestion on the Internet is caused not by the lack of the communication bandwidth, but rather by the limited processing capabilites of routers on the Internet. Numerous technological developments designed to alleviate this routers' overload problem are now taking place, including the development of new generations of faster routers, as well as completely new technologies like the so-called "IP switching".

> Much of the congestion on the Internet is caused not by the lack of the communication bandwidth, but rather by the limited processing capabilites of routers on the Internet.

Entire industries, including cyber-accounting will make external infomation available on-line. Internally, their Intranets will publish financial reports, databases of human resources, technical manuals, and will provide the communications infrastructure for the corporate community.

Internet backbones and providers

Website
Internet access
providers

Although one can hear very often about the co-called "Internet backbone", such a concept does not make any sense any more. It is inherited from the days when the major part of the Internet was funded by the Federal Government. At present, numerous firms own and operate relatively small segments of the Internet. In addition to relatively few "big boys" in the Internet business, there are thousands of small, if not tiny, operators. Over the next few years a major restructuring is very likely. An enormous number of companies within many industries are attempting to obtain market share. In addition to traditional Internet and telephone companies, cable TV companies are now considering this market very seiously. Cable modems make it technically possible to bring to households industrial speed Internet connections (the so-called "ethernet to the home"). It will require some major investment in creating infrastructure capable of supporting two-way cable modem communication and the ability to switch data signal simultaneously with video signal.

These new developments create additional uncertainties for the old-line commercial on-line services, such as Compu-Serve, Prodigy, America Online, and Microsoft Network. The explosive development of the Internet created new business opportunities for them. They can provide their subscribers with a safe home from which to explore this evolving environment. However, a new set of access providers, such as AT&T's EW3 (Easy World Wide Web) and ETS (Easy Transaction Services) illustrate some of these new markets.

To diversify and prosper on the Internet, many telecoms are venturing out of their traditional domain of providing connectivity into the brave new world of content creation. However, the long term commercial viability of such enterprises is uncertain. Various kinds of alliances with more traditional content companies are likely.

Internet telephony is another manifestation of changes to come. It will further blur the boundaries between voice and data communications. Current technology already makes it possible to use the Internet to make regular telephone calls. It is presently possible to make long distance telephone calls over the Internet without paying long distance charges provided that the caller and the recipient have Internet access from their computers and the appropriate (relatively cheap) software. At the same time companies are turning an increasing amount of their telephone traffic into digital data and sending it through private data networks, saving up to a large percentage of their data transmssion and telecommunication costs. However, the quality of these calls is variable and their reliabiltiy is sporadic. Future technological developments will make Internet telephony a close substitute to regular telephone service. It is already possible now to use the Internet to broadcast news, to transmit video (although there are major bandwidth limitations), and to use the Internet to bank and shop. The spread of multimedia PCs, network PCs, and faster Internet connections could make this commonplace. All the companies in those traditional business areas have no choice but to start providing Internet versions of their services.

Telephone companies, banks and publishers will have to follow the rule: "if you cannot beat the Internet, join it".

While at the moment the Internet is not large and powerful enough to meet world wide telephone demand, it may acquire the capacity to do so within a decade (or even sooner). However, even then it will not be universal enough to accommodate all telepone calls. As a result, two telephone systems are likely to develop: one that serves all those who have access to the Internet, and the other that serves those unable or unwilling to access cyberspace. Picture-phone will be considerably cheaper to provide over the Internet than over the conventional telephone network. It now looks like the much awaited video phone will eventually become commonplace thanks to the Internet. Thus, the regular telephone service outside the Internet will become a no-frills service devoid of any access to data or images. Despite the rapid pace of the Internet today, this will not happen overnight. After all, most of the local loop is still copper wire, most equipment in user premises is still analog, and more than 15 years after the PC's launch it is still not considered an appliance. Faxes were developed in the sixties and saw ubiquity in the late eighties. The Internet will become a ubiquitous medium simply because without it the communications needs of modern economies will not be met.

For accounting, the Internet opens new and bold vistas. Companies want flexible accounting data, provided in real-time, representative of their orgaizations, and inexpensive to purchase. Investors, on the other hand, want much information, customizable at will, reliable and attested to by a third party, diagnostic of company problems and available at the fingertips. These requirements from companies and investors may be provided by cyber-accountants and the Internet.

CONCLUDING REMARKS

This chapter examined the many facets of the accountant's forthcoming Internet role and features of future technology with particular emphasis on the electronic commerce over the Internet. Accountants, being information providers, are natural agents for information technologies as well as users of great import. In an environment of continuous contact with customers, electronic care of customer interfaces, and continuously changing costs and benefits, new roles and activities are emerging. In a computer environment that will link many processes, intelligent agents performing many functions, deskbound and distributed, monitoring features will emerge to facilitate accounting practice and enable on-line auditing. Risks and exposures, particularly of intrusion and viruses, will present new challenges to accountants.

Disclosure will present additional facets both in scope and frequency. Broader and deeper financial statements, with drill downs and user-based presentation, will push the limits of the current standards and acceptable practices. Managers, as well as accountants, will have to get used to this environment and adapt their practices to a new world.

As the spread of the Internet revolutionizes access to and retrieval of information and spawns electronic commerce, it is bound to profoundly change accounting information systems and professional practices in auditing, financial reporting, management accounting, tax accounting, forensic accounting, and business intelligence and counter intelligence. Many of these developments will be affected by future legal changes relating to electronic transactions, on-line contracts, and intellectual property rights.

Problems

Auditing

1. Describe the concept of on-line auditing.
2. Why is there a controversy surrounding on-line auditing? Are detractors correct in maintaining that on-line auditing is supervision, not auditing?
3. On-line auditing views itself as being "audit by exception." Explain.

Financial Accounting

4. Find five financial statements on the World Wide Web. How do these compare with their correspondent statements issued on paper?
5. Choose one of the above statements and expand it, using HTML, inventing additional numbers as necessary, to show how you would like to see a statement presented on the Web and what additional features you may find.
6. Invent a model of on-line disclosures that could be the model for the future of statements that are continuously updated.

Managerial Accounting

7. Search the Web for management accounting items that may be of value to you in your classes. List also items that you would like to find. Do not forget to visit the site of the Institute of Management Accountants.
8. In our new information society, what are the cost factors that will affect the practice of management accounting?

Other

9. What are Intranets? How are these different from the Internet?
10. Discuss the evolution of Internet Access Providers and their relationship with Online Services
11. Evaluate the AAA illustration in the chapter, in particular Table 10-1. Discuss the numbers used and how you would modify the assumptions in light of different circumstances.
12. Surf the net looking for tax information.
13. Find five instances of on-line accounting education on the Internet.
14. Draw your own analogies between the evolution of traditional telephone services and the current developments of the Internet.

How to Transfer Financial Data from the Web to a Spreadsheet

As was described in chapter 3, most current financial statements are available on the Web site of the SEC (Edgar project). The readers of this book may find it handy to use data from financial statements on the Web for their personal analysis on their local PC. This would require a smooth transfer of financial data in plain text form on the Web to an analytical spreadsheet format on a PC. This cannot be done by simply using the cut and paste commands because the data pasted in the spreadsheet would not convert automatically into the grid form. The column structure of a text table, evident to a human eye in a Web browser, would not be understood by a spreadsheet. As a result, complete rows of text would be placed into single spreadsheet cells.

The problem described in the previous paragraph can be resolved easily by using an intermediate step. The step consists of saving the data from the Web in a plain text file. Then, this file can be opened in a spreadsheet and converted to the grid structure. Consider, for example, how this is accomplished with the data found in Microsoft Corporation's quarterly 10-Q filing with the SEC for the quarter ended March 31, 1996, located at

`http://www.sec.gov/Archives/edgar/data/789019/0000891020-96-000492.txt`

The income statement of that filing is shown in Figure A-1.

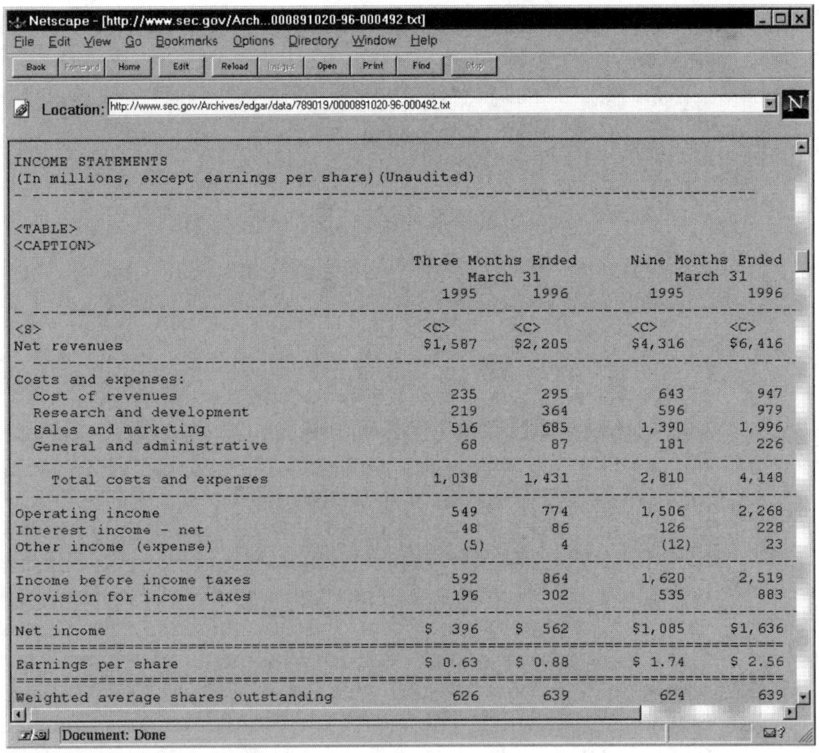

FIGURE A-1
Microsoft's 10-Q
Filing (from Edgar)

The table in the figure can be selected by dragging the mouse and then copying it to the clipboard by **Edit | Copy.** It should now be pasted in a text editor. The standard text editor coming with MS Windows is Notepad. The income statement pasted in Notepad is shown in Figure A-2.

```
 Untitled - Notepad                                                _ □ ×
File  Edit  Search  Help

                         Three Months Ended      Nine Months Ended
                              March 31                March 31
                          1995       1996         1995       1996
 -  ------------------------------------------------------------------
<S>                       <C>        <C>          <C>        <C>
Net revenues              $1,587     $2,205       $4,316     $6,416
 -  ------------------------------------------------------------------

Costs and expenses:
  Cost of revenues           235        295          643        947
  Research and development    219        364          596        979
  Sales and marketing         516        685        1,390      1,996
  General and administrative   68         87          181        226
 -  ------------------------------------------------------------------

     Total costs and expenses 1,038      1,431        2,810      4,148
 -  ------------------------------------------------------------------
Operating income             549        774        1,506      2,268
Interest income - net         48         86          126        228
Other income (expense)        (5)         4          (12)        23
 -  ------------------------------------------------------------------
Income before income taxes   592        864        1,620      2,519
Provision for income taxes   196        302          535        883
 -  ------------------------------------------------------------------
Net income                $  396     $  562       $1,085     $1,636
 ==================================================================
Earnings per share        $ 0.63     $ 0.88       $ 1.74     $ 2.56
 ==================================================================
Weighted average shares outstanding 626      639      624        639
 ==================================================================
```

FIGURE A-2 Plain Text Copy of the Income Statement

The text in Notepad is saved in a file named MSFT96Q.TXT. This file is then opened in Microsoft Excel (either by directly typing the file name in the **File | Open** dialog box or by changing the **Files of type:** to **All Files (*.*),** and then double-clicking the file name). This makes Excel for Windows 95 pop up its **Text Import Wizard.** In Step 1 of this Wizard the file should be defined as **Fixed Width** (the Wizard may erroneously assign **Delimited**). Clicking the **Next>** button advances to the next step. In Step 2 the user has to set column breaks as explained in the window shown in Figure A-3. The figure shows the column breaks already set. Advancing to the next step (3) allows one to change the format of data. The default General format is appropriate for most situations. Clicking the **Finish** button will complete this process and produce a spreadsheet, shown in Figure A-4. This spreadsheet captures the essential column structure. It requires minor editing to adjust the width of columns and reassemble a couple of titles broken in the column creation process. Ultimately, the cleaned up version of the document should be saved as a Microsoft Excel Workbook (.xls) using **File | Save As. . . .**

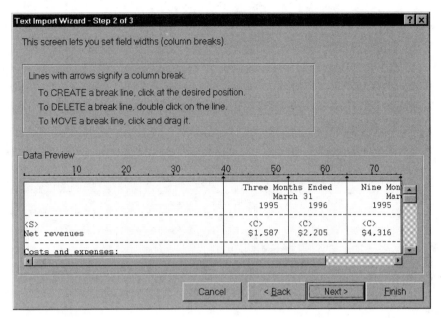

FIGURE A-3 Microsoft Excel's Text Import Wizard

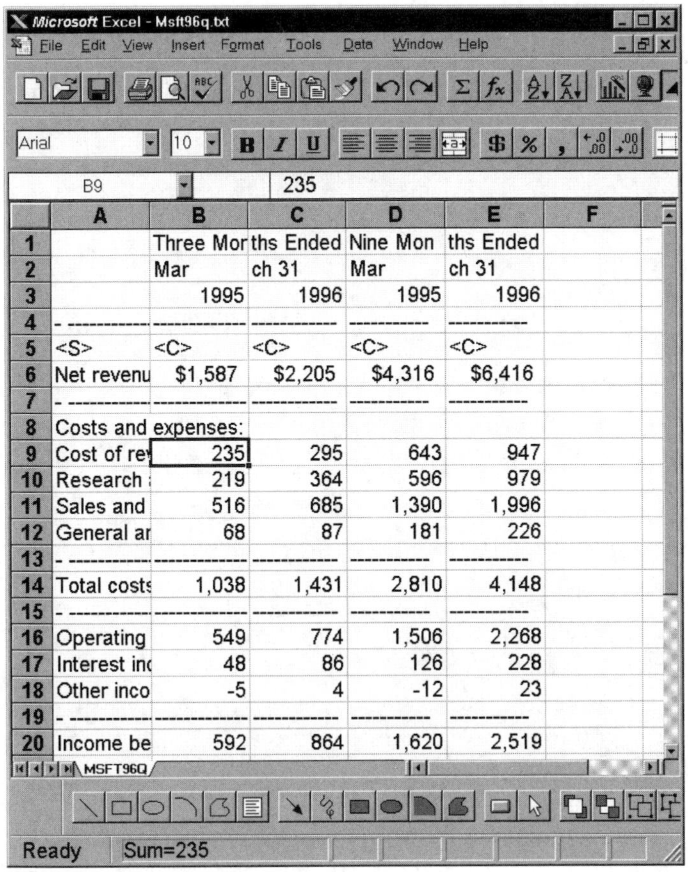

FIGURE A-4 The Income Statement in a Spreadsheet

Viruses

Like biological viruses, computer viruses attack unexpectedly and are contagious. In some cases they can also be fatal (e.g., by wiping out all the data from your hard disk). According to the "Antivirus Terminology" by McAfee Associates, Inc., a virus is "a software program that attaches itself to another program in computer memory or on a disk, and spreads from one program to another. Viruses may damage data, cause the computer to crash, display messages or lie dormant."

Being programs, computer viruses are man-made and developed intentionally. Why do people produce viruses? One answer is that some people have uncontrollable destructive impulses. When such impulses are acted out by computer hackers, they become dangerous viruses. Another answer is megalomania. Some people take pleasure in affirming their intellectual superiority by being successful in "outsmarting" sophisticated antivirus defense systems. The greater the destruction, the more complete is the satisfaction.

Floppy diskettes have been the most common conduit for the spread of computer virus epidemics. An infected floppy would spread the virus to hard disks of all the computers in which it was used. In turn, the afflicted computers spread the virus to other floppies that were used in them. Since computer users frequently exchange information on floppy disks, virus infections tend to spread around very quickly. As long as virus transmission was limited to floppies, users could reduce the chances of contracting an infection by being "monogamous," that is, by restricting their use to manufacturers' floppies. However, the latter practice did not offer fool-proof protection, because even some of the most respected manufacturers of computer software inadvertently distributed infected floppies.

The age of computer networking and the Internet has increased dramatically the means and routes through which virus epidemics spread. Numerous computer viruses have been constantly discovered in various public ftp sites. Computers can now infect computers through direct network connections. It is therefore advisable not to download anything from an obscure ftp site.

What is the best protection against a virus? Fortunately, the answer to this question is relatively simple and straightforward. Any computer user should install an antivirus software. Installation of an antivirus software is analogous to vaccination. It will protect the user against certain common viruses but may be ineffective against new "mutations." Therefore, it is necessary to update the antivirus software regularly.

Most high-quality antivirus programs can be downloaded for evaluation over the Internet. A very good example is programs developed by one of the oldest companies in this area—McAfee Associates, Inc., whose Web site is located at `http://www.mcafee.com/`. McAfee antivirus programs are available for all the popular platforms: MS Windows 95, MS Windows 3.1, MS DOS, etc. They come with an automated installation procedure, so all the trouble of installing them is reduced to downloading a file and running it. The McAfee Web page with the links to evaluation copies of their antivirus software (see Figure B-1) is located at

`http://www.mcafee.com/down/downeval.html`

A very interesting new antivirus product from McAfee is WebScan, "designed to provide virus protection for the most popular Internet services, Web browser and E-mail." It integrates McAfee's ViruScan software with a Web browser (Spry Mosaic browser is included) and an E-mail program (Pegasus Mail is included).

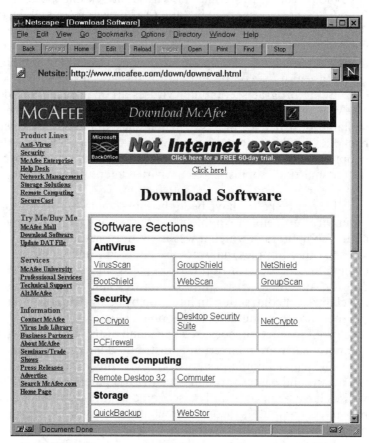

FIGURE B-1 McAfee Download (Reprinted with permission by McAfee Software)

What if despite all the care and protection your computer catches a virus? Be familiar with some common symptoms. Your computer may become "incoherent" by printing on the screen some strange and garbled messages. It may stop responding normally to common actions. Some files may disappear from your hard disk without ever being deleted. Software programs may all of a sudden lose some capabilities. If these mishaps persist, be prepared to fight back. You should get the newest antivirus software, reboot your computer from a clean system startup diskette, and then run your antivirus software (also from a clean floppy diskette). Hopefully, the program will detect malicious intruders and exterminate them.

If the newest program does not detect a virus, then you have either run across a newcomer to the virus family, or your problems may be attributable to some other causes (faulty hardware). In the former case, get in touch with the developer of your antivirus software. In the latter, contact the manufacturer of your computer.

Extracts of the Communications Decency Act of 1995

TITLE V—BROADCAST OBSCENITY AND VIOLENCE
Subtitle A: Obscene, Harassing, and Wrongful Utilization of Telecommunications Facilities.

SEC. 501. SHORT TITLE.
This title may be cited as the "Communications Decency Act of 1995."

SEC. 502. OBSCENE OR HARASSING USE OF TELECOMMUNICATIONS FACILITIES UNDER THE COMMUNICATIONS ACT OF 1934.
(1) in interstate or foreign communications—

(A) by means of a telecommunications device knowingly—

(i) makes, creates, or solicits, and
(ii) initiates the transmission of, any comment, request, suggestion, proposal, image, or other communication which is obscene, lewd, lascivious, filthy, or indecent, with intent to annoy, abuse, threaten, or harass another person;

(B) by means of a telecommunications device knowingly—

(i) makes, creates, or solicits, and
(ii) initiates the transmission of, any comment, request, suggestion, proposal, image, or other communication which is obscene or indecent knowing that the recipient of the communication is under 18 years of age regardless of whether the maker of such communication placed the call or initiated the communication;

(C) makes a telephone call or utilizes a telecommunications device, whether or not conversation or communication ensues, without disclosing his identity and with intent to annoy, abuse, threaten, or harass any person at the called number or who receives the communication;

(D) makes or causes the telephone of another repeatedly or continuously to ring, with intent to harass a person at the called number, or

(E) makes repeated telephone calls or repeatedly initiates communication with a telecommunications device, during which conversation or communication ensues, solely to harass any person at the called number or who receives the communication;

(2) knowingly permits a telecommunications facility under his control to be used for any activity prohibited by paragraph (1) with the intent that it be used for such activity,

shall be fined under title 18, United States Code, or imprisoned not more than two years, or both; and

(2) by adding at the end the following new sub sections:

"(d) Whoever—

"(1) in interstate or foreign communications knowingly—

"(A) uses an interactive computer service to send to a specific person or persons under 18 years of age, or

"(B) uses any interactive computer service to display in a manner available to a person under 18 years of age,

any comment, request suggestion, proposal, image, or other communication that, in context, depicts or describes, in terms patently offensive as measured by contemporary community standards, sexual or excretory activities or organs, regardless of whether the user of such service placed the call or initiated the communication; or

"(2) knowingly permits any telecommunications facility under such person's control to be used for an activity prohibited by

(1) with the intent that it be used for such activity,

shall be fined under title 18, United States Code, or imprisoned not more than two years, or both.

(1) No person shall be held to have violated subsection (a) or (d) solely for providing access or connection to or from a facility, system, or network not under that person's control, including transmission, downloading, intermediate storage, access software, or other related capabilities that are incidental to providing such access or connection that does not include the creation of the content of the communication.

(2) The defenses provided by paragraph (1) of this subsection shall not be applicable to a person who is a conspirator with an entity actively involved in the creation or knowing distribution of communications that violate this section, or who knowingly advertises the availability of such communications.

(3) The defenses provided in paragraph (1) of this subsection shall not be applicable to a person who provides access or connection to a facility, system, or network engaged in the violation of this section that is owned or controlled by such person.

(4) No employer shall be held liable under this section for the actions of an employee or agent unless the employee's or agent's conduct is within the scope of his employment or agency and the employer (A) having knowledge of such conduct, authorizes or ratifies such conduct, or (B) recklessly disregards such conduct.

(5) It is a defense to a prosecution under subsection (a) or (d) that a person—

(A) has taken in good faith, reasonable, effective, and appropriate actions under the circumstances to restrict or prevent access by minors to a communication specified in such subsections, which may involve any appropriate measures to restrict minors from such communications, including any method which is feasible under available technology; or

(B) has restricted access to such communication by requiring use of a verified credit card, debit account, adult access code, or adult personal identification number.

(6) The Commission may describe measures which are reasonable, effective, and appropriate to restrict access to prohibited communications under subsection

(d) Nothing in this section authorizes the Commission to enforce, or is intended to provide the Commission with the authority to approve, sanction, or permit, the use of such measures. The Commission has no enforcement authority over the failure to utilize such measures. The Commission shall not endorse specific products relating to such measures. The use of such measures shall be admitted as evidence of good faith efforts for purposes of this paragraph in any action arising under subsection

(d) Nothing in this section shall be construed to treat interactive computer services as common carriers or telecommunications carriers.

(f)(1) No cause of action may be brought in any court or administrative agency against any person on account of any activity that is not in violation of any law punishable by criminal or civil penalty, and that the person has taken in good faith to implement a defense authorized under this section or otherwise to restrict or prevent the transmission of, or access to, a communication specified in this section.

(2) No state or local government may impose any liability for commercial activities or actions by commercial entities, nonprofit libraries, or institutions of higher education in connection with an activity or action described in subsection (a)(2) or (d) that is inconsistent with the treatment of those activities or actions under this section. Provided, however, that nothing herein shall preclude any State or local government from enacting and enforcing complementary oversight, liability, and regulatory systems, procedures, and requirements, so long as such systems, procedures, and requirements govern only intrastate services and do not result in the imposition of inconsistent rights, duties or obligations on the provision of interstate services, nothing in this subsection shall preclude any state or local government from governing conduct not covered by this section.

(g) nothing in subsection (a), (d), (e), or (f) or in the defenses to prosecution under (a) or (d) shall be construed to affect or limit the application or enforcement of any other federal law.

(h) For purposes of this section

(1) The use of the term "telecommunications device" in this section

(A) shall not impose new obligations on broadcasting station licensees and cable operators covered by obscenity and indecency provisions elsewhere in this Act; and

(B) does not include the use of an interactive computer service.

(2) The term "interactive computer service" has the meaning provided in section 230(f)(2)

(3) The term "access software" means software (including client or server software) or enabling tools that do not create or provide the content of the communication but that allow a user to do any one or more of the following:

(A) filter, screen, allow, or disallow content;
(B) pick, choose, analyze, or digest content; or
(C) transmit, receive, display, forward, cache, search, subset organize, reorganize, or translate content.

(4) The term "institution of higher education" has the meaning provided in section 1201 of the Higher Education Act of 1965 (20 U.S.C. 1141).

(5) The term 'library' means a library eligible for participation in State-based plans for funds under title III of the Library Services and Construction Act (20 U.S.C. 355e et seq.)."

SEC. 507. CLARIFICATION OF CURRENT LAWS REGARDING COMMUNICATION OF OBSCENE MATERIALS THROUGH THE USE OF COMPUTERS.

(c) INTERPRETATION. The amendments made by this section are clarifying and shall not be interpreted to limit or repeal any prohibition contained in sections 1462 and 1465 of title 18, United States Code, before such amendment, under the rule established in United States v. Alpers, 338 U.S. 680 (1950).

SEC. 508. COERCION AND ENTICEMENT OF MINORS.

"(b) Whoever, using any facility or means of inter state or foreign commerce, including the mail, or within the special maritime and territorial jurisdiction of the United States, knowingly persuades, induces, entices, or coerces any individual who has not attained the age of 18 years to engage in prostitution or any sexual act for which person may be criminally prosecuted, or attempts to do so shall be fined under this title or imprisoned not more than 10 years, or both."

SEC. 509. ONLINE FAMILY EMPOWERMENT.

Title II of the Communications Act of 1934 (47 U.S.C. 201 et seq.) is amended by adding at the end the following new section:

"SEC. 230. PROTECTION FOR PRIVATE BLOCKING AND SCREENING OF OFFENSIVE MATERIAL

(a) FINDINGS. The Congress finds the following:

(1) The rapidly developing array of Internet and other interactive computer services available to individual Americans represent an extraordinary advance in the availability of educational and informational resources to our citizens.

(2) These services offer users a great degree of control over the information that they receive, as well as the potential for even greater control in the future as technology develops.

(3) The Internet and other interactive computer services offer a forum for a true diversity of political discourse, unique opportunities for cultural development, and myriad avenues for intellectual activity.

(4) The Internet and other interactive computer services have flourished, to the benefit of all Americans, with a minimum of government regulation.

(5) Increasingly Americans are relying on interactive media for a variety of political, educational, cultural, and entertainment services.

(b) POLICY It is the policy of the United States

(1) to promote the continued development of the Internet and other interactive computer services and other interactive media;

(2) to preserve the vibrant and competitive free market that presently exists for the Internet and other interactive computer services, unfettered by Federal or State regulation;

(3) to encourage the development of technologies which maximize user control over what information is received by individuals, families, and schools who use the Internet and other interactive computer services;

(4) to remove disincentives for the development and utilization of blocking and filtering technologies that empower parents to restrict their children's access to objectionable or inappropriate online material; and

(5) to ensure vigorous enforcement of Federal criminal laws to deter and punish trafficking in obscenity, stalking, and harassment by means of computer.

(c) PROTECTION FOR GOOD SAMARITAN BLOCKING AND SCREENING OF OFFENSIVE MATERIAL.

(1) TREATMENT OF PUBLISHER OR SPEAKER. No provider or user of an interactive computer service shall be treated as the publisher or speaker of any information provided by another information content provider.

(2) CIVIL LIABILITY. No provider or user of an interactive computer service shall be held liable on account of

(A) any action voluntarily taken in good faith to restrict access to or availability of material that the provider or user considers to be obscene, lewd, lascivious, filthy, excessively violent, harassing, or otherwise objectionable, whether or not such material is constitutionally protected; or

(B) any action taken to enable or make available to information content providers or others the technical means to restrict access to material described in paragraph (1).

(d) EFFECT ON OTHER LAWS.

(1) NO EFFECT ON CRIMINAL LAW. Nothing in this section shall be construed to impair the enforcement of section 223 of this Act, chapter 71 (relating to obscenity) or 110 (relating to exploitation of children) of title 18, United States Code, or any other Federal criminal statute.

(2) NO EFFECT ON INTELLECTUAL PROPERTY LAW. Nothing in this section shall be construed to limit or expand any law pertaining to intellectual property.

(3) STATE LAW. Nothing in this section shall be construed to prevent any State from enforcing any State law that is consistent with this section. No cause of action may be brought and no liability may be imposed under any State or local law that is inconsistent with this section.

(4) NO EFFECT ON COMMUNICATIONS PRIVACY LAW. Nothing in this section shall be construed to limit the application of the Electronic Communications Privacy Act of 1986 or any of the amendments made by such Act, or any similar State law.

DEFINITIONS IN THE COMMUNICATIONS DECENCY ACT OF 1995

(f) DEFINITIONS. As used in this section:

(1) INTERNET. The term "Internet" means the international computer network of both Federal and non-Federal interoperable packet switched data networks.

(2) INTERACTIVE COMPUTER SERVICE. The term "interactive computer service" means an information service, system, or access software provider that provides or enables computer access by multiple users to a computer server, in-

cluding specifically a service or system that provides access to the Internet and such systems operated or services offered by libraries or educational institutions.

(3) INFORMATION CONTENT PROVIDER. The term "information content provider" means any person or entity that is responsible, in whole or in part, for the creation or development of information provided through the Internet or any other interactive computer service.

(4) ACCESS SOFTWARE PROVIDER. The term "access software provider" means a provider of software (including client or server software), or enabling tools that do any one or more of the following
(A) filter, screen, allow, or disallow content;
(B) pick, choose, analyze, or digest content; or
(C) transmit, receive, display, forward cache, search, subset, organize, reorganize, or translate content."

Accounting Resources on the Internet

THE BIG SIX

Arthur Andersen

International	http://www.arthurandersen.com/newhome.HTM
USA	http://www.arthurandersen.com/offices/indx/na.htm
UK	http://www.arthurandersen.com/offices/indx/europe.htm
Canada	http://www.arthurandersen.com/offices/indx/na.htm
Recruiting	http://www.arthurandersen.com/firmwide/recruit/c10.htm
Worldwide offices	http://www.arthurandersen.com/offices/ofc0.htm
Consulting	http://www.arthurandersen.com/BUS_INFO/SERVICES/BC/INDEX.HTM
Business Links	http://www.arthurandersen.com/cgi-win/imap32.exe/newhome?461,166

Coopers and Lybrand

International	http://www.colybrand.com/clwww03.html
USA	http://www.colybrand.com/
UK	http://www.coopers.co.uk/coopers/index.htm
South Africa	http://www.coopers.co.za/Welcome.html
Recruiting	http://www.colybrand.com/clwww30.html
Worldwide offices	http://www.colybrand.com/clwww03.html
Consulting	http://www.colybrand.com/clc/clwww0.html
Hot Topics	http://www.colybrand.com/clwww02.html

Deloitte & Touche

International	http://www.dttus.com/dtti/home.htm
USA	http://www.dttus.com/home.htm
UK	http://www.deloitte-touche.co.uk/
Canada	http://ftn.net/DT/
Recruiting	http://www.dttus.com/dttus/hr/dthr1.htm
Worldwide offices	http://www.dttus.com/dtti/home.htm
Consulting	http://www.dttus.com/dttus/aboutf/mc/mc0001.htm
Hot Topics	http://www.dttus.com/dttus/hot/hotlist.htm

Ernst and Young

International	http://www.ey.com/
USA	http://www.ey.com/us/
UK	http://www.worldserver.pipex.com/ernsty/
Canada	http://www.informp.net/y/
Recruiting	http://www.y.com/us/uscareer.htm
Worldwide offices	http://www.y.com/yi/sites.htm
Consulting	http://www.y.com/us/usmc.htm
Tax World	http://www.y.com/yi/itax/

KPMG

International	http://www.kpmg.com/
USA	http://www.us.kpmg.com/
South Africa	http://www.kpmg.co.za/
Canada	http://www.kpmg.ca/
Recruitment	http://www.us.kpmg.com/career/
Worldwide offices	http://www.kpmg.com/
Consulting	http://www.us.kpmg.com/ssc/
Financing Services	http://www.us.kpmg.com/fs/

Price Waterhouse

International	http://www.pw.com/
USA	http://www.pw.com/us/
UK	http://www.pw.com/uk/
Canada	http://www.pw.com/ca/
Recruiting	http://www.pw.com/us/2232.htm
Worldwide offices	http://www.pw.com/wo/location.htm
Consulting	http://www.pw.com/us/215e.htm
Global Industries	http://www.pw.com/wo/global.htm

PROFESSIONAL ACCOUNTING FIRMS

USA	http://www.rutgers.edu/Accounting/raw/internet/usafirms/usafirm.htm
UK	http://www.rutgers.edu/Accounting/raw/internet/ukfirms.htm
Abell Morliss, Chartered Accountants	http://www.demon.co.uk/morliss/
Blakemores, Chartered Accountants	http://www.demon.co.uk/blake/
Edward Ryan and Company	http://www.compulink.co.uk/~edward-ryan/
Gregory Micheals and Company	http://www.gold.net/users/hi29/index.html/
Hacker and Young	http://www.avonibp.co.uk/hyoung/index.html
Hazlewoods	http://www.hazlewoods.co.uk
John Gale Associates	http://www.atlas.co.uk/jgacs/
Kidsons Impey	http://www.kidsons.co.uk/kidsons/

Micheal Lewis and Company	http://www.innova.co.uk/innova/home.htm
Moores Rowland, Chartered Accountants	http://www.moores-rowland.co.uk/moores-rowland/
Rees Pollock	http://www.demon.co.uk/rees-pollock/index.html
Robert Whowell & Partners	http://www.webleicester.co.uk/customer/rwp/
Saffery Champness	http://www.saffery.com
Canada	http://www.rutgers.edu/Accounting/raw/internet/canfirms.htm
BDO Dunwoody	http://www.bdo.ca/
Bruce W Hutton and Company	http://icewall.vianet.on.ca/pages/hutton/
Doane Raymond	http://www.drgt.ca/
Fred Blauer and Associates	http://www.cam.org/%7EFblauer/serv_bus.htm
Hyde Houghton— Toronto Home Page	http://www.interlog.com/~hyde/hhtor.html
McConnell Galloway Botteselle	http://www.helinet.com/MGB/
Hayes, Debeck, Stewart & Little	http://www.islandnet.com/~hdsl/hdsl.html
Mintz & Partners, Chartered Accountants	http://www.mintzca.com
Ormsby & Mackan, Chartered Accountants	http://www.interlog.com/~fmackan/
Patrick Lett, Inc.	http://mindlink.bc.ca/Shawn_VanderMeer/patlett.htm
Sands & Associates	http://www.sands-trustee.com/
Other Countries	http://www.rutgers.edu/Accounting/raw/internet/otfirms.htm
Claus C. Securs	http://www.widd.de/securs/
Costanzo and Verense—Online Accounting Firm from Milan, Italy	http://www.icenet.it/cosver/home_uk.html
Gilligan & Co., Chartered Accountants at Auckland, New Zealand	http://www.gilligan.co.nz/
Hugo Schouten, Chartered Accountants at Adelaide, South Australia	http://www.ozemail.com.au/~dutch/
Interfisk: Accountancy and Tax in Belgium, Chartered Accountants	http://www.innet.net/~pub00693
Robert M. Kennedy & Co., Chartered Accountant at Adelaide, South Australia	http://www.kennedy.com.au

Patrick J. Kissane, LLB, FCA	http://www.taunet.net.au/pat/
Paul Bryne and Co., Chartered Accountants at Ireland	http://gate1.internet-eireann.ie/proll/byrne

ACCOUNTING ASSOCIATIONS

State CPA Associations	http://www.rutgers.edu/Accounting/raw/internet/assapa.htm
California Society of CPAs	http://www.calcpa.org/
The Credit Union Committee of the California Society of CPAs	http://websites.earthlink.net/~cpacu/
Oklahoma	http://www.icon.net/commercial/account/index.html
Oregon	http://www.bus.orst.edu/cob/acctng/prof_org/oscpa.oscpa.htm
Pennsylvania	http://www.picpa.com
Utah	http://www.uscpa.org
Washington	http://www.wscpa.org
US Accounting Associations	http://www.rutgers.edu/Accounting/raw/internet/usassoc.htm
Academy of Accounting Historian	http://weatherhead.cwru.edu/Accounting/
Accountants for the Public Interest	http://www.accountingnet.com/asso/api/index.html
Accounting Association on the web	http://128.175.20.100/web/actass.html
American Accounting Association	http://www.aaa_edu.org
AI/ES Section of AAA	http://www.bus.orst.edu/faculty/brownc/aies/aieshome.htm
ARAF LOBBY	http://www.homecom.com:80/araf/home.html
Association of Chartered Accountants in USA	http://www.ourworld.compuserve.com/homepages/acaus
BETA ALPHA PSI— The National Accounting Fraternity	http://www.ecnet.net/users/miactg/wiu/bap/bap.htm
Chartered Institute of Management Accountants	http://www.demon.co.uk/cima
Financial Management Association International	http://www.webspace.com/~fma
NALGA-National Association of Local Government Auditors	http://www.libertynet.org/~nalga
NASBA-National Association of State Boards of Accountancy	http://www.nasba.org

Professional Accounting Organizations	http://www.bus.orst.edu/cob/acctng/prof_org/prof_org.htm
Washington Account-ants' Network (WAcc)	http://www.eskimo.com/~earl/
Accounting Associations in the World	http://www.rutgers.edu/Accounting/raw/internet/aaworld.htm
UK	http://www.rutgers.edu/Accounting/raw/internet/
Canada	http://www.rutgers.edu/Accounting/raw/internet/
Other Countries	http://www.rutgers.edu/Accounting/raw/internet/

ACCOUNTING JOURNALS AND OTHER PUBLICATIONS

Account—The Journal of CTI-Accounting, Finance and Management
http://www.sys.uea.ac.uk/cti/account.html

Behavioural Research in Accounting
http://hsb.baylor.edu/html/davisc/abo/bria/briahome.htm

Controller Magazine   http://www.duke.com/controller/index.html

Details of Accounting Journals
http://www.rutgers.edu/accounting/anet/research/

Double Entry from ANET
http://anet.scu.edu.au/anet/lists/adble-1

Management Accounting Research
gopher://ukoln.bath.ac.uk:7070/11/Link/Tree/Publishing/

Academic Press/AP Journals/APJ15

International Journal of Intelligent Systems in Accounting, Finance and Management
http://www.bus.orst.edu/faculty/brownc/isafm/isafhome.htm

I.O.M.A. Business Page   http://www.ioma.com/

KRL Consultants & Publishers, Inc.-Complete Financial
& Information Systems Consulting & Publications
http://www.poweradz.com/kricp/

Oil & Gas Tax Quarterly   http://http.tamu.edu:8000/~crumble/

Coopers and Lybrand's Tax Publication
http://www.colybrand.com/tax/tnn/taxpub.html

Other Accounting and Finance related magazines
http://sunsite.nus.sg/wiley-text/bus/bus-index.html

EDUCATIONAL RESOURCES FOR ACCOUNTING

Major Areas of Accounting	**http://www.rutgers.edu/Accounting/raw/areas/areas.htm**
General	gen_acct.htm
Financial Accounting	fin_acct.htm
Management Accounting	mgt_acct.htm
Auditing	audit.htm
Management and Accounting Information Systems	actinfsy.htm

Tax Accounting	tax_acct.htm

Major Courses in Accounting	**http://www.rutgers.edu/accounting/Accounting/raw/courses/courses.htm**
General Courses	gen_cour.htm
University Accounting Courses Web Site	http://nsns.com/Syllabits/acc/
Principles of Accounting	prin_act.htm
Intermediate Financial Accounting	int_fina.htm
Advanced Financial Accounting	adv_fina.htm
Basic Management and Cost Accounting	bas_cost.htm
Advanced Management and Cost Accounting	adv_cost.htm
Management and Accounting Information Systems	m&ais.htm
Auditing	aud_cour.htm
Tax Accounting	ctax_acc.htm
Accounting Information Systems	infor-cour.htm
Other Accounting and Accounting-Related Courses	oth_cour.htm

Accounting department pages of some universities in the USA
http://www.rutgers.edu/accounting/raw/internet/usuniv.htm

Arizona State University—The School of Accountancy
http://www.cob.asu.edu/acct/

Baylor University Accounting Department
http://hsb.baylor.edu/html/dept/acc/

Bryant College   http://www.bryant.edu/

California State University at San Marcos
http://www.csusm.edu/CBA/undergraduate_program/acct/home_pa ge.html

California State University at Stanislaus
http://panoptic.csustan.edu/

Case Western Reserve University
http: //weatherhead.cwru.edu:80/dept/acct

Cornell University—Johnson School
http://www.gsm.cornell.edu

Elaine and Kenneth Leventhal School of Accounting at USC
http://www.usc.edu/dept/accounting/graphics/index.html

James Madison University at Virginia
http://www.jmu.edu/accounting/

Accounting Department of King's College
http://www.kings.edu

Macquarie University   http://www.macq.edu.au/accg/index.html

Ohio State University   http://www.cob.ohio-state.edu/~acctmis/acctmis.html

Oregon State University at Corvallis
                         http://www.bus.orst.edu/cob/acctng/acctng.htm

Rutgers—The State University of New Jersey
                         http://www.rutgers.edu/accounting/

Stanford University   http://www-gsb.stanford.edu/

University of Delaware College of Business and Economics
                         http://www.udel.edu/raker/acct/accthome.html

University of Illinois   http://www.cba.uiuc.edu/~accy/intro.htm

University of Iowa   http: //www.biz.uiowa.edu/acct/index.html

University of Massachusetts at Amherst
                         http://www.umass.edu/acctg

University of Mississippi—The School of Accountancy
                         http://sunset.backbone.olemiss.edu:80/accountancy/
                         acc-main.html

University of North Texas at Denton
                         http://www-lan.unt.edu/cobabak/www/acct

University of Oregon   http://darkwing.uoregon.edu/~ actg/actghome.htm

University of Texas, Austin
                         http://www.bus.utexas.edu:80/~accounting

Virginia Tech University http://acctserver.cob.vt.edu/

Wharton School   http://www.wharton.upenn.edu/wharton/acctdept.html

Wiley College   http: //www.wiley.co/Guides/Accounting/Accounting.html

Accounting department pages of some other universities in the world

Aberdeen University—UK
                         http://www.abdn.ac.uk/~acc025

Chinese University of Hong Kong
                         http://www.cuhk.hk/acy/home.htm

Laval University Department of Accounting
                         http://www.fsa.ulaval.ca/dept/ctb

Swedish School of Economics and Business Administration
                         http://nan.shh.fi/Depts/Redovis

University of East Anglia http://www.sys.uea.ac.uk/cti/cti-afm.html

University of Canterbury—New Zealand
                         http://www.afis.canterbury.ac.nz/afishome.htm

Other Educational Resources

List of all colleges in the World
                         http://www.mit.edu:8001/people/cdemello/univ.html

Yahoo's list of all colleges in United States of America
                         http://www.yahoo.com/Education/Universities/
                         United_States/all.html

Accounting Change Archive
                         gopher://mcmuse.mc.maricopa.edu/1m/acchange/archive

CIA—Certified Internal Auditor

Gleim's CIA review cources
                         http://www.gleim.com/Accounting/CIA.html

CMA—Certified Management Accountant

IMA Home page   http://www.rutgers.edu/accounting/raw/ima/ima.htm

California State University, Chico Accounting Society—The Student chapter of the national organization of the Institute of Management Accountants
http://www.csuchico.edu/accsoc/index.html

CMA information from San Francisco State University
http://www.sfsu.edu/~acct/cma.htm

Gleim's CMA review cources
http://www.gleim.com/Accounting/CMA.html

CPA—Certified Public Accountant

AICPA Home Page   http://www.rutgers.edu/accounting/raw/aicpa/home.htm

CPA weekly news update http://www.hbpp.com/weekup/weekup.html

CPA Exam Home Page   http://www.ais-cpa.com

CPA Web Page from Accounting Department at San Francisco University
http://www.sfsu.edu/~acct/cpa.htm

Kent Information Services—Internet Bulletin for CPA's
http://www.kentis.com/ib.html

CPA Internet Reference Guide
http://www.kentis.com/cparefgd.

Becker CPA review   http://www.beckercpa.com

Bisk CPA Review   http://www.bisk.com/cpa.html

Gleim CPA review   http://www.gleim.com/Accounting/CPA.html

Kaplan CPA review   http://www.kaplan.com/accounting

Wiley CPA review   http://www.wiley.com/PRT/cpa-cpa-home.html

WISEGUIDES   http://www.wiseguides.com

CPE—Continuing Professional Education

CPENet Home Page   http://uu-gna.mit.edu:8001/~compass

Gleim's CPE cources   http://www.gleim.com/Accounting/CPE.html

Western CPE 1996 Catalog
http://www.umt.edu/cesp/wcpe

ISWorld Net   http://129.119.80.101/isworld.html

Research in Accounting Regulation
http: //weatherhead.cwru.edu/dept/rar/

COURSE INFORMATION AND SOME PAGES OF ACCOUNTING PROFESSORS

Accountant's Home Page http://www.computercpa.com

Advanced Management Accounting and Cost Accounting at the Vanderbilt University
http: //www.vanderbilt.edu/owen/boer/mgt413/mgt413.html

AMIS Faculty Home Pages at The Ohio State University
http://www.cob.ohio-state.edu/ ~acctmis/fac/homepage.html

and their On-line Courses http://www.cob.ohio-state.edu/~acctmis/class/online.html

Faculty of Management at Rutgers
http://www.rutgers.edu/accounting/Accounting/raw/
gsm/faculty.htm

Barry Rice's Bookmarks from Loyola University
ftp://pacioli.loyola.edu/pub/ricemark.html

Germain Boer at the Vanderbilt University
http://www.vanderbilt.edu/owen/boer/boer.html

Prof. Brown of Oregon State University
http:/www.bus.orst.edu/faculty/brownc/vita/home.htm

Prof. David R. Fordham from the James Madison University's School of Accountancy
http://falcon.jmu.edu/~fordhadr

Prof. David Spiceland from University of Memphis Intermediate Accounting
http://www.people.memphis.edu/~spicelandjd/acct3120.html

Prof. Glenn Owen's Intermediate Accounting I
http://www.mcl.ucsb.edu/classes/econ136a/136ahome.html

Intermediate Accounting II
http://www.mcl.ucsb.edu/classes/econ136b/136bhome.htm

Advanced Accounting Pages
http://www.mcl.ucsb.edu/classes/econ139/139home.html

Prof. Joey Styron of Augusta College
http://www.csra.net/jstyron/

Prof. Larry Tomassini's   http://www.cob.ohio-state.edu/~acctmis/fac/tomassini.html

Introduction to Financial Accounting
http://www.cob.ohio-state.edu/~tomassin/amis211/lat211.html

Introduction to Accounting II (Honors)
http://www.cob.ohio-state.edu/~tomassin/h212/w96/
lat2_h212.html

Prof. Laura Ingraham from California State University, San Marcos
http://www.csusm.edu/CBA/faculty/ingraham/
home_page.html

Dr. Gray of California State University
http://www.csun.edu/~vcact00f/index.html

Neil Fargher (Fargs) at the University of Oregon
http://darkwing.uoregon.edu:80/~afargher/index.html

Prof. Gerald M. Myers, Pacific Lutheran University, School of Business
http://www.plu.edu/~myersgm/

Professor Leslie Turner's Home Page, Northern Kentucky University,
Cost Accounting & AIS   http://www.nku.edu/~turnerl

FINANCE

Investment Houses

Accel Partners	http://www.accel.com
Allied Capital	http://www.cyberserv.com/alliedcapital
GE Capital	http://www.ge.com/gec/index.html
Gruntal and Co	http://www.gruntal.com
J P Morgan	http://www.jpmorgan.com
Meryll Lynch	http://www.ml.com
Morgan Stanley	http://www.ms.com/MS.html

Stock Exchanges

American Stock Exchange	http://www.amex.com
Arizona Stock Exchange	http://www.azx.com/azx.htm
Asian Stock Exchange	http://www.euro.net/chinacom/STOCKS1.html
Australian Stock Exchange	http://www.asx.com.au
Bombay stock exchange quotes	http://money.com/exchanges/e_bom.htm
Canadian stock exchange quotes from Telenium	
	http://www.telenium.ca
Chicago Stock Exchange	http://www.chse.com
Geneve Stock Exchange quotes	http://www.bourse.ch
Korean Stock Exchange quotes	http://korea.directory.co.kr/daily/daily.html
London Stock Exchange quotes from ESI	
	http://www.esi.co.uk
NASDAQ Stock Exchange	http://www.nasdaq.com
New York Stock Exchange	http://www.nyse.com
New Zealand Stock Exchange quotes	
	http://www.charm.net/~lordhill
Rio de Janeiro Stock Exchange	http://www.embratel.net.br/infoserv/bvrj
Santiago (Chile) Stock Exchange	http://www.bolsantiago.cl/bolsain.htm
Singapore Stock Exchange quotes from FISH	
	http://www.infront.com.sg
Singapore Stock Exchange quotes from NCB	
	http://www.livewire.ncb.gov.sg
Tel Aviv Stock Exchange quotes	http://www.globes.co.il/stock.html
Zagreb (Croatia) Stock Exchange quotes	
	http://www.zse.com.r

Stock Market Quotes and Portfolio Management

MIT Experimental Stock Market Data	
	http://www.stockmaster.com
NYSE Quotes from Aufhause	http://www.ai.mit.edu/stocks/graphs.html
NYSE Quotes from Interquote	http://paragon.interquote.com
NYSE Quotes from PCQuotes	http://www.pcquote.com/cgi-bin/namelook.exe
NetWorth Stock Quotes	http://quotes.galt.com
Quoteline's affordable stock exchange quotes	
	http://www.ping.ch:80/quoteline
Security APL's Quoteserver	http://www.secapl.com/cgi-bin/qs
Wall Street Journal Home Page	http://update.wsj.com/
Yahoo's stock market information	
	http://www.yahoo.com/Economy/ Markets_and_Investments/Stocks

Forex converters

Olsen & Associates Currency Converter	
	http://www.olsen.ch/cgi-bin/exmenu
Chicago Merchantile Exchange's Forex quotes	
	http://www.cme.com/market/hotquote.html

Banks

The World Bank	http://www.worldbank.org
Bank of America	http://www.BankAmerica.com
Banque Nationale De Paris	http://www.calvacom.fr/BNP/ukindex.html
Barclays Bank	http://www.barclays.co.uk
Chemical Bank	http://fstc.poly.edu/Chemical/Chemhp20.html
Citibank	http://www.citicorp.com
Imperial Bank	http://imperialbank.com
Yahoo's list of banks	http://www.yahoo.com/Business/Corporations/Financial_Services/Banks

Finance Journals and Newsletters

Barrons	http://www.enews.com:80/magazines/barrons
CNN's Finance network	http://cnnfn.com
Financial Times	http://www.ft.com
Mutual Funds online	http://www.mfmag.com
Money Magazine Online	http://www.money.com
Nasdaq Financial Executive Journal	http://www.law.cornell.edu/nasdaq/nasdtoc.html
Syndicate of Money Pages	http://www.moneypages.com/syndicate
Wall Street Journal	http://update.wsj.com

Financial Services

Annual Reports Library	http://www.zpub.com/sf/arl
Ballou Internet Services, Inc.	http://www.ballou.net
Canadian Investor Protection Fund, Toronto	http://www.cipf.tcn.net/~fcpe
Commercial Finance Online	http://www.cfonline.com/cgi-win/cfonline.exe
CorpFiNet	http://www.corpfinet.com/first
Finance Hub	http://www.financehub.com/vc
Financial Management Service of The Department of the Treasury	http://www.ustreas.gov/treasury/bureaus/finman/finman.html
Finance Net Home Pages	http://128.150.195.85
Financial Data Finder from Ohio State University	http://www.cob.ohio-state.edu:80/dept/fin/osudata.htm
Finance Watch	http://finance.wat.ch/default.htm
FINWeb—Network service for Finance and Economics	http://www.finweb.com
International Business on the Web	http://ciber.bus.msu.edu/busres.htm#trade
Internet Hong Kong Star	http://www.hkstar.com
Investment Exchange	http://ultimate.org/2743
NETworth By GALT Technologies	http://networth.galt.com
Smith Barney's Wall Street watch	http://nestegg.iddis.com/smithbarney

UK Business directory	http://www.milfac.co.uk/milfac/
Other Finance related links	http://www.lib.lsu.edu/bus/finance.html
Other Finance Resources	http://www.berkley.edu
World Economic Window	http://nmg.clever.net/wew

The World Wide Web Virtual Library: Finance
http://18.23.0.22/hypertext/DataSources/bySubject/
Finance/Overview.htm

TAXATION

Tax Analysis

FedTax Archives	gopher://Niord.SHSU.edu:70/1ftp%3ANiord.SHSU.edu@/fedtax-1
Miscellaneous Taxes FAQ's	http://www.cis.ohio-state.edu/hypertext/faq/usenet/taxes-faq/part1/faq.html
Net Tax '96	http://www.vni_net/~nettax
On line Tax News	http://www.cls.com.au/tax
Tax and Accounting Directory	http://www.uni.edu/schmidt/bookmark.
Tax Analysts	http://www.tax.org
Tax Digest	http://www.unf.edu/students/jmayer/taxdig
Tax Logic	http://www.taxlogic.com/
Tax Web	http://www.taxweb.com
Tax World	http://omer.actg.uic.edu

Tax Associations

Miami Tax board	http://ids.net/~dsmith/mtb.html

National Association of Tax Practitioners (NATP)
http://www.natptax.com./

Tax Services

1 800 FILE TAX (on line tax preparationservice)
http://www.filetax.com/

1 800 TAX LAWS (on line tax preparationservice)
http://www.5010geary.com

IRS	http://www.irs.ustreas.gov/prod/
and their Online tax magazine	http://www.irs.unstreas.gov/prod/cover.html

J.K. Lasser's Your Income Tax 1995
http://www.mcp.com/bookstore/jklasser/jklhome.html

Tax Savings Site	http://www.angelfire.com/free/taxsave.html

TAXATION AND BUSINESS SERVICES
http://www.taunet.net.au/pat/

Tax Sites—Intern Income tax Information
http://www.best.com/~ftmexpat/html/taxsites.html

Taxing Times 1995	http://www.scubed.com/tax/tax.html
Tax in Australia	http://www.csu.edu.au/faculty/commerce/account/tax/tax.htm

UK Tax Model on the Internet	http://wwwl.ifs.org.uk
US Tax Code—On Line	http://www.fourmilab.ch/ustax/ustax.html
Larry M. Elkin & Co.	http://www.elkin.com
COMTAX	http://www.comtax.com

Other Tax sites from

Yahoo	http://www.yahoo.com/Business_and_Economy/Taxes/
Best Internet Communications, Inc.	http://www.best.com:80/%7Eftmexpat/html/taxsites.html
Johnson from University of North Florida	http://www.unf.edu/students/jmayer/tax.html

AUDITING AND LAW

Audit agencies and associations

Air Force Audit agency	http://www.afaa.af.mil
Chicago Chapter of Information Systems and Audit Control Information	http://www.isaca-chicago.org
and their Year 2000 survey	http://condor.depaul.edu/~ysurvey/
Government Auditors	http://www.netaxs.com/~edoig/GARP.html
Institute of Internal Auditors—UK	http://www.iia.org.uk/
Institute of Internal Auditors—USA	http://www.rutgers/Accounting/raw/iia/
Mississippi Office of the State Auditor	http://www.its.state.ms.us/home/osa/
Office of the Inspector General (OIG), Tennessee Valley Authority	http://www.tva.gov/oig/
Office of Inspector General at the University of Western Florida	http://www.uwf.edu/~oig/oig.htm
Office of Internal Audit in Albuquerque—New Mexico	http://www.cabq.gov/aud/home.html

Auditing Softwares

Audit Command Language (ACL)	http://www.acl.com/
The Barefoot Auditor from Pathfinder Other Audit links	http://www.u-net.co/pathfinder/
Other Audit Things	http://www.rutgers.edu/accounting/raw/internet/aulalink.htm
Audit Net Resource List	http://www.unf.edu/students/jmayer/arl.html
Audit Net—Denmark	http://inet.uni-c.dk/~kimrolf/
Audit Net Home Page	http://users.aol.com/auditnet/karlhome.htm
ASAP—AuditNet Auditors Sharing Audit Programs	ftp://ftp.unf.edu/pub/auditnet/programs/
Audit Serve, Inc.	http://www.auditserve.com/

Employment Opportunities with Fortune 500 Organizations
http://www.lainet.com/audit/

Internal Auditing WWW   http://www.bitwise.net/iawww

Michael P. Cagemi—Home Page
http://www.rutgers/accounting/raw/isaca/cangemi/mpc.htm

Quality Auditor Home Page   http://www.lookup.com/Homepages/56694/qa-home.htm

Law

Villanova Center for Information Law and Policy
http://www.law.vill.edu/

National Association of Estate Planning Attorneys
http://www.netplanning.com/

The Legal Research Centre   http://www.insync-corp.com/LRC/index.html

GOVERNMENT AGENCIES

Canadian Government home page
http://canada.gc.ca/main_e.html

Canadian Government's Department of Finance
http://www.fin.gc.ca/fin-eng.html

Commonwealth of Australia   http://www.nla.gov.au/finance/budget95/budget95.html

Department of the Treasury   http://www.ustreas.gov/treasury/homepage.html

FedWorld   http://www.fedworld.gov/index.html/#usgovt

Federal Trade Commission Home Page
http://www.ftc.gov

Finance Net's Electronic Library
gopher://gopher.financenet.gov:70/1

General Accounting Office of USA
http://www.gao.gov/

General Accounting Office Report
http://www.rutgers.edu/accounting/raw/internet/GAOreport.htm

GAO High Risk Reports   http://140.174.164.191/Gopher/Gov/GAO-Risk

GAO Miscellaneous   http://140.174.164.191/Gopher/Gov/GAO-Report

GAO Technical Reports   http://140.174.164.191/Gopher/Gov/GAO-Tech/

GAO Transition Reports   http://140.174.164.191/Gopher/Gov/GAO-Trans

Internal Revenue Service   http://www.ustreas.gov/treasury/bureaus/irs/irs.html

IRS Phone Directory by IRC section
http://www.timevalue.com/irsindex.htm

NASA's HomePage   http://www.gsfc.nasa.gov/NASA_homepage.html

The National Performance Review
http://sunsite.unc.edu/npr/nptoc.html

Social Security Administration   http://www.ssa.gov:80/SSA_Home.html

The Whitehouse, Washington DC   http://www.whitehouse.gov/

U.S. Business Advisor—Federal Government information, services, and transactions
http://www.business.gov/

U.S. Department of Labor http://www.dol.gov/

U.S. House of Representatives http://www.house.gov/

US International Trade Commission http://www.usitc.gov/DEFAULT.HTM

CORPORATE SEC FILINGS

US Securities and Exchange Commission
http://www.sec.gov/

EDGAR Online http://www.edgar-online.com/

SEC EDGAR Database http://www.sec.gov/edgarhp.htm

EDGAR Project: A Case Study in Disseminating Financial Data on the Internet
http://www.ncsa.uiuc.edu/SDG/TT94/Proceedings/
Fin/ginsburg/edgar.html

New York University EDGAR Project
http://edgar.stern.nyu.edu/

The Securities Exchange Act 1933
http://www.law.uc.edu/CCL/33Act.index.html

Securities Exchange Act 1943 http://www.law.uc.edu/CCL/34Act

Disclosure provides almost any need for corporate filing information
http://www.fact.com.sg/

FINANCIAL ACCOUNTING STANDARDS BOARD

FASB's Home Page http://www.rutgers.edu/accounting/raw/fasb

FASB's Proposed Stock Options Rule
http://www.law.cornell.edu:80/nasdaq/v3n4/skaff.html

INTERNATIONAL ACCOUNTING NETWORK

Anet People Database http://www.scu.edu.au:80/anetpeople/anet/
ANetHomePage.html

University of Hawaii's Accounting Network
http://www.soa.cba.hawaii.edu/

Nordic accounting Network http://www.nan.shh.fi/nan.html

ACCOUNTING PUBLISHERS

US Accounting Publishers

Addison-Wesley Business & Economics—Accounting
http://www.aw.com/he/BE/BECategories/ac.html

Bisk Publishing—Accounting http://www.bisk.com/

Carswell Publishing—Accounting/Auditing

> http://www.carsell.com/areas-of-interest/
> Accounting_Auditing_Library.html

and Taxation

> http://www.carswell.com/areas-of-interest/
> Taxation.html

CCH Incorporated—Accounting

> http://www.cch.com/bks-cpe/school/accounti.htm

Gleim Publications—Accounting

> http://www.gleim.com/accounting.html

Gremwood Publishing Company—Accounting, Auditing and Taxation

> gopher://ns1.infor.com:5400/11.browse/Business/
> Accounting%20%26%20Taxation

McGraw-Hill College Division   http://www.mhcollege.com

Practitioner's Publishing Company—Accounting

> http://www.ppcinfo.com/aa-1st.htm

and Taxation

> http://www.ppcinfo.com/tx-1st.htm

Prentice Hall—Online Reference Center

> http://w3.phdirect.com/phdirect/

Richard D Irwin—   Accounting

> http://www.irwin.com/rdiprinf.html#acct

and Finance

> http://www.irwin.com/rdiprinf.html#finance

South West College Publishing—Accounting

> http://www.thomson.com/swcp/acct/accounting.html

Finance

> http://www.thomson.com/swcp/bef/finance.html

and Great Ideas for Teaching Accounting
http://www.thomson.com/swcp/acct/gita/gita.html

Thomson Publishing—   Accounting

> http://zelda.thomson.com/catalogs/
> srch_allcats?accounting

Auditing

> http://zelda.thomson.com/catalogs/
> srch_allcats?accounting

and Tax

> http://zelda.thomson.com/catalogs/srch_allcats?tax

Warren Gorham & amp; Lamont—Accounting

> http://www.wgl.com/acct/acct.html

and Tax

> http://www.wgl.com/tax/tax.html

West Publishing–   Accounting/Auditing

> http://www.westpub.com/cpea/cpecacc.htm

Wiley Publishers—   Taxation

> http://www.westpub.com/cpea/cpectax.htm

Accounting

> http://www.wiley.com/Guides/Accounting/
> Accounting.html

and Finance

> http://www.wiley.com:80/Guides/Finance/
> Finance.html

Accounting Publishers from other countries

Accounting and Taxation   http://www.ca.cch.com/cat95/account/account.html

Index—WWW Virtual Library Publishers

http://www.comlab.ox.ac.uk/archive/publishers.html

ACCOUNTING AND COMPUTERS

Accounting and Finance InLine Resources

http://www.bus.orst.edu/tools/other/acc_fin/acc_fin.htm

Accounting Courses Online, Ohio State Univ

http://www.cob.ohio-state.edu/dept/acctmis/
class/online.html

Accounting Education Using Computers and Multimedia

http://www.csun.edu/~vcact00g/acct.html

Computer Guidance & Support's Activity-Based Costing
and Open Systems Accounting Solutions

http://www.csn.net/~rab/

Some Accounting Softwares

ACL-Data Analysis, Audit and Reporting Software

http://www.acl.com/

Automotive Accounting Software by R*KOM

http://www.Web.InfoAve.Net/~rkom/

Check Mark softwares   http://www.bigsoftware.com/

Check Mark softwares   http://www.checkmark.com/

CTS's Guide for Accounting Software purchase

http://www.accounting.org/cts/

FACT Software International Pte Ltd

http://www.fact.com.sg/

Genovation   http://www.genovation.com/

Great Plains Software   http://WWW.GPS.COM

Students Trial Balance by DeRespinis

http://www.rutgers.edu/Accounting/raw/internet/
stb/main.htm

Flagship's Managerial Accounting software

http://www.wn.com/biz/flagship/

A Guide for Accounting Software purchase

http://www.accounting.org/index.html

I-Trac from Execware   http://www.radix.net/~execware/welcome.html

Navision & Navision Finanacials http://www.openix.com/~eernst/navision/

New Data Systems   http://people.mne.net:1234/7706/2ndcats.htm

Small Business Manager from Systems Research Inc.

http://www.pacificrim.net/~sysr/

Timeline Financial Reporting   http://www.tmln.com/

Heritage Inc   http://www.halcyon.com/cpelog/

Accounting Software Seminar   http://www.cpassoc.com

Clarisys' Accounting Software   http://www.clarisys.ca

CAPP * Computer-Aided Profit Plan for Professional Services
http://cust.iamerica.net/jmburson

Computerized Accounting　　　http://www.accounting.org/

Computers in Teaching Initiative—Accounting, Finance and Management
http://www.sys.uea.ac.uk/cti/cti-afm.html

Macola Software　　　http://www.macola.com

Research and Development Survey of Software Companies
http://www.dttus.com/dttus/publish/r&dsurv.htm

Time Value Software's Home Page
http://www.timevalue.com/

Training for Accounting softwares
http://rampages.Onramp.net/%7Edavecpa/

Woolworth Accounting Service—Macintosh Accounting Software Consultant
http://www.sonic.net/~rickw/

SUNSYSTEMS INTERNATIONAL SOFTWARE
http://www.gcg.ch/p04.htm

P&L—Pro Modifiable Accounting Software
http://www.plpro.com

STF Services Corp　　　http://www.stfservices.com

OTHER ACCOUNTING SITES

Directory, Index and Search

Audit Net, Accounting Audit and Financial Management E mail directory
http://www.cowan.edu.au/mra/home.htm

Index to Some Accounting Resources
http://www.servtech.com/re/aoct.html

K2 Enterprise's Hotlist of Internet sites
http://www.k2e.com/hotlist.html

Internet's Accounting Directory　http://www.tradenet.it:80/links/arsocu/accounting.html

Site Seeker: An online directory of accounting resources.
http://www.kentis.com/siteseeker.html

Some interesting Web sites for Tax and Accounting from Prof. Dennis R. Schmidt of the
University of Northern Iowa　　http://www.uni.edu/schmidt/bookmark.html

and Virtuocity　　　http://www.vxr.com/business/accounting.html

General Resources

Accounting Resumes　　　http://www.career-pro.com/index.htm

AAA Accounting, Behaviour & Organizations Sections
http://hsb.baylor.edu/html/davisc/abo/home.htm

Accountants Center　　　http://antares.prodigy.com/acctgcoi.htm

Accounting Hall of Fame, Ohio State Univ
http://www.cob.ohio-state.edu/dept/acctmis/hof/hall.html

Business Plan Workshop for a Retail Store
http://harbor.ptd.net

Careers in Accounting	http://www.cob.ohio-state.edu/dept/fin/jobs/account.htm
Career Opportunities	http://www.accounting-jobs.com
Cogent Information Systems, Inc.	
	http://www.access.digex.net/~cogent/welcome.html
Controller magazine's Weblinks	http://www.duke.com/controller/WebLinks.html
Count—Resources for accounting students, educators and professionals	
	http://www.users.interport.net/~avea/
Drake University—School of Accounting	
	http://www.drake.edu/acctg/accounting.
European site for Accounting Resources	
	http://www.cybco.be/acc/
Mercon Web, from Merchant Consulting Network, Inc	
	http://www.mercon.com/mercon/index.html
Practice Building Systems Corporation	
	http://www.wwdc.com/~pbs/
Small Business Accountants of America	
	http://www.sbaa.com
Smart Business Supersite, The How-To Resource For Business	
	http://www.smartbiz.com
and their Dr. HTML	http://www.smartbiz.com/doctor.htm
Virtual Accounting Library from Bloomsburg University	
	http://acwww.bloomu.edu/~acct/account.html

Research Resources

AMIS Research Colloquim, Ohio State Univ	
	http://www.cob.ohio-state.edu/dept/acctmis/papers/coll.html
University of San Diego Accounting Society	
	http://pwa.acusd.edu/~bay/

ARTS AND ENTERTAINMENT

Art History Images, Australia	http://www.ncsa.uiuc.edu/SDG/Experimental/anu-art-history/home.html
Children's Museum	http://www.cmcc.muse.digital.ca/cmc/cmceng/cmeng.html
Discovery Channel	http://www.discovery.com
Electronic Visualization Laboratory	
	http://www.ncsa.uiuc.edu/EVL/docs/html/homePage.html
Hollywood Online	http://www.hollywood.com
Museum of Paleontology	http://ucmp1.berkeley.edu/
Virtual Tour of the World	http://www.vtourist.com/vt

Index